MANDARIN RED

JAMES CAMERON was born in Scotland and educated in France and England. He has been a professional journalist for more than twenty years, lately specializing in international affairs. His work has taken him to every continent in the world and more than fifty countries. His articles have appeared in this country in *The Reporter, Atlantic Monthly,* and *The New York Times Magazine.* Mr. Cameron is married and has three children. As Chief Correspondent for the London *News Chronicle,* he is not often home but when in England he lives in Chelsea.

James Cameron

MANDARIN RED

RED

Rinehart & Company, Inc.   NEW YORK

LIBRARY OF CONGRESS CATALOG CARD NUMBER: 55-9463

AUTHOR'S NOTE

THIS book is the story of a visit made to China in the last months of 1954. Like most expressions of a personal experience, it is probably far from consistent; I am not, after all, a particularly consistent person, especially when confronted with conflicting and sometimes troubling situations. But the China trip was one I had sought for a long time—indeed I had almost despaired of making it, having no outstanding qualifications or, better still, affiliations to ease the awkward path. In the end I went, as I had asked, on my own terms. I am a journalist, a Western journalist; though I have become deeply fond of Asia over the years, I am a European even by inclination. I went to China as a Western journalist, and I think I was the first of my trade from London to be so admitted in that simple unattached capacity. I went for the *News Chronicle* of London, to whom I am indebted, as for many things, for permission to amplify here the observations made on their behalf.

This narrative, readers may be sure, does not pretend to be the last—or even the first—word on contemporary China; I have bucketed about the world enough to know that two months in a country much bigger than Europe is hardly likely to produce a heavy crop of the eternal verities. Nevertheless, I traveled some seven thousand miles within the borders of China; I did not see everything I might have wanted to see, but I saw a great deal more than has been seen for some years.

v

I went there bearing several things rather self-consciously in mind as a means of escaping prejudice as far as was possible: Item—that a tremendous number of inhibitions and frustrations might not be Communist, but Chinese; that many perversities and equally many enchantments might not be political, but simply Asia. Item—that I was nobody's guest and nobody's delegate, and had therefore neither obligations nor responsibilities. Item—that the Chinese were a great and cultivated people for a thousand years before there was any Russia, America or Britain; also that the Chinese had been, and indeed still technically were, at war with the United Nations, which I profess to support. Item—that one did not believe all wisdom lay in the Orient because Confucius lived there, but that one did not necessarily oppose Peace because Picasso invented the Dove. Item—that neither side ever lost or found a pennyworth of face by pretending things to be otherwise than they are. Finally, if there was any fun to be got out of the trip, I proposed to find that, too.

When I put that viewpoint up to the Chinese they said, "Go ahead." But of course one never knew. So I put it down on paper as I went along.

J. C.

CONTENTS

CONTENTS

MANDARIN RED

(1)
Over the Line

FOR once the border was more than a strand of wire, a face through a grille, a change of flags and a visa. The border was where everything paused, caught up for a moment of doubt between the banal and the unknown. One said, "Don't dramatize the commonplace," but it was inescapable, here on the dusty bridge beside the almond trees and the guardhouse, with the prim official voice murmuring into the telephone, "The party in question, sir . . ." To whom? Somebody must care, I supposed. The border is always the end, or the beginning.

At eleven every morning the train leaves Kowloon Station for the next world. For two dollars it trails you along from the edge of Hong Kong—all that congested prosperity petering out so quickly among the green hillocks and paddies of the mainland—until it comes to the little bridge, and there it stops. From then on, you walk.

It is not much of a bridge, over a trifling river, but exactly across its middle runs (you compromise with the phrase for the last time) the Iron Curtain. Like a traveler changing trains, you cross the tracks, turn away from the English signs and the English words, the polite expressionless official faces, and walk over into China.

All frontiers are facts, and this one more than most. On the other side everything would be different: hopes

3

higher or despair deeper, men greater or more diminished, some sort of fulfillment or disenchantment—it all lay just across the bridge, invisible among the rice fields. For the curious, mystery; for the anxious, fear; for the Communist, a shrine; for the spy, a bullet. A hundred yards was not too far to walk for such a revelation.

I picked up my bag and crossed over between the observation posts, the binoculars glinting and staring at each other like strangers in a narrow street. The sentries idled watchfully; the stiff-starched shorts of the Hong Kong police, the red stars of the Chinese—they had seen it all so often before. It was like the looking-glass journey.

The frontier control was ridiculous, almost casual— one waits three years for a visa, and then nobody seems to bother. Clearly *someone* knows all about it, and manifestly no one but a lunatic would embark on a proposition of this kind without his passport watertight. . . . The passport! Never had it seemed more valuable and vulnerable; one fingered it like a talisman.

But nobody wrangled or peered; the soldier at the barrier merely nodded—he was guarding the gate of the biggest and most controversial country on the face of the earth, and he merely nodded. In a moment I was in the other station among the Chinese soldiers and the Chinese people and the Picasso doves and the portraits of Chairman Mao, and the old life was on the other side, either a hundred yards or a thousand miles behind.

There had been something enigmatic even about my visa—somewhere in Switzerland the gears had unexpectedly meshed, long after I had given up all hope. Abruptly, there it was—a telephone call from Berne: everything was at last in order, *if* I could arrange to be over the frontier by the twenty-ninth. But this was the twenty-fourth—in London, England; the other side of the world.

I decided then that it might yet be necessary to modify the old conception of the timeless Orient.

From that moment on life began to buzz like an alarm clock; a familiar feeling. I am not wholly unaccustomed to moves of maniacal suddenness; for some time past I have been very nearly reconciled to living less as a person than as a projectile. Moreover, part of my working assets as a writer—some would say the major part— is that my blood stream is maintained in a condition of more or less permanent corruption with the dead organisms of typhoid, typhus, paratyphoid, yellow fever, smallpox, plague, all the amenities that are held to stave off the more repulsive inconveniences of tropical travel. The airport authorities no longer raise their eyebrows when I arrive hurriedly, demanding a passage to Asia—anywhere in Asia. In a word, I was mobile. I was off next day.

There is no point in recounting the inexpressibly tedious details of a long trunk flight. One after another international airfields appeared, lingered, sank away behind, indistinguishable one from the other in their faded plywood and chromium; growing warmer, damper, darker, lighter; peopled with a shifting sequence of faces that varied occasionally in color but never in their expressions of settled, harassed melancholy. Nothing is to be gained by elaborating this. It is the sort of journey characteristic of a peculiar trade where to travel hopefully is of vastly less importance than to arrive—if possible safely; better still quickly. But somehow.

Hong Kong—with nine hours to spare. Then there was the rather numb surprise of finding, even here, someone at every turn completely informed of one's purpose

—who knew where, and knew when, and knew how. The Republican China Travel Service operates its Hong Kong headquarters, as I soon found out, with the same frank and open efficiency as does the solid organization of Thos. Cook. There is very little that is sub rosa or furtive about the C.T.S. They are accepted, they have an ear to the ground, they are in the Book, and any traveler with a hint of China officially on the wires need not cast awkwardly around for the end of the pipeline.

I will say this, before any inference of subversion creeps in: the China Travel Service—having few customers, indeed, and with only one objective—is superbly efficient. Through an arrangement of circumstances that had all the air of inevitability, I fell in with an earnest young executive in dapper white shorts and rimless spectacles who said, with an almost imperceptible tone of reproof, "You cut it pretty fine. However, leave it all to me."

I drove to the station, trying not to think of all the indispensable things I should require that I had now lost all hope of buying, past the shops and the bars and the cinema posters for American films, arrestingly erotic attitudes and mammary revelations—the last I should see of *that* for some time.

At Kowloon the man in white shorts was there, debonair and composed. He gave me some pieces of paper, assured me he had sent the necessary telegrams, and shook me by the hand. I said, "Do you come to the frontier?" and he laughed, just a trace too lightly.

"No," he said, "that is where *you* walk."

And thus I came to the platform at Shum-chun, over the edge at last.

The first station in New China was smart as a new toy, all vivid green paint and red, plastered with phrases

and exhortations in the elaborately beautiful characters
with which I was to live surrounded, and which somehow
invested the ponderous slogans of Marxism with a sort of
bizarre grace, all appearance and no meaning. It was odd
to be precipitated so abruptly into illiteracy. I leaned for
a moment against a wall with a sign that should have
said, "Long Live the Solidarity of the People's Republics"; but what it really said was, "Wet Paint." I moved
into Red China streaked with green.

The difference in everything was so enormous, so
powerful, that it was some time before I realized how
completely indefinable it was. On either side of this line
the people were of the same stock, the same blood; the
little tiled houses were identical; over the paddies the
same peasants moved with the same timeless industry under enormous hats of woven straw, fringed like lamp-
shades. The line drew through them, this arbitrary line—
and God knows you could have examined the political
world for a line of tougher temporal significance!—as one
demarcates the territorial waters of a maritime state: how
do the fishes differ this side or that?

And yet, one saw—they *did*; there was no mistak-
ing this railway station for the other, on the other side of
the bridge. It was not just the uniforms, or the banners,
or the sudden crowded quiet activity of it all; I think it
must have been the sense of arrival into an almost pal-
pable order and method, a feeling of people moving in
rows, an air haunted by the same inexorable purposeful-
ness that now, one knew, ran like a rod through the life
of China. Such feelings as I have about it are wholly emotional and by no means moral; it was an impression unfamiliar to me in Asia—admirable, perhaps; in a way
formidable; in any event it was abruptly exciting. The
implications could wait. For the moment the change was

simply tangible; from that moment on I knew I was right to have come; this was something new.

In the frontier sheds people were going through the most tremendous customs examination I ever saw—the inspectors unfolding undervests, probing into teapots, shaking out shoes—yet when they came to me they merely asked if I carried a camera or a weapon, and barely glanced at my bag. It seemed a curious case of inverted privilege, and—perhaps unwisely and certainly impertinently—I mentioned this. The officer smiled and said, with a vagueness by no means reflected in his eyes, "You are not a frontier person. Please proceed."

There were two hours to wait for the train to Canton, so they offered me lunch—four simple dishes, the chopsticks were decorated with the inescapable dove. They changed some money for me—I gave them a handful of Hong Kong dollars and they returned with a stack of rather ragged notes nine inches thick: the J.M.P., the People's Money, which henceforth one must call *yuan*. It rated at approximately twenty-three thousand to the dollar and forever more padded one's pockets with vast disintegrating wads, to be counted in pennies.

To the end of my stay in China one simple point baffled me: I was able to analyze certain Marxist deviations; I was able to accept, if not approve, certain variants on the general ethical code; I was able to appreciate occasional aberrations of foreign attitude and policy; but I was never able to understand why, with a firm and viable currency stabilized at a rate that made it impossible to buy anything for less than five hundred *yuan*, it was necessary to make use of a currency involving such perverse and astronomical quantities of paper. Even, ultimately, to the Minister of Finance did I put the question: "If you knocked the last two zeros off all your units, would it affect the economics of public expenditure?" He said, "I shouldn't think so." So I said, following up my point with a rapier logic, "Then why don't you?" To which he replied—scoring the final point, as ever, "Why should we?"

They never did. I lasted out to my final day sorting out damp tattered rags into collections ample enough to purchase, for example, a box of matches.

All that was in the future.

This, in the meantime, was a station—and also, it seemed, a recreation hall, and a library and a cafeteria. A group of soldiers were playing Chinese pool, which looks in a way like billiards played with draughtsmen on a card table and calls for loud and repeated cries of "Ha!" at every stroke. The man selling little cakes and bottles of gaseous soda pop wore a gauze mask. I put this down as a very desirable hygienic reform, until I found out later that it was a purely personal and Chinese whim that had somehow spread irresistibly over the nation. Everywhere there were people masked like surgeons; the things were sold in the markets, by peddlers in the street; rickshaw drivers wore them and so, not infrequently, did politicians; even the policemen directed traffic masked as though they were about to perform a difficult appendectomy. Someone had claimed long ago that the masks prevented colds and kept away the endless dust that drifts for months over North China; many more took them up at the time of the germ-warfare story, still most faithfully and implicitly believed by those who recall it. It was as well I noted the masks during my first absorbing hours in Shum-chun Station; after a while they became so commonplace that I would as likely have encountered a street cleaner without his trousers as without his mask.

The bookstall was crammed with benches for those

who simply wanted to read, sitting there among the poster reproductions of earnest young people doing worthy and admirable things: driving tractors, killing flies, joining the army. On the platform were rows of cots in which women passengers had deposited their solemn, enchanting, self-possessed, black-eyed babies. A few people looked up in surprise as I passed—but only momentarily; throughout China the odd thing was the absence of any expressed or impolite curiosity; the scrupulous courtesy of the Chinese forbade their embarrassing the stranger; one passed through avenues of averted eyes. There was a moment at the station—the inevitable blunder: faced with twin toilet doors, unhesitatingly I chose the wrong one. Confronted by two sets of equally unidentifiable characters, I had taken an even chance. When I lost, I hurried out and copied the "Male" and "Female" characters on a piece of paper, to a gratifying round of applause and appreciative laughter from everyone standing by. There was a sort of mnemonic anyhow: the "Woman" sign looked like a drawing of a bidet; the "Man" looked simply like a tangle.

By the time the train arrived, the patient passengers, without any prompting from anyone, had already formed themselves into neat lines opposite the proper doors. The crowds filtered in with complete decorum.

I found myself beside a young man who by chance spoke English, who was by chance going to Canton, who by chance knew both my name and my mission, and who by chance was in a position to stand by me until the end of the ride. He was more than amiable; in the end I was sorry to lose him, but somehow he was always replaced.

Unluckily we happened to be sitting beside the imperative accessory to all forms of Chinese life and activity: the loud-speaker. For some time before the train moved off the instrument kept up a steady flow of what

sounded very like indignant and vituperative Chinese—
it was in fact only official proposals to the passengers
that they pass along the car, that they sit down, that
they behave with propriety—which they did, with every
appearance of docility and co-operation.

The tenor of the announcements became more fer-
vent and declamatory; then, as we began to move, the
machine broke into the national anthem. One felt one
was on some historic mission, instead of merely aboard
the two-forty from Shum-chun. I glanced quickly at my
companion, to see whether some dramatic gesture would
be considered proper, but he was busy extricating a
dried preparation of edible seaweed from a cellophane
bag—he had madly bought it on the Hong Kong train how
many years ago? Three hours.—He looked up absently;
the anthem squealed to its end unacknowledged by us:
we were on the way.

And so at last we were inside China. We rolled
along beside the minute fields of rice and sugar, through
the lush and abundant South China that gave three
crops of paddy a year, with the buffaloes drowsing in the
pools and the peasants in their immense rice-straw hats
turning the old irrigation treadmills. Suddenly it all
seemed too traditionally Chinese to be true; the hills and
the houses were out of some old wash drawing, somehow
even the clouds had escaped from a nineteenth-century
silken screen. I do not know how this could have been so,
but it was. There are times when every country looks like
its standardized sentimentalization; this was such a time
for the province of Kwantung.

The stations came and went anonymously, and at
each one a curious miracle took place. The porters, who
had rushed around organizing minuscule pieces of bag-

gage and gigantic indeterminate crates with equal energy and aplomb, saw the train off at attention, in accurately dressed and rigid rows. No one ordered this to take place, and at no time did it happen that one single man was out of line. It was clear to me that these people had a sense of discipline unexampled anywhere—or perhaps it was just a sense of symmetry. Never, at any rate, on that journey (or indeed at any time) did I see a man, woman, or child in China behaving in a fashion that could be called random or ill-considered or graceless. That could have been a good thing or a bad; I was in no position to be sure of *that*.

Inside the coach, however, a small sort of hell was breaking loose, based as usual on the loud-speaker. In most forms of human behavior the Chinese have a delicate and scrupulous sense of gentleness and sensitivity, but they have one disastrous characteristic: they appear to be wholly invulnerable to noise. We shall almost inevitably refer back, too, to *this*, since it is possibly a factor in the contemporary Chinese scene that shares top place with dialectical materialism. The machine, at our very ears, roared and screamed and quacked—sometimes a sort of demented bagpipes from Mongolia and sometimes it was a Slavonic march—usually, in fact, since communism requires military music and the old Chinese, most reasonably, composed nothing especially martial. However, no variation made the slightest difference to the passengers, who chatted in an animated way throughout it all, and frequently broke into separate songs of their own whenever the impulse came, producing a chaotic mélange of sound to which in the end I became, by some providential dispensation, almost immune.

It was far from a new train, but it was without doubt the most impeccably clean train I ever saw in my

life. (This again was something that was to weigh upon
me with an almost philosophic importance as time went
on.) There was a man whose job, throughout the entire
journey, was to drift about the coaches dusting things
off and picking things off the floor. When I dropped a bit
of cigarette ash on the ground, he would be there in a
flash, pointedly scraping it up and nudging my attention to the ash tray. Every ten minutes the tea-man appeared to refill our glasses with hot water; if a drop was
spilled, someone would appear to mop it up; it was as
though one was toping old ale in an operating theatre.
This, I felt sure, was some absurd overemphasis for the
benefit of new arrivals from the Other Side; it could *not*
go on everywhere. . . .

Well, I was to see.

Dusk fell over this enormous country and we still
rocked along. Every now and again the man would come
along with his fragrant green tea. At one halt we loaded
a pile of brand-new English bicycles. At the next great
wicker baskets came aboard, crammed with live ducklings, protesting and shrilling like machinery. I asked
my chance-met cicerone where we were. He didn't know;
he never did.

Then, as we came crawling into the dim lights of
Canton at last, the tea-man came round to be paid—
something like a nickel for about forty glasses of tea. He
produced the receipt—you get a receipt for *everything*
in China; even a box of matches goes on the record. And
a peculiar receipt it was, with a printed message on the
back.

I asked my friend what aspect of democracy those
characters advertised, but he laughed and said, "No—
on train receipts, always get printed riddles."

He read me one, some fearfully intricate Oriental

merrythought about how to light a candle in a dark room so that no one can see it. I couldn't get it at all, and I asked for the answer, but he shrugged again.

"Give riddles," he said. "Not give answers. Answers got to find."

As we ground into Canton station—as the loudspeakers roared and the brakes howled and the ducklings squealed and everyone began shouting at once, as the new Government man appeared with superlative timing precisely at my window—I began to feel the man was right: Answers got to find.

(2)
Peking

THERE were, of course, few mysteries in China for those who had never been there; everything could be learned through the diligent cultivation of illusions. It was a country, everyone knew, composed in the main of curiously carved bridges and formal attitudes, elaborate gates and seamless steel tubing mills; it was inhabited chiefly by Mandarins, War Lords, Sages and Commissars, who dwelt in Pagodas, and subsisted on complicated preparations of the nests of birds and the fins of sharks, while reading the Book of Odes, Mencius, and Marx. These people, one was well aware, conveyed themselves from place to place in palanquins; their prime diversion was the incessant consumption of opium, the administration of intricate tortures, and the dilettante painting of water-color bamboos.

The picture of this ancient but only too familiar civilization was clear enough; one was well aware that the Chinese were numerous and, of course, inscrutable. There were many reliable accounts of their personal eccentricities of behavior: they were given to shaking hands with themselves, wearing white for mourning, and completing their meals with unusual but significant soups; they devoured dogs and tended to make philosophical observations while they drowned their girl children. They

had, some said, no proper word for "no. . . ." Everything one heard added to the rich and engaging variety
of that absorbing nation. I had, in fact, often tried to
equate these fascinating values with the simple natures
of my Chinese friends in Singapore, Hong Kong, or Saigon.
Clearly these decent people had been subjected to some
alien influence, for my Chinese friends had always
seemed, ridiculously, very much the same as myself, only
perhaps more rational. In China, one knew, they would
be Chinese—kowtowing, and writing upside down.

These lasting truths were latterly overlaid by a new
index of national practices: the washing of brains, the
collection of germs, the sacrifice of feudal landlords on
the altar of Mao Tse-Tung. The Chinese, in 1954, had
finally combined in their enigmatic persons the characteristics of two sets of eternal verities: they were aggressive and passive, cunning and supine, warlike and cowardly, artistic and illiterate, reliable and corrupt, devious
and dull, doomed to economic disaster and about to
overwhelm the world; they were Communist and Confucian, a social liability and an international threat; a
nation of laundrymen, poets, coolies, moneylenders, generals, sing-song girls and female engineers; of hordes, her-
mits, oafs, Talleyrands, brigands, Boxers, conjurers. . . .

The enormous city of Canton, it seemed, lived somehow on an economy of water; a place wholly aqueous,
built on damp—floods, rivers, ferries, sea food, boats,
ducks, rain, the still-tremendous colony of sampan dwell-
ers called, mysteriously, the Family of the Egg; rice-paddies
everywhere. Even the airport—it was called the Sky River.

There was a special plane leaving in the morning,
and a seat for me. It had to be a special aircraft; there was

no other kind. The Skoga Airline ran excellent connec-
tions from Shanghai to Chungking, from Peking to Mukden, from Hangkow to Kunming—indeed everywhere—
but for some reason that to the end of my stay remained
unexplained there was no scheduled service between
Canton and Peking. Yet, for some equally curious reason,
there was almost always a special plane on the runway,
waiting at the right time for the right people; a very good
Russian-built version of the DC-3, Chinese crewed, and
on the bulkhead, where less socially conscious airlines
carry the seat-belt light, there were two framed pictures,
one of Georgi Malenkov, the other of Chairman Mao.

To save three days, I flew eight hours. . . . up to
the North, up to the heartland, up over Kiang-si and An-
whei and Shan-tung, through the cloud and the mist,
trailing an erratic shadow over the crumpled cardboard
of the endless country: vast. How vast?

At last this was China, and what was China? You
could ask, but nobody knew; nobody's figures agreed, nobody's statistics matched. Down there lay some part of
the minimum guess—four million square miles, perhaps
half a million more than all of Europe, and even then the
boundaries faded into speculation. Take China proper
alone, the Eighteen Provinces; assess it on a tangible
basis—from Harbin in the North to Canton in the South
is from London to Tripoli; from Shanghai in the East to
Tibet in the West is from Moscow to Liverpool. A lot of
country. The product of four thousand years of continu-
ous history, of a national entity—no nation on the records can match it; they were old and settled when ancient
Greece was young; Solomon was born and Plato died,
Shakespeare came and went; Jesus was conceived, born
and crucified; the world saw Alexander and Charlemagne,

the Crusades, the French Revolution, a hundred wars; from the death of Nebuchadnezzar to the birth of Adolf Hitler—China was the same nation, one people.

How many, no one knows. At the time of the Magna Carta there were more Chinese than the rest of the entire human race. Today there are more Chinese under ten years old than there are British of any age. Down there below the wheeling wings—perhaps six hundred million people, and ten million more each year. A quarter of the world's people. . . . How do you examine the fourth part of all humanity?

"If you glance down to the left," said the Chinese official beside me, "you can see the Summer Palace—there beside the lake, just outside Peking. A remnant of the old feudal days. Nevertheless," he said, leaning across the seat, "so very pretty, you must agree."

Morning began with music; a flock of awakened pigeons wheeled over the curving roofs, fluting mournfully through the little bamboo whistles strapped to their legs. In Peking even the pigeons go to work. On festivals and the holy days of Marxism they trailed long ribbons of pastel silk, carving arabesques against the decorated eaves, for the Chinese obstinately continued to invest the Revolution with at least a few of the pleasantly useless fantasies of feudalism.

Then abruptly, all over the chilly city, the loud-speakers brayed into the morning with an urgent howl —always the same tune, vaguely reminiscent of some fugitive hillbilly theme of the 'forties—and in the gray streets the citizens assembled, with a kind of desultory diligence, for the first of the day's Three Physical Interludes. ("The Modern China is a Healthy China.") For fifteen minutes the population bent and creaked in its blue cotton-padded suits, while the enormous map of China came to life all around.

Far away among the paddies of Kwantung, the mountains of Szechuan, the pits and forges of Manchuria, much the same thing went on, with a zeal in inverse ratio to the distance from the center. Here under the walls of the Government City the Chairman's eye seemed closer. The round avuncular face gazed down in ten thousand representations, from the immense likenesses in the streets to the pocket version that was always slipped under the glass tops of office desks; it was bland and smooth, with the famous wart touched in affectionately; Chairman Mao had a Cromwellian streak. After a while it ceased to be the face of a man; it became somehow that of a Buddha. (When I saw Mao Tse-Tung for the first time at close quarters, I was startled to see him human—old and almost frail, with the smooth polished preservation of a nun. He stood in the Hall of Purple Light that had been built by the Mings, the one-man dynasty of the new age; the Surrogate-Emperor dressed up as a garage hand; the most equal man for three thousand miles. . . .)

". . . . And so," said my friend Shen, waiting at the airport, "you did get here after all. You said you wouldn't. . . ." We had met at Geneva, among a negative flurry of shrugged shoulders and dubious hopes. "What do you make of it?"

Some time had passed; what did I make of it?

When the political Great Wall of China yielded a crack momentarily wide enough to slip through, the initial impression was oddness itself—like breaking with enormous effort into a Pharaoh's tomb and finding yourself instead in the middle of Brooklyn Heights. Was this

what all the somber mystery had been about—just someone reciting an ancient scroll in the chilly, sensible accents of the London School of Economics? And then one
day you found that inside the box was another box, and
another and another; you never found the last one. All
you reached was the alarming conclusion that Marx was a
Mandarin all the time.

But it was Peking at last. I suppose the mind still
groped around for Oriental glamour on the one hand and
reigns of terror on the other, while the body continued
wearily to wrestle with forms and oblique courtesies and
peculiar plumbing. If the fear were there, as doubtless it
once was, it had long since ceased to show (this was a
rather merry country) and had taken the glamour with
it (this was a bleak country, too). What were left were
the walls, everywhere walls.

Some were visible. Five centuries ago, when London
was a village, the Emperor Yung Lo had laid out Imperial
Peking behind the enormous ramparts that still contained
the three million people who live there now. It was then,
and may yet be again, one of the greatest cities in the
world, and surely one of the most beguiling. Behind the
Big Wall was another, and still another, ringing the Tartar City, the Chinese City, the Forbidden City, box
within box of curving colored fantasy, and threading
throughout were the windowless gray streets where the
Pekinois lived in inward-facing houses, most gracefully
preserving their final measure of privacy.

This curious and splendid place was inhabited by
the race of Martians of whom for the previous five years one
had known practically nothing, except from the special
pleading of the pros and antis, the noisy overstatements
of the wild men on both sides. (The tedium of descrip-

tive propaganda, the weariness of the old subjective song.)

And then finally the drive towards it all—through a landscape the color of ashes, through a clattering riot of new construction, towards the Great Gate—and there they are; you feel the six hundred million of them pressing and surging invisibly around, forming at the least excuse into queues and lines of the inescapable drab navy blue cotton suit that is China's badge of the new orthodoxy, so useful, so economic, so ideologically correct, and so dull. Everyone makes too much of this first impression— does one expect embroidered silk in a revolutionary society? Should one ask gaiety from a nation abruptly faced with the imperative necessity of clothing itself without help of any kind? Nevertheless, it seemed fair to remark that nine hundred and ninety-nine out of every thousand were in uniform, either military or this sadly practical livery that made everyone, men and women, from the Prime Minister to the postman, look like boilermakers. The cloth shortage that had created this need was easing fast, but necessity had inevitably become a cult; it would be a long time before a comrade showed up again in brocade. So long as Chairman Mao dressed like a well-tailored engine driver so would his Government, and the Government servants, and all those who wished to stand well with the Government, which not unnaturally was everyone not at the time under psychiatric care.

Nobody shared these regrets. They agreed: "The clothes are not pretty. But they are clothes. Not long ago *that* was a luxury to most of us."

There was no defining this strange effect of unanimity, which so clearly went below the boiler suit to where the Chinese kept his heart, which was very deep indeed. I grew out of the practice of believing my eyes some time ago, but there was no escaping the feeling of millions of people consciously enjoying the novelty of *not* being kicked around. It is possible that there is never any need to kick when there is only one way to go. . . . Yet these were early impressions; it was necessary to hang on to almost anything; the pressure on the senses of this extraordinary Chinese puzzle was initially so great, so rapid the alternation of delight and despair, that everything got lost in a sort of baffled fatigue.

Where were the bans and barriers? They were there all right, one might be sure, but one brought most of them in oneself. There were times, here in China, when I felt that I had unfettered liberty to do and see anything they wanted me to—but that, too, was unfair. No one at any time interfered in any way with my random wanderings around Peking (though it tended to be a very different matter outside). On the contrary, I was loaded with suggestions and help of every kind—except the kind they had no power to give: the gift of speech. So long as the Mandarin language remained Greek to me, then I had to seek out the aid of the helpful young interpreters, and if they chanced to have a Foreign Office connection on the side, then that was part of the game we daily played.

It was delightful that the chief seat of Asian anti-imperialism should be the Imperial City. The thought of that cheered many dismal days for me, when it seemed that nothing would ever make sense. It put the thing in order; it hinted at the frustration of a new China, violently grasping at the future, which could still not wholly forget that the rejected past was not only feudal and reactionary but uncommonly beautiful too, and that the old tyrants had a good eye for a summerhouse. . . . For Peking was still enchanting to the eye as few of the world's great cities are, in spite of the new cranes and derricks, in spite of the strident hortatory billboards ("We Shall Liberate Taiwan!" they said, and "Comrades, Work Only for Peace!"). Why does one say "in spite" of a thing one must find unexceptional? They were encircling Peking with new building of surpassing starkness, punctuated with some outstanding horrors. The new Government blocks in the Tien An Men Avenue were of a barren ugliness so striking that even hardened Party cadres winced and averted their eyes. The sight of an eight-storied building topped automatically by a little fluted pagoda roof was an almost pathetic illustration of the Chinese dilemma, living on two planes at once—the dialectical materialists who yet could not restrain themselves from building little ceramic monsters on the rooftrees to scare away the devils.

Outside the city walls, the new Peking rose almost before your eyes. The pace of building was, unless you watched it yourself, unbelievable—by Asian standards, supernatural. The Chinese delegates who went to Geneva returned to find that four new hospitals, six factories and eleven full-scale ministerial blocks had been laid out, started, completed, and inhabited during the time it had taken them to divide up Viet-Nam—a matter of weeks. Wherever you looked was a back cloth of scaffolding, slashed diagonally by great conveyor ramps; it looked like a city of scenic railways—a roller-coaster museum. As you watched this beelike construction, with its uncounted multitudes of workmen swarming and scurrying over the bamboo joists, manhandling great stone blocks, conveying tons of material on the end of a shoulder pole—then, indeed, you were conscious of living in a land endowed almost without limit with hands, and backs and sinews.

Yet somehow it was all invisible from within the Inner Walls; behind those great red barricades the silence fell as it always did around the architectural fancies with the strange reflective names. . . .

"China looks ahead," said the *People's Daily*, "forsaking the feudal roots of an unconstructive past. . . ."

Within the walls the Administrative Bureaus and Protected Places of the Communist State remain officially listed:

The Gate of the Meridian. The River of Gold. The Gates of Supreme, Middle, and Prosperous Harmony. The Palace of Exalted Harmony. The Palace of Military Glory, and that of Perfect Peace. The Gate of Unity Within Harmony. The Palace of Literary Distinction. The Palace Where One Honors the Masters. The Separate Palaces of Intellectual Honor, of Powerful Fertility, of Earthly Tranquillity, of Purity in Affection. The Separate Palaces of the Southward View, of Celestial Favor, and of Normal Delights. The Gate for the Distribution of Rewards. The Gate of Quietude in Old Age. The Palace in Which One Gives Thanks for the Birth of Sons. The Pavilion of Melodious Sounds, and the Tower in Which One Finds Truth. The Pavilion of the Jade Shell, and the Wells of the Precious Concubine. The Palace of the Passing of Time. The Pavilion of Favorable Winds, the Pavilion of the Danger of Fire, and the Pavilion of Vigor in Old Age. The Palace of the Ultimate Certainty of Reasonable Happiness. The Palace of the Cultivation of Serene Character. The Palace of Supreme Elegance. The Pavilion of the Public Well-being. The Gate of Mixed Harmonies. . . .

The Forbidden City itself is now a park, or museum, open to anyone with five hundred *yuan* to spare—at the rate of twenty-three thousand to the dollar, not a ruinous toll for the place that once cost so many earlier visitors their necks.

Outside, in the great wide avenue, the little policemen wear red megaphones for shouting at people ("The lady comrade with the basket is asking to be run down if she continues to ignore the crossing!" . . . "That scandalous pedicab driver will be in trouble unless he keeps to his right!") over the endless racket of bells and horns and the resounding expectorations. There were new red buses from Hungary and great black Zim limousines from Russia, and Skodas from Czechoslovakia, and Warzwas from Poland, and glossy Buicks and Packards from somewhere or other that no one could ever quite remember—but some were only a year old.

The superb Tien An Men—the Gate of Heavenly Peace—now wore its peace with indifference, in the form of Picasso's dove; it was everywhere, completely replacing the dragon. The colossal slogan across the gate said, "Long Live the Unity of the People's Republics," and somehow the beautiful elaborate characters took the curse off the arid phrase. The byways—Fine Spirit Street, or the Street of the Happy Phoenix—glowed and rippled with red flags. But for three thousand years red has been China's color of prosperity.

How did one reconcile anything in China? How did one equate the old lady hobbling on bound and crippled feet (the shops still sell the little triangular hooflike shoes) with the pig-tailed tomboy driving the streetcar? The Street of the Lantern Makers—crawling with miniature dealers in everything, from cabbages and goldfish to violins and aphrodisiacs, caged linnets and pictures of J.V.Stalin—with the State Shops and People's Stores? In the once-European street that was called Morrison Street (and is now most sensitively called "Former Morrison Street") the Co-operatives have taken over from the silk shops of the old White Russians, but you can still turn a corner and buy a costly speck of the *jing-pen* root for longevity, "for the enduring upstanding of the Sex"; or you can buy a cricket in a cage, or a gong to play at weddings, or a vast carved and colored coffin like an inlaid man-o'-war. How did one equate the Revolutionary State with its own Capitalists' Association? How did one square Chinese individualism with the extravagant fact that three times a day the radio shouted all over town and everyone stopped in the street for those fifteen minutes' PT?

The shopkeeper was selling an electric computing machine—but he reckoned the bill on a bead abacus. The Street Leader was a Party cadre from away back, but she lived in a house with a board across the door to keep the devils out. Wherever one looked were the posters: "We Must Fight for Taiwan!" and "Long Live Peace!" What was the answer to that?

One talked literature in salons plastered with red stars—how did one identify those kindly scholarly theoreticians with the dark and terrible events of 1950? Above all, how did one reconcile this virile and apparently happy people, who were cultivated when the Russians wore skins and the British, blue paint, with the dreary unpersuasive platitudes of the Communist written word?

You did not, of course. What you did was cling desperately to your reservations, keep your brain from reeling at the overload of information and spend uncounted hours in People's Ministries in search of one unchallengeable fact, make friends and influence no one, respect the many good things you could see and reflect on the other things that you could not, and thank God for bedtime.

Everyone had said that China would be a mystery on two formidable levels at once: the enigma of democracy imposed on the labyrinthine processes of the East—it would be a proposition far too tortuous to resolve in less than a lifetime. All this turned out to be true; I cannot imagine why I did not resent it more. I decided that in Peking I had access to everything—except of course the simple things. Soon, I thought, I should be able to present the perplexed story of the new China with statistics so lucidly exposed that they convinced no one, with conclusions so elegantly balanced that they changed around with every new persuasion.

"You will naturally never get near anyone," they had told me, or "Nobody gets within sight of the top men," they said, and "For obvious reasons, the Administration seldom reveals itself." There were so many friends who, having secured the Soviet visa that I had not, had roosted in the plush Edwardian comfort of Moscow's Nationale Hotel and never clapped eyes on anyone over the rank of undersecretary. It was worse than England, everyone said.

I bore this in mind, therefore, coming in over the glorious roofs of the city in a very new Russian-built, Chinese-manned version of the DC-3, having no idea that within a few hours of touching down I should see Mao Tse-Tung *and* Chou En-Lai, and not only them but Kruschev from Moscow, and Bulganin and Shvernik, with Beirut of Poland and Kim Il Sung from North Korea, and indeed all the leaders of every People's Democracy on the Cominform list; in fact possibly the entire top level of the Communist world.

Lest it be thought, however, that the most luminous existing galaxy of Marxists had turned out to a man to welcome me to Peking, it has to be said that in those sociable days in which China celebrated her Revolution it was extremely hard *not* to be at least partially surrounded by the godlings of the new order. October began in Peking with a superb extravagance; it was the observation of a holy rite, the sanctification and endorsement of those extraordinary years that had transformed China from a vast dinosaur of a country into—whatever this was; something enormously exciting and oddly depressing, admirable and challenging, neurotic and friendly and hostile all at once.

Very soon it became clear to me why I had been brought with such tremendous haste across the world to Peking: it was to be present at the Big Parade. When this dawned upon me I was inclined to be slightly resentful. I had not argued and agitated for so long to be admitted into China as an independent being in order to assist at the least characteristic of her public observances; I am not a fanatical amateur of public ceremonies, and this lunatic scramble across the earth in order to watch a military fiesta filled me with a sudden pettish desire to have nothing whatever to do with it. In China, however, these wayward attitudes are neither understood nor condoned. The dawning of the First of October found me up, and shaved, and clad, with a watchful comrade at my side; an hour later found me standing in my appointed position among what seemed to be about three quarters of the population of the world.

As it turned out, the procession was phenomenal.

I am no hand at describing such things. I have seen them almost everywhere in the world where they take place, and without enthusiasm. I have a personal, and probably psychologically revealing, distaste for men walking in parallel rows; I have no love of multitudes; I try very hard to equate a theoretical affection for humanity with a very practical dread of swarms, which of course leads to commonplace but troublesome conflicts. If there is one engagement that lowers me *aux bas fonds* quicker than another, it is standing inside one crowd while another crowd tramps past. However. . . .

Somehow this was different.

Not in content or in purpose; only in method. The October March was as tremendous a demonstration of the old upon the new as, I dare say, was ever produced. It is not impossible that this was the biggest crowd of human beings ever assembled anywhere on earth. As I stood there, watching this unbelievable profusion of people plodding by—singing, playing, marching, dancing, offering every manifestation of the public human's behavior—there was a sudden, rather terrifying mental flashback to the old childhood analogy: if all the living Chinese should march past a given spot, they would *never* stop, so endless is their number. . . . There were moments, here in Peking, when I felt with an abrupt alarm that this was exactly what was going to happen. One saw this colossal mass receding out of the avenue, out of the city, receding into the gigantic secret hinterland of a Gargantuan country, six million people revived and consolidated by some magic that few of us, at the moment, could either understand or share. . . . For a little while it was necessary to retreat into all manner of personal memories and fantasies to avoid being visually overwhelmed. They might find, with a numbing, well-schooled horror, that they had set into motion something that indeed *couldn't* stop. . . .

Obviously, nothing of the kind. The huge and intricate production was due to start at ten and finish at three. It started at ten, and it finished at three. All the illimitable Chinese in the world stayed at home, pounding their water wheels and scratching at their paddies. Here in Peking was merely, as they most carefully refrained from calling it, the greatest show on earth—half a million people, watched at some point or other on the route by something like another three million; everything one had ever seen multiplied by three.

To this extraordinary concentration of people the Minister of Defense, Peng Teh Luan, made an opening address. He gave thanks, he said, for the easing of international tension since the armistice in Korea and the cease fire in Indo-China. "But," he solemnly added, "one unfinished task remains for the Chinese Army. This is the liberation of Taiwan. It shall be the glorious duty of our people to free Taiwan from the American Imperialists and the traitorous clique of Chiang Kai-Shek. I give you these orders," he said, his words crackling from the loud-speakers throughout a Peking which, perhaps for the only time in a year, was almost supernaturally still; "from now on hold yourselves constantly, and hourly, prepared for combat."

These were disturbing words for me, who felt singularly vulnerable to threats and was, moreover, in no situation, as it seemed, to regard these challenging attitudes with composure. If Peng Teh Luan meant what he professed to mean, I thought, then I have come a remarkably long way in order to arrange for myself a wholly inextricable position. I was to adjust myself later to this endless third-act rhetoric; one lived forever on the edge of this sort of crisis. Familiarity made it no more satisfactory, but after a while one became numbed. The day will surely come, of course, when some successor of mine in just such a position will emerge from the anesthetic just a moment too late.

Meanwhile, there was something to see that could scarcely be seen elsewhere. For hours, then, the Chinese paraded every aspect of their manifestly growing resources, in iron and steel and flesh and blood. There were, inevitably, the twin emphases on the great contemporary paradox: the demonstration of might beside the call for peace —the great *pons asinorum* of the time, the contemporary rationalization so blandly shared by both contending sides. There were, therefore, the big battalions and the dancing girls with fans; the rumbling heavy tanks and the endless ranks of workers waving olive branches; the four-engined bombers and the screaming Migs high over the vast fluttering multitude of doves, suddenly and symbolically released above the soldiers, trailing silk banners with the double message: "No More War!" and "Taiwan!"

Probably no city anywhere had a better tribune for such a show than the superb Tien An Men, the Gate of Heavenly Peace that stood so dramatically—that colossal ponderous grace, that delicate gross immovability—at the entrance to the Forbidden City. It was arguable whether the sublime proportion of its blood-red walls and the imperceptibly subtle curl of its tiled and sculptured roof was improved by the enormous portrait of Chairman Mao— but it was that they had come to cheer, not the elegance of the Imperial Gate; that, and the tiny round speck high above the picture, which was Chairman Mao himself, benign and bland, the eternal uncle of this strange, new, wonderful and awful world.

I was placed, with a rather chilling aptness, in the Minorities Section, among the Mongolians and Tibetans, who looked very rakish and liberated and who smelt most terribly of garlic. There were also Koreans and a squad of the Chinese People's Liberation Army. I shared a step with a bemedaled veteran of about thirty who, doubtless, had helped to chase me out of Seoul some years before. There was also a posse of Russian women soldiers, very blonde and booted. It is perhaps pertinent to remark here that the only Russian women I ever encountered in China who were worth pursuing even across a street were in the army; a striking contrast to one's experience in, for example, one's own country.

Even the Soviet celebrities on the mammoth tribune looked somehow subdued and muted by the performance below. I am readily prepared to believe that there have been bigger military processions—as I say, I am an unreliable judge—but the drilling was of a fabulous accuracy; even the tiny Mongol ponies of the cavalry trotted precisely in step, like an articulated clockwork toy. The tanks and rocket launchers crawled deafeningly below and the aircraft howled overhead; at intervals the doves and balloons spattered a random pattern across the sky; there was even a section of elastic-driven model airplanes that climbed and buzzed and stalled among the banners. The whole thing may have been contrived and spurious, but it has to be said that it did not look it.

There were hours of it—because after the People's Army there came the People's People: tens of thousands of the new aristocracy, workers at this and at that, unions and federations, trades and associations; gigantic pictures of everyone from Chairman himself to Stalin and Lenin and Gorki and all the unidentifiable Balkan patriots with pursed-up, querulous expressions and small mustaches; vast teams of drummers and dancers and artistes with what was happily named the "walking fan"—beguiling and beautiful tapestries of pastel colors among the steel gray, everything brutal leavened by something almost fey; only too suggestive of the dilemma of our times.

It may be hard to believe, but at one point there was, for Revolution's Day, a section of Roman Catholic nuns, with a banner saying, "Christians for Democracy!" and—to stretch credulity until it creaks—a group among the "minorities" labeled the "New Chinese Capitalists' Associ-

ation," behind the huge characters which read "Long
Live Private Enterprise in the Glorious Revolution"—at
which point it has to be confessed that I for one surrendered my grip on reality, standing pop-eyed among the
Tibetans.

"Ho Ping Wan Tsei!" shouted the tens of thousands
of soldiers and miners and factory workers and peasants
and little children—"Long Live Peace!"—and the monstrous banners marched endlessly by, saying, "Taiwan
Must Be Ours!" Another great cloud of multicolored balloons climbed upwards, drifted to the west, high over the
curved and colored walls of the Imperial City. The high
anointed of the Communist world waved and bowed for
the last time and disappeared behind the walls, but the
crowds kept moving on through the streets of Peking, on
and on; when dark came the fireworks soared and rattled
in the sky, and the crowds began to dance. All through
the evening they danced, while the rockets sprinkled the
night with colored stardust and the politicians retreated:
once a year, the people of Peking in their good blue suits,
celebrating the age of uniformity by becoming people once
again.

(3)

Under the Roofs

I LIVED in an establishment rather grandly called the Press Club, a three-storied building in a side street off the Hata Men Road, of such extreme newness that my friend Shen, who conducted me there from the airport, expressed a mild surprise at finding it there at all. When he had last passed that way, he said, that part of the Pei Chi Ko had been a vacant lot. To be sure, that had been some weeks before. That was the way things were going on these days in Peking, said Shen, never one to miss the opportunity of making a valid point.

Newness, however, did not imply opulence. It would have taken more than the few days it had been in existence to have mellowed the austere lineaments of the Press Club, which at first sight had aspects suggestive of a railway-station waiting room, the municipal offices of some English provincial town, and a rather up-to-date monastery, combining the less convivial characteristics of all three. It was not at first sight a place where one would linger in some splendid leather easy chair beside the fire, with whisky and soda to hand and a copy of *The Times* on one's knee. The chairs were, in fact, built of some unresilient material resembling concrete and covered with green serge; in place of a fire were radiators capable only of outrageous extremes, now casting a glacial chill, now burning like a furnace. For the whisky and soda it was possible to substitute a ferocious and corrosive Chinese vodka, and for *The Times* there was either the *People's Daily*—which, being in Chinese, had serious limitations as a diversion—or a selection of illustrated Russian magazines portraying illimitable and apparently identical groups of lady welders in dedicated attitudes and with faraway, confident smiles.

It was not, in short, a very clubbable club.

However, one would need to be unambitious indeed to spend one's time in the Press Club. The beds were excellent; the best in China. It does not occur to the energetic builders of new China to build bathrooms into their latest hotels, so we soon fell into the habit of marching up and down corridors to communal ablutions reminiscent of an army mess. Moreover the Chinese had not forgotten that a press club would be used by the press; they had established downstairs a branch of the Foreign Office information section, which worked admirably, and a telegraph and cable office which—once one grew adjusted to the formality of identifying oneself by documents five times a day to the young woman operative who greeted one most cordially by name—worked with an efficiency that can only be called superb.

There was, as I may have occasion to mention again, no censorship.

In these circumstances I lived for some time in the most welcome and good companionship of my two friends, fellow space-travelers in this mysterious world, fellow Western guinea pigs in this Chinese experiment in professional coexistence—Zig, the Frenchman, and Bill, from Canada. I could scarcely have been better served for colleagues. But for one another's presence, none of us would have done any work at all.

From time to time we would be joined by other drifting groups from overseas—a handful of Indonesians, a large and compact body of Japanese, monuments of zeal and industry; they would appear abruptly round corners in unexpected places—the Summer Palace, the Temple of Heaven, the Ministry of Agriculture, a nursery; they wore their caps back to front in a rather dashing way and carried small expensive cameras with which they unremittingly photographed each other. There were some Indians, who took profuse notes about everything in enormous exercise books. There was, for all too brief a time, an extremely pretty girl photographer from some Communist magazine in Paris; she was immovably escorted by a handsome, somber welterweight whose suspicions, one felt, went deeper than politics. Sooner or later they would disappear, all of them; they were always guests or delegates, and however much closer a rapport that gave them with their hosts, we maintained a perverse sense of privilege in that we were not.

Life was both eased and complicated by the conscientious help of our Chinese colleagues. The senior members of the group, either from the Government or the All-China Journalists' Federation (a distinction perhaps academic), were courteous, helpful, efficient and, in at least one or two cases, genuinely friendly. The varying and opposing temperaments of the squad of interpreters was a matter of great fascination to me, and will come up in the proper sequence. But these experts were served at a lower level by a bureau most misleadingly called "Information," which was staffed by a little group of young men who constituted one of the most serious hazards of the trip. Few people in the world could have been more well-meaning. It is difficult to imagine any who could have been more ineffectual. Their desire to please was in directly inverse ratio to their powers of expression. It was they who were generally charged with the task of liaison between ourselves and whoever was in charge of the day's events. On some principle hard to determine it had been decided that they could speak English. It was, moreover, apparent that they did in fact know *how* to—it was just that they could never actually *do* it. It led to situations of desperate frustration.

At given intervals the phone would ring. "Is—that —Mister—Kamalloh?" With a sinking heart I would recognize the Information, who would ask if I were going to such-and-such a place that day, and who would proceed to put the question. "I—must—inform—you. The—programme—for—the—day—shall—be—as—follows." This could take up to several minutes, but there was no way of interrupting it, nor could the formula of the phrases be interfered with. The slightest interjection would throw the poor young man completely out of his stride; it would then be necessary for him to begin again. "I—must —inform—you. The—programme——" until the introductory bars had come to their predestined conclusion. "There—will—be—a—demonstration—of—glass— polishing (or shuttle-shifting, or tube-blowing, or whatever it chanced to be)—at—fifteen—thirty. If—interested— will—gather—in—lobby . . ." and so on. It was harrowing; one felt as great a sympathy for Information as for oneself. Sometimes it would entail a disappointment: "We aren't going to the People's Court after all?" But Information would say, "Yes, yes!" Many were the fatiguing misunderstandings until one caught on to the meaning of the Oriental positive-negative, which is, "Yes—you're right; we aren't going."

There were times when one felt that *nothing* was ever going to happen; in those early days—when, I expect, our presence was so novel and the nature of our requests so unusual—life seemed to be an endless procession of concentric circles. There was nothing extraordinary in this for anyone who knew something of Asia; in the end things began to move with an expedition that left one breathless.

There were whimsies, too. One day an Indian correspondent had complained—a little overzealously, we thought—that some item of news had been kept from the denizens of the Press Club until some hours after it had been released to the Tass Agency. The complaint was noted gravely. That night, or rather shortly after three the next morning, every living inhabitant of the establishment was aroused from sleep, instructed urgently to dress and be ready to attend the Foreign Office forthwith. I scrambled dazedly into my clothes with a growing and rather horrified apprehension; I could think of nothing that could have happened of such great emergency other than the final one; through my mind flashed a detailed memory of the thousand posters I had seen demanding the liberation of Taiwan. As we were formally ushered into cars and driven through the black streets, I considered with some melancholy the alternative prospects before me: ten years in a Manchurian internment camp, or a job as war correspondent on the Amoy front; no two possibilities had ever struck me as more repellent.

When we reached the Foreign Office numbers of solemn people were sitting about in the hunched, disordered attitudes of people aroused from sleep. We waited twenty minutes, sipping scalding tea. Then at last a very senior member of the staff entered with a sheet of foolscap paper, and proceeded to read out a wholly trivial and tiresome item of intelligence about a new railway.

When this was done, the officer rose brightly, thanked

us for our assistance, and closed the meeting. As she went, she said, "As you see, this is issued *simultaneously* to Tass."

Whether this elaborate—and, on reflection, not unfunny—performance was offered as a reproof or merely as a *jeu d'esprit* is one of the things one was unlikely ever to find out. It threw an interesting light on the Chinese official character. But as we drove shivering back to our tousled beds the Indian cut a sheepish figure.

Nor, however, was that all. We had not been in bed another hour before once again the establishment was invaded by groups of official messengers, who knocked on everyone's door, entered everyone's room, switched on everyone's light, and politely laid on everyone's bed table a copy of the official, verbatim version of the meaningless railway story we had just heard.

It occurred to me then that it was perhaps possible to underrate the tongue-tied personnel of Information.

Information, too, was responsible for the provision of passes, and accreditation cards, entailing the production of untold numbers of photographs and the signature of multitudes of forms. Here again everything was done to ease the way for us; Information himself would fill in the forms. Since he then had to ask us the questions, and translate the answers, this made the process not more than eight times longer than it might otherwise have been. To leave the city in any direction—even to visit the nearby Western Hills, or the Ming Tombs—required a permit, the permit in turn requiring, for some unfathomable reason, the repeated registration of such facts as that my telephone number, during the daylight hours, was London Central 5000.

A characteristic day in the Press Club was compounded of all these things.

But there was so much to see, to absorb, in this superb city that very soon the administrative mazes did not matter. To walk around the streets was a perpetual pleasure—a visual delight, in its curious way a social delight; after the blank clinging stares of India, the persistent curiosity of Siam, the edgy resentful glances of Indonesia, there was something uncommonly civilized about the casual acceptance of Peking. If they were interested, they looked; if they were not, they didn't; and when you caught an eye, it usually smiled. I lived not far from the Tung Tan—the Eastern Market; there was endless diversion in its crowded alleys, its stalls of junk and charm and sensible clothes, with the little stick of incense smoldering on the counters. Nothing was very dear, nothing was noticeably cheap; for almost everything that could be considered a necessity prices were roughly on a par with those of the outer fringes of London. Now and again one bought something, fetching from the pocket a shapeless tattered wad of disintegrating thousand-*yuan* notes— three thousand for an exercise book or a small cigar: ten cents.

There were some odd aberrations: although you could see at a glance the absence of imports, the home-made character of everything consumable, there would be, among the great variety of Chinese-manufactured cigarettes, one package manifestly designed to resemble Camels (only with an elephant); things like tomato sauce and razor blades had labels clearly copied from European counterparts. There were alleys of book dealers, exhibiting for once not the collected works of J.V.Stalin and Mao Tse-Tung, but English books—solid editions in decaying morocco, the relics of some old library liberated from a vanished diplomat or a dispossessed Old China Hand, queer memorials to other people's taste: *The Bird Life of*

Southern Hampshire, How To Make a Crystal Set; War
wick Deeping, Wells. On a front shelf, plain to see between a dog-eared Mrs. Beeton and Mediterranean
Baroque, was the title: *Red Hands, the Menace of Communism.*

Sometimes it grew very difficult.

Then one would walk back along Former Morrison
Street and look at the pedicab drivers—long rows of
them, reclining on the back seats of their vehicles with
every appearance of relaxation, smoking very small pipes
with very long stems, engaging in desultory arguments
among themselves, or merely lying back in a gentle stupor. The pedicab drivers of Peking appeared to represent
the final redoubt of complete professional individualism
in the city; they were private enterprise at its most private
and rugged. As a group they were very far from the silent
dignified Chinese of the legends. In appearance they were
superbly ruffianly and *dégagé*; they had escaped regimen-
tation in a fashion that was clearly not accidental. They
were probably the only adult people in Peking who did
not wear the uniform blue suit. On the contrary, they
had equipped themselves with the most elaborately various sets of padded rags from undetectable sources. On
their heads they wore old trilbies, cloth caps, huge helmets of rabbit fur, and, more often than not, a simple
cloth of quite exceptional filthiness which, when not
serving as a turban, was useful for sundry incidental purposes: cleaning the back axle, blowing the nose, wiping
the brow, wrapping up the steam-bread for lunch, dusting
off the seat for any passenger held to be sufficiently fas-
tidious.

What would possibly have surprised a Peking native
most, however, was the fact that, independent as they
seemed to be, they now worked to a very meticulous rule:

a map of the city hung at each stand, divided into colored areas which denoted the accepted and accurate fare. There was no bargaining.

But if the pedicab drivers were a variegated lot, their machines were infinitely more so. It would scarcely be possible to imagine that vehicles so broken down, so patched up, so intricately held together by bits of string and old wire, could be capable of another day's service. It seemed that the policy of the Government was explicit in this matter. The profusion of pedicabs in China was undesirable from every point of view. On the other hand, the elimination of the profession would abruptly throw many thousands of untrained men into the urban labor market. They could be absorbed, but only gradually. On the other hand again, the anarchical spirit of the pedicab driver prevented his going voluntarily into industry. Therefore, the Government was deliberately allowing the pedicab business to drop, like the pedicabs themselves, to bits. No more spare parts were issued.

The machines, then, were by this time holding together by guess and by God, and quite a few were *in extremis*. One day I was riding down the Tien An Men Avenue beside Bill (and there is no more satisfactory or companionable form of city travel) when my chain broke. On swerving to avoid us, the other rickshaw braked. His wheels fell off. There was a faint ripple of applause from the passers-by. The pedicab drivers pushed their wreckage to the roadside, sat down on the curb, lit their pipes, and continued their discussion where it had been interrupted.

In a pedicab you had still to direct your driver in the classic geographical sense. China has no "left" nor "right"; you had to say "*Wang tung!*" which is "Go East," or "*Wang Pei!*" which is "Go North."

The Chinese geography has five cardinal points: North, South, East, West, and Middle. The Chinese call their country *Ching Kuo*, which means "The Middle Country." They say this is because they are *in* the middle, and because they take the middle way. That has not latterly been true, but that is what they say.

One searches for the one adjective that would describe the Chinese character—not the cadre's character, or the politician's character. One is driven always back to the word that has been used for so long—for the pedicab drivers who sit down in the street, for the officials who get you up in the middle of the night because you asked for it—*reasonable*. I suppose, the Chinese are a *reasonable* people. I wonder for how long.

When all else failed there was always food.

I suppose that by now everything has been said and written that could be said or written about the endless pleasures and mysteries of the classic Chinese kitchen. I do not propose to add much to the already vast and occasionally sentimental bibliography of this only too-rewarding subject, except to say that by the time I got there you could still eat sublimely in Peking.

There is a grim temptation to elaborate a gastronomic anthology of the many wonderful eating places in China, a kind of Club des Sans-Club of Cathay. It could be done; the land is vast; there is after all no more an identifiable "Chinese food" than there is "European food." Peking cooking does not resemble Cantonese cooking; neither of them has much in common with the food of Hunan or Szechuan. I have had to eat a half-tortoise with sea slugs in Shanghai, and a dish of curried frogs in Shao-San. There exists no such thing as chop suey. Rice is a separate course almost everywhere, and traditionally a signal for a toast (as indeed what is not). There is a special fish in the Southwest which, when served towards the end of a meal, means "Let's start again," because the fish's name is a homonym for the word "more." There is a restaurant in Peking where the soya sauce is served in old Coca-Cola bottles. I have a friend who invented a pair of *hollow* chopsticks, to save having to bother with a spoon for his soup. The only aperitif known to China is tea.

And I traveled seven thousand miles through China without ever once meeting with a dish that in any way resembled anything I had ever seen produced in Europe as "Chinese food."

On the fourth day there my other friend, Li Ping, took me to a Muslim restaurant. Theirs was held to be very famous and desirable local food, because it resembled Chinese food even less than anything else. So we went to the most celebrated of all, called "Kao Jou Wan," which means "Roast Meat Man." It was recognizable by a phrase from the Koran over the door; the liquid Arabic script looked curious and rather sensual among the elaborate Chinese characters. The door was tightly shut.

"Extraordinary," said my friend. "It must be Friday." But it was Monday, and it is fair to add that although I returned on many subsequent occasions to Roast Meat Man, I never once found a day when the establishment was open, though my friends were repeatedly coming back to me with entrancing stories of its excellences.

So we hurried some distance to another restaurant, similarly protected by the Koran, which was called "You I Shun," meaning "Another Going Smoothly." It was by the Hsuan Wu Men, or Gate for the Promotion of the Military Sense, so called because it balances another, the Ch'ung Wen Men, or Gate for the Respect of Culture. It is part of the Chinese gastronomic tradition that the worth of an eating house is basically assessed by the unpretentious squalor of its outside appearance, on the sound principle that the better a restaurant is, the more will its fittings have been knocked about. On this basis, the establishment of Another Going Smoothly was the La Pérouse of Peking; from the outside it resembled a truckman's diner in the English Midlands that had fallen upon evil days; almost wholly without charm of any kind.

The excellences of this restaurant challenge description. It was what was known as a "fire-pot" house, where one ate *shuan yang jou,* which meant "instant-boiled mutton." The fire pot itself was placed on the table; it could be defined as a shallow round bowl with a charcoal-burning chimney through its center, or perhaps more accurately as a sort of conical kiln surrounded by a trough. It was of a design most awkward to define in words, though wholly satisfying in appearance; the principle behind it was to keep this round trough of water boiling hard. All around were cooks at wooden tables, slicing legs of mutton into wafer-thin rashers. What seemed to be a quite excessive amount of this sliced meat was placed before us. A waiter produced the ingredients for mixing the sauce; his tray was a wonderful sight, like a painter's palette: scarlet pepper sauce, brown shrimp oil, green minced leeks, bean-curd cheese, hemp-seed paste. We ladled these things into our bowls in varying proportions; the permutations of these flavors could produce a sauce either bland or immensely piquant. The meal then began.

It was simplicity itself. One took the slices of mutton in one's chopsticks, held them momentarily in the bubbling pot, plunged them into the sauce to cool and flavor them, and ate them. There may be more delicious ways of preparing mutton, but I have never met with them anywhere. Nor do I know of a more convivial fashion of dining—the group around the circular table, the comfortable warmth from the burnished bronze fire pot, the gentle hiss and bubble of the water, the reaching around for some especially attractive sliver of meat, some additional dash of flavor from the bowls of sauces. About halfway through the meal someone arrived with plates of sliced cabbage and spinach, squares of bean curd and transparent green-pea noodles; these were hurled into the boiling water, which by now had become a rich and splendid mutton stock. When we had finished all the meat, we ladled this magnificent liquid into our bowls: it was a pungent and rewarding soup.

Around the bare wooden walls of the room hung old pictures of reflective and peaceful scenes, embellished with legends done in characters of even greater beauty. "The essence of literary peace can be described as the grace of a fish in a pond." "Tranquillity is the silence of a piece of jade, still undiscovered in the heart of the hills." "The breeze sighing through the bamboo rolls up the empty autumn in the cloth of the year"—gentle or even vapid pieces of imagery, but beautifully done, and most sympathetic to the process of fire-pot eating.

The cost of this incomparably delightful meal, expressed in Western money, was about twelve cents, for each person.

There were many such meals. There were also others in the more familiar Chinese style, infallibly good, and occasionally superb. They left, as Chinese food has always left, one lasting mystery unexplained. The Chinese though at their best with vegetables, are great carnivores too, yet in a strange sense. Whenever they killed a sheep, or a pig, I would ask myself, what *happened* to it? I knew what happened to the tripes and the lungs and the viscera and the feet: one ate them; one also ate, in variously pleasant forms, the hearts and the livers and the testicles and the brains. What one could never discover was the Chinese process for the disposal of the *flesh*. Outside the Muslim eating places one encountered no recognizable meat, in the recognizable European sense. There was one noted establishment in Peking, specializing in pork, where one was said to eat one's way through a pig from the tip of its tail to the end of its snout—and very good it was, but at no stage in this gross process did one find much more solid than entrails and curiously shaped organs; it was, I found, best to inquire the nature of each dish some time after completing it.

The exception to all this rather allusive eating was the traditional meal that no one in Peking can escape nor should ever wish to: the Peking Duck.

At the risk of being momentarily semiprecious on a more or less recondite matter, I feel I should at least outline the great qualities of this meal; there will be others who will follow in happier days to Peking without, I fear, any better mock-Michelin than this. I must say, therefore, that it is necessary to make a reservation at the restaurant Fong Tze Yuen (translated, since this time I was with my French interpreter—a nice touch!—as the "Jardin Richement Favoré") in a magnificently elaborate alley known most casually as Mei Shih Chien, or the Coal Merchants' Street. There one eats Peking Duck at its best, and its best is quite exceptional.

The party must not be for more than twelve people —not because there is any ritual or superstitious significance in thirteen, but because the circular Chinese table can accommodate a dozen; its circumference is considered exactly proper for that number. There are few other niceties. It is important to remember that the chief guest must be seated directly facing the door. It is even more important to remember, after pouring the tea, that on no account must the teapots be returned to the table with their spouts facing one another—that is a quarrelsome sign, as bad as leaving one's shoes on the ground toe to toe. Otherwise the meal is a free-for-all, with courses served in an accepted sequence but thereafter to be consumed at will, and in any convenient order. I list them merely for the record.

The dinner begins with *pinh-pa*, which is, as they say, wine-food, and serves as an excuse for commencing the drinking, since it is held improper in China to drink liquor unaccompanied by food. This, on all the occasions when I enjoyed this meal, consisted curiously, but not too unpleasantly, of the feet of the duck. Divorced from their associations, these are no worse than many Western hors d'oeuvres; one does no more than play about with them in a conventional way. There follows *tcha-ya-kan*, which is the creature's liver, served scalding hot, with a powdery preparation of condiments into which to plunge it before eating; I can recommend this in any circumstances. Simultaneously arrives the *la tze-chi*, which is a spiced preparation of chicken—the one digression from the duck theme; I do not know why it is introduced always at this point, but it is; moreover it is accompanied by *tung suen shon kou*, a kind of ragout of mushrooms and bamboo shoots, the delight of which is beyond reasonable comparison. As a kind of parenthesis, there is now insinuated the *tsu-chio-yu*, or fish soup, which arrives on the table a short head in front of the evening's summit, the *chiao-ya-tze*, or lacquered duck itself. For those accustomed to the Western, or commonplace, duck, there is no adequate method of describing the satisfactions of this dish—a duck prematurely brought to fulfilment; it is no more than ninety days old but some fantastic method of concentrated upbringing has given it the stature of an Aylesbury of ripe years; it appears at the table lacquered, as its name implies, with some substances that give exceptional flavor to the really superlative part of any roasted duck, which as everyone knows is the skin. A waiter then appears with the little hatchet that is the Chinese equivalent of a carving knife and, with a series of gestures almost invisibly swift, hacks the bird into convenient morsels, which are then wrapped, with a portion of young onion, in a wafer of unleavened bread, and devoured at a mouthful. Disliking gastronomical ecstasies as I do, I can say no more than that mankind has perhaps developed no better way, so far, of consuming his servant, the duck.

Throughout this process, which takes a great deal longer than one would imagine, one is drinking *huang-chou*, the rice wine which is served from porcelain pots like tea, and tastes like a rather thin Amontillado sherry, hot. As a concession in the new social system prevailing in the country, it is necessary to propose a toast every five minutes or so. There are two varieties: For salutations of especial importance—such as toasts to guests, democracy, peace, Chairman Mao, or indeed anything else that strikes the fancy as emotionally apt—the call is *"Gam-pei!"* which, since it implies bottoms-up, demands the reversal of the wine cup after drinking. Those who maintain an attitude of prudence throughout the meal have a saving-clause expression: *"sui-bien."* This means "As you wish to take it," and permits of a token sip; it is considered to be rather caddish until at least three quarters through the meal.

The meal finishes—or so they say; there are not many authentic records—with *pinh tan lian tze*, which is a dessert made of lotus seeds. It also finishes with *mao-tai*, the formidable spirit made from sorghum, or *bai-gar*, which is a coarser and even more lethal variety of the same thing.

Wherever it may be found, it rates three stars.

There was a great deal of hospitality of this kind.

Between meals—indeed several times a day— I made an earnest and considered effort to grasp the details of the contemporary situation in China, the results of which may appear in the more evidently painstaking parts of this book. These cultural efforts were devoted to many ends, but took invariably the same form.

Early in the morning the telephone would ring; it would be Information, presenting the program in his usual relentless formula: "It—is—arranged—that . . ." And in a little while one would be conducted to this or that Ministry, or Group Headquarters; they were all indistinguishable in appearance. It would be a room that had clearly never in any circumstances been used for any purpose other than conferences or interviews. The furniture would be of the kind normally acquired in America for a modest down payment; there would be a glass-topped table for each chair, equipped with a newly opened packet of Tien An Men cigarettes, which were excellent, and a tall cup of fragrant tea, which was also excellent. The official in question would receive one with every evidence of pleasure, which is a great deal more than one could say of similar encounters elsewhere; he would sit down and, through the interpreter, ask for questions.

When the question was asked, the official would

nod, and note it down, and wait. One of the eccentricities of these meetings was the fact that questions were never answered as they were put; it was the practice to have *all* the questions put first, and all the answers delivered in a string at the end. This I took at first to be a shrewd way of evading supplementaries, until I found that they welcomed supplementaries just the same; it was merely one of many inexplicable aspects of the Oriental technique.

After a while, however, I found that the inextricable similarity of these meetings numbed and confused me to the point where I would sit in a sort of trance, arousing myself with a start, desperately seeking for some clue that would tell me whether I was listening to the Minister of Waterworks or the Chef de Protocol. The words droned on, practiced, fluent, hypnotic, Chinese, pausing for a moment here and there for translation, which itself was compounded, whatever the context, in phrases of such timeworn familiarity that they were equally applicable anywhere. I would wake in the morning obsessed with the necessity of being alert and gleaning from the day's collection of platitudes some crumb of novel information. As time went on it became more and more difficult until, after several weeks, I found myself falling into a profound sleep the moment the conversation began, while my fingers deceitfully kept up a kind of twitching movement over the paper, simulating the taking of notes. I recognize that this is a shameful thing to confess, excusable only by virtue of the fact that all the information imparted at these sessions was readily available in printed literature; the valuable things were acquired elsewhere.

The question of sleep, of course, haunted this expedition as it has haunted every other for many years. For some reason doubtless buried in an undesirable subconscious, I find sleep easy only in the most unfortunate and inconvenient circumstances—in the rear seats of cars that are being driven through scenery of incomparable magnificence; in the presence of extremely important people whose favor I have been at great pains to cultivate; at the final stages of banquets where it is imperative that I produce a good impression. The one situation where I find sleep eludes me completely is at night, in bed. I have tried to remedy this by every means available to me, without any really satisfactory result; it is not, I think, the fault of medical science but of my own technique in using it. There are, of course, pills. I have been a careful dilettante of the several delightful soporifics, with no especial success—it was my experience that unless I consumed them in a really alarming quantity they would not *send* me to sleep; they would only *keep* me there. After a hearty nightcap of these sinister capsules I would lie in an alert and vigorous wakefulness until about half past five. I would then doze—at which point the pills would seize their opportunity and hold me fiercely under, so that the morning would find me in a stupor from which I could barely extricate myself. To some people these devices are saviors; to me they are jackals, not daring to strike me low, but awaiting their chance to tie me down.

This is an especially tiresome situation in remote places, at the time when the first novelty has worn off, for those who can find no particular reason to stay and who sometimes feel, in those white nights in the hotel room, with the tap that drips like a clock and the desolate taxi hooting in the street below, that there was not much to return for either.

The mornings were better. True, the Press Club was favored by the presence, immediately outside the courtyard, of a musical academy, the students of which were under some compulsion to start work in the very early hours. For those who have never greeted the dawn to the accompaniment of the *erh hu*, or two-stringed Chinese violin, the *san hsien* guitar, and the common or garden saxophone, I can only say that they have missed no particularly soothing experience.

There were also the street vendors. They, at least, were full of charm. In their established intervals the peddlers would pass up and down the street—the Noodle Man with his piercing rattle: *krrrraaa! krrraaa!* and his wailing call: *"Chieh Mien!"* the man with the sesame cakes crying, *"Chao Ping!"* and tap-tap-tapping on a minute bamboo drum; the vegetable dealer with his swinging gongs, his baskets of cabbage and lotus root, beans and sweet potatoes. They did not look very Communist. They were not very Communist. "Why should they be?" the officials used to tell me. "There is plenty of time, plenty of time."

It was in the new tradition to arrive in Peking and exclaim, "But it is *clean!*" And then to say, "But it is true —the flies *have* gone!" And the stark facts of the case were that this was indeed so; the place was *clean*—in a scrupulous and self-conscious and almost unreal way; North China was swept and brushed and dusted; people were forever scurrying about the streets picking up odds and ends, tidying things up. To throw away a cigarette end in public became a feat of considerable embarrassment; someone was always sure to whip it into a container, drawing one's attention reproachfully to one's casual, doubtless Western, disregard of decency. There were times when I went around for days with my pockets gradually filling with match ends. Similarly, then, and as part of the same *mystique*, the flies *had* disappeared. I offer this as the considered observation of one who not only knows a fly when he sees one but who has frequently spent the greater part of the year in more recognizable Asian circumstances, *very* much more than outnumbered by flies.

This, I imagine, was a by-product of the germ-warfare story (still widely discussed and, it seemed, implicitly believed). It had resulted in a state of affairs where any stray fly that somehow had evaded the primary pogrom was hounded and harried remorselessly, like an English fox in a Leicestershire field. Children in North China carried fly swatters as regularly and casually as British Guards officers carried canes.

(Yet some weeks later, in Hunan Province, I moved impulsively off the road and came upon a memorable sight: a little walled town of such insignificance, or remoteness, that the whole contemporary stream of history seemed to have swirled around it, leaving it untouched. There they were still wearing the Long Gown; there the Classical Apothecaries still maintained their intricate stores—and furthermore the place was infested, swarming, vibrating with the densest multitude of flies I ever saw in my life, which is no trifling assessment. I marked that little town down as the last outpost of the persecuted flies of China—the refugee center; headquarters of the Free Fly Movement: a sort of biological Formosa.)

In some sort of way this anti-fly campaign was characteristic of the new impulse towards the absolute, observable in all contexts: with cleanliness as with sexual virtue (I made some effort to determine later) and with honesty—it appeared, for example, hard to get one's pocket picked in Peking; one knew that a room boy who lifted a cigarette or a pair of socks would find himself in the People's Court within a day. The consequence of this was that it became almost impossible ever to throw anything away. . . . It might have been a trap, or perhaps their standards of values differed. I was pursued over three provinces with a packet of old razor blades left in a guest-house bathroom. When I left the country, to rid myself of a worn-out pair of shoes I had to make special representations to the management. . . .

All this would seem to have given life in Peking an inhibited not to say somber quality. Strangely, that was not quite the case. It was true that there was not, in all the city—outside of Shanghai, I am prepared to say, in all of China—one single bar. It is true that the new Peking experiment in social life, called "dancings," were grim, halfhearted and flinty proceedings by the possibly more licentious Western standards; they were as poor and unnecessary an imitation of the less-admirable aspects of European culture as, for example, a Western copy of the Peking opera would have been. I could not help feeling that this reflected credit on them, rather than otherwise, though it made for personal tedium in one's more abandoned moods. But the prevailing atmosphere in the streets of Peking was of relaxation and amusement; essentially it seemed to me that the Chinese were a merry people, and the easiest thing to do, in a country where so many things were not easy, was to tempt them to a smile.

Sometimes, to be sure, it went a little too far; on sponsored visits to public places the more zealous bystanders tended not only to greet the Westerner but actually to applaud him, under the doubtless understandable impression that everyone with a long nose—known as a *Kao pi tze*—permitted to roam around Peking these days must be an Elder Brother—that is to say, a Russian. The practice became extremely tedious after a while, since while there can be few more gratifying experiences than to be applauded by groups of strangers, there can equally be few more irritating reflections than to realize that it is being done under the impression that one is someone else.

The really odd thing, however, was that even when I emphatically denied any Elder Brother claims and insisted, in the bizarre and corrupted phrase I had learned to make effective—"Niet Tovarich—Ying-Kuo"—it seemed to make no difference at all; they still beamed. Without any doubt the contemporary Chinese could not get it into their heads that a European *could* be in China without being an official guest, or a delegate, *ipso facto* on the Party line, and therefore worth a few minutes' of anyone's clapping time. It is also one of the curious modifications of Chinese courtesy that anyone who is applauded must applaud back. For public figures, appearing on platforms to storms of clapping, this no doubt solves a very awkward problem—no need for the deprecating gesture, the modest smile, the affected astonishment: important people in Peking appear in public applauding themselves like billy-ho, with evident relish.

The basic principle of driving a car through Peking was easy to learn, though hard to endure: the chauffeur steered a course exactly down the middle of the street, with his foot on the accelerator and his finger on the horn. No other controls were required, except a watchful hand on the steering wheel to ensure that the vehicle does not deviate any farther than is absolutely imperative towards the correct, or right-hand side, of the thoroughfare.

When two cars approached each other, traveling in opposite directions, this gave rise to a very nice point of detail. Since they were both occupying the precise center of the highway, which was the honorable position and not lightly to be surrendered, the passengers in both cars were subjected to several moments of electric suspense, while the two cars surged towards each other's radiators, with increasingly furious shrieks of the horn. It appeared to be a factor of considerable chivalry among the Peking drivers that he who first edged off towards the side of the road conceded a damaging point; this was a matter of importance since there were practically no cars in Peking other than official cars, and it seemed to be inimical to a chauffeur's chances in the State garage if he acquired a cowardly reputation. Since, however, it was held to be in nobody's interests to obstruct the streets with repeated head-on collisions, a compromise had been arrived at: when both cars were within a few feet of each other there would be a simultaneous, almost imperceptible swerve; nobody actually retreated to his legal side of the road, but disaster was avoided. There have been occasions when the thing has been so close that both door handles have been torn off, and there were tales of less-robust Government guests who have arrived at their destination pale and prostrated. After a little while in Peking one picked up a valuable tip: never to sit in the front seat beside the driver. If one did, without nerves of stretched steel, one felt the black wing of the Angel of Death whistling by half a dozen times between the Avenue of Tranquillity and the Gate of Heavenly Peace.

But nobody was worried by *mian tseh*—there was no loss of face.

Policemen in Communist countries are notoriously brutal, callous, sinister and overbearing. There were doubtless many such in Peking. They did not allow those to direct traffic.

The traffic police stood at the intersections striking attitudes of tremendous efficiency and grace; a car had only to be observed on the horizon and the officer would spring into a position that would have given satisfaction to the late Diaghelef. From time to time the policemen would call instructions through their little red megaphones to errant pedestrians. Only once or twice was I ever in a car that was involved in a difference of opinion with the police—passing a streetcar on the wrong side, or some violation of the traffic rules so flagrant that it could not be overlooked. The policeman would approach the car, and the dialogue would follow roughly this course:

"It seemed to me that you were impetuous, Comrade."

"It is possible, Comrade."

"Perhaps I should not have mentioned this?"

"No, by all means, Comrade; you have your duty to do."

"It causes no offense if I suggest you were driving in a disgracefully careless way?"

"In the circumstances, no, Comrade. I freely offer you the right to say this."

"Very well; I have said it. I shall return to my post."

"Certainly, Comrade. Let us both return to work."

Face is a wonderful thing. Among many irrelevant musings the question occurred to me many times: How was the disastrous effect of losing face equated with the equally serious modern Marxist necessity of self-criticism? That self-criticism was a very real factor in the day-to-day life of China was evident: one observed it in action after every railway journey, among the train crew; I saw hints of it among the guides and counselors after every day's work. How did a man retain face if, being lazy, he was compelled publicly to acknowledge the fact; if having been that day a little short on honesty, he had to admit it?

I asked them this, and they said, "We have reconciled the two facts. In any case, *mian tseh* is an old-fashioned conception, and not a genuine factor against the greater contemporary values."

Diversion. One day the phone rang; this time it was not Information, but a senior official with whom I was on good-morning terms; a very likable man just perceptibly inhibited by the strains of his office, which I was never able to identify. He said, "I have an urgent request. Will you please be at home at six tonight, as we wish to see you?"

Nobody had been quite so brusque before; my reaction was as it automatically is in countries where one tends to be identified in a political sense: I went back over my modest file to see what I could have written to cause offense. So far, nothing—it was no particular case of discretion; I just had not cabled very much after the first ebullient days when, overlooking the astronomical cable tolls from China I had quickly run up a bill of some five hundred dollars for a few thousand words of quite exceptional triviality and unimportance.

At six o'clock they came—my acquaintance, with two other gentlemen. With them they bore, as if it were some document of ritual significance, a letter to me from my wife, posted in London more than three weeks previously. It had, in fact, been opened. This, in the personal circumstances of the time, caused me certain misgivings; I loathe receiving opened letters wherever it may be and although (as it turned out) this one was almost disappointingly harmless, it was nevertheless a bore.

My friend said, "This is Mr. Somebody, of the Postal

Service, and this is Mr. Someone Else, of the Foreign Language Press. We have come personally to deliver this letter because of a most unfortunate and deplorable error. It was addressed correctly, as you see. The address is however new, and the post office did not recognize the European characters in which it is written. In such circumstances, they tend to send such mail automatically to the Foreign Language Press which inadvertently opened the envelope. It has not been read. I deliver it to you with the deep apologies of the Chinese Government."

I thanked them, and said, "This is a lot of trouble to take."

"No trouble," he said flatly. "It is possible you might consider this accident was part of some system of which you might not approve. As a matter of fact, it is not. We are, as I say, intensely embarrassed, and we hope you will not consider this a normal occurrence."

It was clearly a most unpleasant moment for everyone concerned. No one, perhaps, especially minds their letters being read if they contain no more intimate intelligence than that Fergus is getting on with his first term, that it rains in London, and that the dining room is being repapered. I was driven into the curious position of trying to ease the impact of the situation. I said, "Never mind. I am only sorry the letter was delayed, because I have already cabled to my home my complaints at being abandoned."

"The letter was from your family?"

"Yes."

"That at least is not so bad. It could have been from your Bureau, or your Administration."

"You do not appreciate," I said, "the peculiar emotional complexities of British domestic life."

"Ah, perhaps," he said, and they bowed themselves out.

I liked the Chinese officialdom. The only difference that ever occurred between myself and my Governmental semi-friend was this trifling incident. It made my heart somehow warm to him more than it had done before; but he never spoke to me again.

Down by the Temple of Heaven there was a most wonderful Fair. It seemed to do business every day, and at most hours of the day too—a broad area, several acres in extent, filled with booths and stalls and eating places and entertainments of all kinds; it was usually congested with people, and another of my perplexities was how, in a tightly disciplined land like this, so dedicated to production, there could be so many *flâneurs* apparently at a loose end at any given time.

However, they added greatly to the attractions of the Fair. It was a place of almost unlimited diversion. There were tents with dancing in various forms, and a marionette show. There were several sets of the famous Chinese sword-and-pike performers, who would go through the motions of a ferocious battle, all superbly timed, with much clashing of steel and hairbreadth escapes. There was an absorbing cross-talk act between two Chinese elaborately dressed in a strange parody of European costume—black coats, straw hats, bow ties. It was naturally wholly unintelligible to me but, since at regular intervals the comedians would stop and belabor each other over the head with paper clubs, I felt that its formula could have differed only slightly from that of vaudeville.

There was a remarkable man whose work it was to recount the history of China before a changing screen of painted representations of classical moments in martial lore. He would describe these events in song, or rather in a sort of musical recitative, accompanying himself on an elaborate system of drums and gongs which he operated with his feet. It was a virtuoso performance. When his narrative reached its climax—which from its stirring illustration I took to be either the beginning or the end of the Long March, since it portrayed Chairman Mao in a prominent position in the van, waving a flag of piercing vermilion—one or two people would throw a few hundred *yuan* into a box.

It was here also that I saw a conjurer performing a trick of such superlatively baffling quality that it remains one of my most vivid memories of China. I never saw it before, nor expect to see it again.

The conjurer was a sturdy man of middle age, with a powerful grin revealing an enviable set of chromium-plated false teeth; he talked remarkably little for a magician, and he was dressed in a pair of blue cotton pants and nothing more. This seems to me relevant. It is also the case that his performance took place not on a stage but on a piece of bare trodden earth, from which indeed he was perpetually being moved on by the pressure of other acts around him. What he did looked possibly more impressive than it sounds.

He took a piece of black cloth the size of a table napkin, spread it on the ground and stamped it flat. Then he stood back; by and by the cloth bulged and stirred. He picked it up, revealing a large white duck, which staggered off in a rather bewildered way among the onlookers. This was the preliminary, occasioning no especial stir.

The conjurer then made what seemed to be two rapid jokes. He clapped his hands sharply together, reached up into the empty air above him and withdrew—quite obviously from nothing at all—a glass bowl brimming full of water, in which swam three goldfish.

I repeat that this admirable man had no properties, no table, no stage, no flowing garments. He merely reached into the air and *found* a completely overflowing bowl of water, complete with fish. I maintain that this is the greatest conjuring trick in the world.

He then placed the bowl carefully on the ground, spread over it his cloth, and equally carefully trod it into the earth, until the cloth was flat. When he raised the cloth, there was no bowl, no fish, only the same piece of trodden earth.

I know nothing whatever about conjuring tricks. To those who do, this performance may be a transparent simplicity, as elementary an affair as pulling Jacks of Spades out of the ears of schoolboys. To me, however, it was and remains magic of the purest sort, and the man in question finally establishes a point long in doubt: that wizards are people with chromium teeth.

So one would walk back through the darkling streets; evening brought the first slackening of the city's noises. But not of the crowds; they were always there, strolling, chatting, forever eating in groups round wooden tables under the hissing oil lamps. The Chinese, it seemed to me, were the greatest possible lovers of communal life; they were gregarious to a degree remarkable even for Asia; their days were full of a bland curiosity in each other's behavior; they had a perpetual warm interest in each other's doings. Even in their own homes they lived in each other's laps, moving through open doors, calling through windows, playing with each other's children, inspecting each other's dinners. It was impossible even for the stranger completely to escape this pervading sociability; one walked among them, attracting no more attention than anyone else but certainly no less; one sat among them to eat, to ride, to rest, to look—until eventually one went back to the aseptic isolation of the retreat in the Pei Chi-Ko.

There was, it seemed, no place in China where one found oneself alone—except, whether one liked it or not, in bed.

(4)
Anything Can Happen

THE first week or two had passed, the initial aston-
ishments had worn off, but there remained a curious sense
of fantasy enduring against a background that was frequently banal, like a circus parading down Bromley High
Street. This was where *anything* could turn up, where *anyone* might suddenly appear around the corner. One got
used to seeing red flags flying from glossy Buicks, to a
Marxist Y.W.C.A., to five-cent tickets for the Forbidden
City, to Communist Capitalists and State-aided lute players, to people with a three-thousand-year-old tradition of
artistic excellence queueing for miles to see a collection of
chocolate-box lids because it was Russian. Yet across this
endlessly monochrome stage, peopled with industrious
and evidently contented Chinese, flitted all manner of
curious deviationists—Soviet citizens in Edwardian suits,
courteous Finns who asked one to lunch, Indians one had
last encountered in Berlin, intensely cultural people from
Java and Japan. There was even Doctor Globo—an engaging, mad Brazilian who wandered around in an agonized
way, seeking everything and finding nothing. He was a
guest of the Government, but he spoke nothing but Portu-
guese, which nobody in Peking seemed ever to have heard
of, let alone understood. He moved around from conference to conference, following not one word for weeks on

end, hurrying home to write enormous diaries on no one knew what. Doctor Globo was engaged on some vast *reportage* for the Latin-American public; always it seemed he was on the point of some momentous revelation on the Chinese character and methods; always it eluded him because he had not been able to understand anything of what was being said around him. He attached himself to me from time to time; he felt some rapport for me since, although he could not speak English, he felt himself always on the verge of doing so. Also I had been one of the first people he had met on his arrival—a shattered man; his plane had been held up for two days in Irkutsk, of all places, and nothing, it seemed, had more closely approached the Brazilian conception of hell than the Siberian winter's night. It appeared that the snow had fallen even on his bed. "Snee," he said, with emotion, "snee on bid! *Nao me agrada.*" (I discovered later the reason for this: Doctor Globo was a health fanatic of the kind that insists not so much on open windows but if possible on *no* windows; as the cold in Peking grew more intense he would fling his bedroom casement wider; he would then put on two pairs of pajamas, three heavy sweaters, two pairs of socks and a scarf. He installed a thermometer by the window and, as a tremendous wind swept and whirled around the room, he would stare at it and announce with satisfaction, "*Quatro* degrees, maybe." When it fell to around zero, he would pile overcoats and rugs on himself and go to bed, his nose flaming scarlet.) He had other hobbies. On his first evening he buttonholed me on the steps of the Press Club and made a wide interrogatory gesture that embraced our little street, the avenues around, and all the city. "Life," he said, and I agreed. "Ah yes— life, indeed." He seemed dissatisfied. "Life—where?" He waved his arms in impatient frustration. "*Onde esta—*

life, *vie?* Where," he said with a difficulty that clearly infuriated him, "is—life—*nocturnale?* Cabaret, please."

I could almost observe his heart sinking as I tried to make clear the truth: that he was in a city without a bar or a dance hall or a *boite* of any kind, where all activities came to an end around nine; where there was not only no cabaret but where the absence of cabarets was actually a positive thing. Peking held many enchantments, but the Life Nocturnal was not one of them. At that moment it was clear that China thudded to the bottom of whatever list Doctor Globo kept of his favorite countries; from then on he cast himself into his work, whatever it was, with a disillusioned and angry determination; I would hear his typewriter chattering furiously away until the small hours, as he sat in his self-made icebox recounting the developments of yet another day spent in the unintelligible wilderness of People's China. He could not tolerate the Chinese food; he was addicted not only to fresh air but to some scrupulous dietary regime, and he viewed the anonymous confusion of most Chinese dishes with the deepest suspicion, uncertain whether or not they were composed of some ingredient outside his catalogue. Instead, he ate fish—always fish; once when I called at his room late at night I found him depositing a plateful actually under his bed. "Fish—good," he said. "Full of matches." I found this observation extremely perplexing, until I arrived at the conclusion that he had confused the word "phosphorus" with "fosforus." He made violent and admirable efforts to translate himself into English, sometimes with ruinously bewildering results. "In China," he said, "no—see—humans——" I thought this was a needlessly harsh analysis, and said so. "No, no," said Doctor Globo, "humans—in punts. As mens. All Chinese pupils in punts. No good." It took what I still consider an inspirational piece of decoding to clarify this; from then on, to Doctor Globo, women were "humans" and people were "pupils" and pants were "punts."

As time went on this speechless life began to tell on Doctor Globo; he became discouraged and went to fewer and fewer conferences, which he put down, rightly, as a waste of time. When some event or other appeared on the schedule, he would come up to me, in some despair, and say, "Is interest—no? I not," and he would go back and throw his window open a little wider, sneezing with satisfaction, pursuing his wind-blown papers about the room. Towards the end of his stay he never left his room at all, but remained enveloped in overcoats and blankets, writing essays about Maxim Gorki.

But Doctor Globo was not the lot, not by any means. Peking had become the headquarters, possibly the world's number one center, for what was almost a new profession: that of the delegate. Probably more Communist-sponsored conferences met in Peking than anywhere else; there was also a steady flow of uncommitted, or at least only partially committed, guests of the Government, a very considerable fluctuating population of international characters of all interests and persuasions who filled the guest houses, monopolized the interpreters, and overflowed the transport. When I arrived—full of a modest *élan* at my success—I found that there were in fact forty-seven delegations present from twenty-six countries, more than two thousand people originating everywhere from Bulgaria to Chile. There were, for example, nearly eighty official guests from India alone. One of Peking's first major building projects was the erection of several huge, barrackslike hotels, of which three were reserved for delegations alone. In one of the biggest, which had three hundred and fifty rooms, there was exactly one paying guest—young G. K. Reddy, who wrote his papers on China to the *Times of India* surrounded on all sides by dedicated disciples, devotees and guests.

This business could not have been an easy matter for the State to organize, since the logistics of guesthood in an enormous place like China are more difficult than for most places. Some four hundred Government cars were set aside for guestly use; these people moved about the country in special coaches. Every big city they visited had the same facilities—in some of the big industrial centers, indeed, whenever a new factory went up they started by building the guest house. Shortly before I arrived a two-hundred-strong Bulgarian Cultural Dance Ensemble had a special train to themselves for the four thousand five hundred miles from Moscow to Peking. From Britain there were Cultural Delegations, Trades Union Delegations and Parliamentary Delegations—mostly, in these cases, one felt they were serious parties whose anxiety to fulfil a useful function of co-ordination was heavily impeded by the hospitable confusion all around. It was interesting but, one felt, futile; how much more usefully could the Chinese have spent their money and their courtesy than on some, at least, of the professional delegates who contrived to cling almost permanently to the band wagon, moving from conference to conference over Asia and Eastern Europe, with what contribution to world understanding, to world peace? Yet the Chinese when they wish can be impulsively generous, quite evidently prepared to maintain a dozen second-raters for the sake of one useful catch, and whether the time and money spent on them was worth while or not was Chairman Mao's worry, not mine.

So the social whirl went on, revolving in a kind of slow-motion deliberation, punctuated by bursts of energy at the arrival of anyone held to be important for this reason or that. It produced many subsidiary encounters—it produced Doctor Globo; it produced a Japanese Cultural Figure who wore square spectacles and a peaked cap always turned backwards, like a motorist of the nineteen hundreds. It produced Burmese trade unionists in silken *longghis* and Indonesians in Harris tweeds and Indians in *dhotis* and Englishmen in corduroys and suede shoes, and Tibetans. . . . I know about Tibetans; that meant something to *me*.

One evening I went to a reception, one of the standard functions offered by the Prime Minister for a visiting celebrity (on this occasion Jawaharlal Nehru, Prime Minister of India). This sort of diversion was frequent enough, indeed, and composed the sum and total of what Doctor Globo wistfully called our life *nocturnale*; its pattern was identical wherever it was held and for whatever purpose.

It was customary never to receive an invitation for anything—dinner, cocktails, a night at the opera—until some twenty-five minutes before the occasion was scheduled to begin. A common sight in official quarters was that of social stand-to around six o'clock, poised for instant departure in any given direction. Having been given the word, great numbers of guests would then converge on the Peking Hotel, or the International Club, and assemble in a vast somber salon reminiscent of the older waiting rooms at railroad stations—an impression made all the more painfully accurate by the uniform evening dress of the company, which was precisely the same as their day dress: the blue boiler suit, differentiating the sexes in no perceptible way. A very small minority of the more daring senior official ladies occasionally appeared in skirts but since these too were of the standard material the impression was that of an evening gown run up out of gunny sacks, though perhaps a little less frivolous. For some time, then—anything up to three quarters of an hour— one would merely stand around, exchanging pleasantries with whoever was at hand, a task that became increasingly difficult as one's experience of such occasions grew; who- ever was at hand was invariably whoever had been at hand the previous evening, and events in Peking do not move with a rapidity that provides more than one new conversa- tional opening a fortnight.

At the moment when a deep and numb paralysis had descended over the room the host and principal guests would appear in the doorway and advance through the crowd. This would be the signal for much enthusiastic applause, partly because the guests were always identified in some way with worthy international causes and partly to restore the circulation. It is the Chinese custom for any- one applauded publicly to applaud back—a most sensible custom too, providing for the honored person an escape from the fixed smiles and deprecatory gestures necessary in the West; he can move into his entrance clapping as though he thinks himself the finest fellow in the world, which as a rule he does.

This arrival would release platoons of waiters bearing drinks, which would be consumed at a tremendous rate— vodka and Chinese champagne, which was very odd in- deed; rice wine, which was agreeable but insufficiently drastic; and *mao-tai*, a white distilled corn liquor which gave every impression of being the really curative emer- gency treatment until perhaps the fourth, when its af- finity to vitriol became abruptly and disconcertingly apparent.

It was at one such point, moving stiff-legged and tongue-tied among the blue uniforms, drifting into the final coma of boredom, that I found my sleeve entangled with a rich silken robe of glowing saffron, turned, and saw with a sense of serious shock that the slim boy inside the brocade was none other, as they say, than the Dalai Lama of Tibet.

Now this may sound from afar like a commonplace enough event. For some, there may be no especial novelty in suddenly hobnobbing with the fourteenth reincarnation of the Divinity, the seventeen-year-old stripling who had officially lived for six centuries, who was never born and who could never die, of whom until the other day everyone had heard but whom scarcely anyone in the world had ever seen. For me, however, it had the most resounding implications, bringing about one of the most vivid personal flashbacks I can recall. This was, in short, the ineffable being I had once spent many weeks trying to track down through South Tibet when his phenomenal Court was in flight from the liberating Chinese Armies. . . . It was a justifiable excuse for a reverie, and perhaps for a digression.

It had been a few months since that first confused news that the Chinese had invaded Tibet; still the world —or that part of it that could spare the time from its own more violent preoccupations—was very little better informed. North India, on the edge of it all, was full of wild surmise and the most unlikely and ever-changing rumor: The Dalai Lama was expected momentarily, plodding over the ridge at the head of a golden-caparisoned caravan of yaks or soaring over the peaks on a pearly cloud; the Dalai Lama was dead; the Chinese were at this moment at the gates of the Pass; the Chinese had been routed by divine intercession on the Chang Tang plains; the Russians, infuriated at their reverses in Korea, were about to land an air-borne army along the Chumbi; the rebellious Tibetan peasantry had risen in Lhasa and were even now storming the walls of the Potala. All these things were recounted solemnly, humorously, fearfully, anxiously, skeptically, or with the mercenary zeal that overcomes many good and simple people at the sight of visiting newspaper men. They meant nothing.

It was an unprecedented business for the Tibetans, whose considered foreign policy had always most rigorously been to have none at all, to get involved in no way whatever with the antics of the outside world—in which, one seemed bound at the time to feel, they showed themselves no fools. Tibet, which had by then reached approximately the condition of social progress achieved by Britain in the fourteenth century, knew that the Chinese could have a walkover whenever they chose. Tibet knew that the days of isolation were gone, emergency had at last arrived, and, as is customary in such situations, the big boys tended to be the most swiftly off the mark. Many wealthy citizens were outside already; many more were fidgeting on the brink, waiting for the correct moment, and passing the time searching the Scriptures in any of Tibet's three thousand monasteries. The peasantry, having nothing to lose, were waiting to see what showed up —or so one supposed; everything in Tibet was supposition, for nobody knew.

I spent my time trying to find out. Yet the baldest and most simply factual account of the Tibetan methods and manners acquired in the telling a curious unreality, a hint of something rather spurious, as of a place self-consciously untouched by any of the developing conventions of the rest of the world. There was, however, no way of improving on the facts as they were. Resist familiar romanticism as you might, there was no simple way of explaining the wholly theocratic nature of a state where

priestly power and temporal authority were inextricably
mixed, where a third of the total male population were
monks and where the ruler was God, and technically several centuries old. There was no short cut definition of
a religion which mingles most aspects of the Shamanist
culture, Tantric mysticism, devil worship, pantheism and
Indo-Tibetan demonolatry, tinged here and there with
the teachings of the Buddha, and involving a really formidable pantheon of gods, saints, demons and canonized
evil spirits. The recognition of these was practically a
life's work by itself from the pinnacles of Boddh, Amitabha and Avalokitesvara, through the tutelary deities,
the familiar Demon Kings, to the countless Brahminical
godlings and angels and the rank-and-file local and country gods; a mind-reeling series of considerations.

But above all there was no simplifying the creature
who sat above it all: the Fourteenth Dalai Lama, the living
incarnation of all before him, free from human error,
all-knowing and all-powerful, the man with, undoubtedly,
the most exclusive job on earth. Under the staggering
hieratic form of government preserved in Tibet—those
were the days—supreme authority over all the land was
wielded by both this excessively holy person and the Panchen Lama, both of whom were regarded as incarnate aspects of the deity, of Amitabha or of Avalokitesvara—
beings who have the power, while remaining themselves in
heaven, of living also on earth in a *Nirmana-Khaya*, or
apparitional body. But the Panchen Lama's sphere was
wholly academic and spiritual; he contented himself with
the title of *Panchen Rimpoche*, "the glorious teacher";
that of the Dalai Lama was not only hallowed, messianic,
almighty and divine, but secular and administrative too;
he was *Gyalpo Rimpoche*, "the glorious king"; he was

ruler and Pope and Almighty; Viceregent of Buddha on Earth.

That is, until the Chinese came.

This position, however familiar, had to be understood before anything that followed made any sense at all.

These ineffable persons, being selected by reincarnation, made their country the only kingdom in the world's history of which the inheritor was chosen, by an inflexible convention, after the ruler's death. Even now, while the Dalai Lama is alive, no one on earth can conceivably even guess as to who might succeed him, since that successor can only be a child born on earth at the moment when the Lama breathes his last, into whom the holy spirit flees for shelter as it is released, because the existence of the Buddha never stops, nor even pauses.

This, as can well be imagined, made the discovery of a new ruler a matter of some complexity. The new Dalai Lama obviously could not be chosen; he had to be divined. It was no easy matter to determine, among the three and a half million inhabitants of such a bleak and impossibly difficult country as Tibet, the correct candidate; even when it was established that an infant existed who had come into life at the holy death-moment, it could be by no means certain that the Spirit had chosen that particular frame for inhabitation; there might be many others. The search, customarily, took years, and that was the business of the Chutukus—the Abbots of the great monasteries, the Cardinals of Lamaism, who themselves are also incarnations of one or another of the celestial Bodhisats of the Great Vehicle mythology. These officials applied for a prognostication from the State Oracles to narrow down the neighborhood of search; then, while more long Regencies took charge of the throne, candidates were selected, sacred marks were perceived on the bodies that reveal the embodiment from simpler mortals —Tiger-Mottled Legs, Divinely Large Ears, the Conch-Shell Print on the palms.

Then the infant Dalai Lama had to prove himself by an intricate series of tests and examinations: he would be set to grope and crawl among a selection of venerated objects; some authentic, some not; some the property of the late Lama, some not; some had exceptional properties of virtue, some had none. The divinely inspired one would unerringly locate the correct article and would prattle words from the sacred books. Ultimately he would be found, but it was rewarding to reflect on the gigantic opportunities for distorting the ritual, for abusing the selective powers, for prolonging the delay, for manipulating the whole bizarre system of succession in the interests of this political possibility or that. It became almost traditional for the poor Dalai Lama to transmigrate very often indeed, usually dying a minor, thus prolonging profitable regencies.

Standing there in a daze in the Peking party, I most vividly recalled the situation as I in my khaki shirt and scrubby beard had waited at the foot of the Pass. Tibet had been without a Panchen Lama for twenty-eight years; the last one had fled to China in 1923 after a political quarrel with the then Dalai Lama, and had died in exile fourteen years later. With his death the Tibetan priesthood found itself up against a seriously tough problem of succession, even for a country historically steeped in intrigues and holy double-crossing. Three youths were put forward as claimants, but no true reincarnation could be found—because, the Tibetans insisted, of the Chinese interference which prevented them from traveling to

Lhasa for what can only be called their Sacerdotal Finals. A young man living in the Kumbum Monastery in Chinese Sikang was being claimed by a number of followers as the true Panchen Lama, but Lhasa refused to recognize him, accusing him of association with the pro-Chinese faction. His time, as it turned out, was to come.

But a Dalai Lama there certainly was, and of course is. The incumbent, a boy of fifteen then—or rather sixteen, since in the Oriental fashion he was born a year old—had been discovered in the family of a small trader in Si-ning, in Northern China, in 1938, after a five-year search following the Thirteenth Dalai Lama's death. He had been enthroned in 1940 and given his names: Jampel Ngawang Lobsang Yishey Tenzing Gyatso, which means "Tender Glory, Mighty in Speech, Excellent Intellect, Absolute Wisdom, Holding to the Doctrine, Ocean Wide." For ten years he ruled through regents, but suddenly in 1950, because of the Chinese emergency, he was given accelerated promotion and invested with full powers.

And he was waiting, and pondering, and beating his gongs just over the border in Yatung—as, they said, he had so often done before.

It was that aspect of the Dalai Lama's personality that was so baffling to the Western mind—the accepted continuity that joined him with the past, not just as one link in an ancestral or dynastic chain, but personally, as an individual. The present Dalai Lama is not the inheritor of his predecessor's functions; he *is* his predecessor, and the predecessor before that, and before that for thirteen times. He is not merely the contemporary bearer of the Yellow Hat; he is the precise personage for whom it was originally created. It is accepted that he has, in simple fact, lived for six hundred years.

Thus when the Chinese Manchu Emperors invaded

Tibet in the eighteenth century, the Dalai Lama was there.
When in the early years of this century the Chinese Imperial Government attempted still greater control over
the land, it was this Dalai Lama, still thirty-seven years
unborn, who fled to India; when the Chinese Revolution
overthrew the Manchus in 1911 it was this Dalai Lama who
had broken the final ties with China. It was he, too, who
had ruled Tibet when the Simla Convention of 1914 had
once again recognized nominal Chinese suzerainty over
Tibet while forbidding her to interfere internally. It was
he who had expelled the Chinese Mission from Lhasa in
1949 ("as we wish to live apart, uncontaminated by the
germ of a highly materialistic creed"); it was he who
waited beside the State Oracle, over the Pass from me,
heavy with the weight of his fifteen years, contemplating a life that had endured six centuries, stretching as tediously into the past as it did into the future. . . .

And now it was he who stood beside me, robed in
orange silk—Tender Glory, Mighty in Speech, Excellent
Intellect, Absolute Wisdom, Holding to the Doctrine,
Ocean Wide—shaking his shaven head like a Methodist
at the waiter with a tray of vodka.

I reflected that this was one of the most singular
things that had ever befallen me, in a life not altogether
empty of incident. I knew—had known all along, I suppose—that the Dalai Lama in the end had compromised
with the inevitable; even an Immortal did not monkey
with Marxism in such circumstances. He did not escape
over the mountain, and when at last he returned to his
Capital, a Chinese general went with him.

His older brother, the Taktser Rimpoche, managed
otherwise. It seemed his rheumatism was troubling him.
He crossed into India to see the doctors. When he

reached Calcutta, there was the Chinese Communist Ambassador, full of concern for his well-being, solicitously recommending—indeed insisting—that the Taktser Rimpoche hasten back to Tibet where they, the Chinese, would undertake his treatment, and not stay a day longer in India. Thoughtfully the Taktser consented; that very night he took an airplane to America, where he had prudently made arrangements in Virginia, from which he has equally prudently never returned.

And so the Chinese won the war at last, without difficulty or bloodshed, without special endeavor; there was in the end neither a bang nor a whimper.

The Chinese Republic said that a military base would be established in Lhasa as in all other Chinese provincial capitals, and that they, the Tibetans, were required not to argue but to sign. The delegates were told, when they protested, that it would be unnecessary to consult the Dalai Lama; the deal was in any case closed. They signed.

As the Viceregent of Buddha on Earth moved north the Army of Liberation moved west, from Cham-do—possibly the smallest Army of Liberation in the history of Cominform: eight hundred men. That chapter was over.

The new chapter began without delay. The circumstances may have been strange and in their way unprecedented, but the pattern was the same the world had seen many times before. The nominal collaborator was not hard to find: the new Panchen Lama, Ngoerhtehni, who received his accolade and his orders in Peking in what must have been a ceremony of some originality, probably the first man to be confirmed in supernatural and divine authority under Marxist principles.

Groups of Chinese technicians—miners, doctors, radio engineers—began to filter into Tibet; a new motor road was begun to link Szechuan with Lhasa. The private armies of the feudal landlords—who had operated for years exactly as they liked, Dalai Lama or no—were disbanded. The Tibetan soldiers were very smartly told that from now on a rifle would be of more use than a prayer wheel. The days of the Mountain Fastness were gone. The Chinese told the Personification of the God Incarnate what to do and when to do it, and that was the end of Shangri-la. When, a little later, they appointed the Dalai Lama and the Panchen Lama to the Chinese Consultative Conference, that at last made Tibet an integral part of the People's Republic, and that brought paradox to its apotheosis. To see the Holy Kingdom of Tibet—feudal, medieval, barbaric, theocratic, with as many pretensions to political democracy as Caligula's Rome—embodied in anybody's People's Republic was like seeing the Pope of Rome carrying a flag in a May Day rally. It was, perhaps the ultimate touch, the wheel full-circle overnight, that the All-Knowing and All-Powerful, Absolute Wisdom, the Only Undefiled, should fetch up at last among the little men in the blue boiler suits.

Well, there he was, looking very young and almost bashful, accepting the casual greetings of the passers-by like a new curate at a garden party. I could see very little of the godling except that he carried more fountain pens in one row in what I suppose must be called his pocket than anyone I ever saw. That put an idea into my head that was never there before; I asked there and then for my first autograph.

Then, as the holy being wrote his name on the back of my invitation, another hand reached out: that of the Panchen Lama, Ngoerhtehni, whom, if you can believe it possible, I had not observed. He, too, signed.

As I took back my piece of paper, now doubly sanctified, the Dalai Lama spoke his only words, pointing to the signature. "Dalai Lama first name," he murmured, "Dalai Lama top man."

(5)
The Women

THE street cleaner was a woman, the duty foreman at the rolling mill was a woman, the head of the Department of Foreign Information was a woman, the streetcar operator was a woman, the house surgeon at the workers' hospital was a woman. A girl was dynamiting rocks on the Chungking Railway; a girl was proclaiming the glories of Socialist Emulation over the Peking radio; a girl was dispatching the trains in the Shanghai station. An old woman sold me cigarettes from a stall at the bleak corner of Pei Chi-ko, where I lived. She was always there at seven in the morning; no matter when I came home she was still there, counting out the little ragged notes by a kerosene flare. The teller in the Bank of China was a woman; a woman had just won the Stalin Prize for literature—Ting Ling, who wrote about virtue triumphant in villages. Down by the Chien Men gate a girl emerged giggling from a crowd around a doorway and darted into a car that was wholly swathed in scarlet draperies—a bride, unveiled; there was even a photographer. Up by the Eastern Market there was a girl soldier in stiff khaki, her army cap balanced on top of her Liberation bob; she carried a baby in her arms, but it only looked strange, not ridiculous. They wore the same clothes as men, they did the same work and got the same pay. It wasn't always easy to identify them as women at all, but they were.

"And you must remember," everyone told me, over and over, "that until four years ago it could not have happened. There used to be two hundred and fifty million Chinese slaves, without rights or advantages or hope in the world. You can say what you like about our economics, but *that* is something nobody can deny."

It was true; everybody had talked and written so much about the new freedom of women that it had to be a fact, and it was. Probably no other single factor in the Revolution was so revolutionary. The old condition of the Chinese woman had of course been brutal—an almost unbelievable destiny, by Western standards, and deplorable even by those of the rest of Asia. There *were* no accepted rights for a woman in the old China—the very birth of a girl was traditionally held to be a misfortune. Many times I asked, "Is it a *fact* that female babies were occasionally drowned?" and they always replied, "Certainly. Not invariably, of course, but often enough. In the case of the river by my own village, for example. . . ." Everyone had an example, recounted with the same gravity as the tales of the bad food and the Western imperialism and the unsatisfactory dams; a curious gloomy satisfaction: "You have only to look to see the change."

The Chinese woman of the old days had been unwanted—not always unbeloved, perhaps, but usually. It was customary for her to be betrothed very young to some child, or occasionally some man, she had never seen. That is not rare in the Orient, but there were not many of the matriarchal compensations of the Hindu wife, and none of the oblivion of the Moslem purdah. After marriage she was to all intents and purposes the slave of her mother-in-law and her husband; she became an integral part of the new family, and could on no account return home. If her husband died, she could not remarry; or if she did—it was occasionally known—the law would automatically protect her relatives if they killed her to save the family face. There were even more curiously barbaric touches: If the affianced man died before the wedding the girl could be traditionally compelled to "marry" his memorial tablet, which provided her with every conceivable legal disadvantage. Until fairly recently there was a great deal of selling into concubinage or the brothels. There was no female right of divorce. An illegitimate child provided no claim on the father. Not one in twenty female children went to school. In the last year of the Kuomintang occupation of Shanghai six thousand five hundred babies were found abandoned in the streets. . . . The melancholy tales went on and on.

On the first of May, 1950, the new Government announced the Marriage Law. It abrogated the old "feudal" matrimonial methods as "arbitrary and imperative, based on the superiority of men, indifferent to the rights of children." The document of the Law itself is quite startling, not for any originality in the system it defines but for the hopeless negations it replaces. It opens with the statement that "The New Democratic Marriage is based on the free choice of partners." It abolishes "bigamy, concubinage, child betrothal, interference with the remarriage of widows, and the exaction of gifts or money in connection with marriage." It states that marriage requires "the willingness of both parties." It gives men the right to marry at twenty, women at eighteen. It says that "They have the duty to love one another, to live in harmony, to engage in useful production, to help each other in the building of a new society." It gives them both the right to retain their own name. Abruptly, in Article Thirteen, it says bleakly, "It is strictly forbidden to drown newborn babies." Children born out of wedlock "have the same rights as those born in wedlock, and are protected from all persecution and insult." Each partner has the right to inherit the other's property. There is a quiet concession to the historic traditions of filial piety: "Neither parents *nor* children shall maltreat or desert one another."

It was all astonishing and somehow pathetic, for all its worthiness and solemnity: "They have the duty to love"—is there such a thing as a duty to love? " . . . to engage in useful production. . . ." they would walk down to the Administrative Office of the *Chu*, the city district, of the *Hsiang*, the rural area (that fulfils all the law asks) and one saw them going off, each preserving his and her own name with steadfast democracy, to the factory for mutual aid in building the new society as required by statute. It seemed very splendid, and a little sad: a gray way to legislate for ecstasy. And then you thought of the exhausted young-old women imprisoned in someone else's kitchen, of the fourteen-year-olds in the Shanghai whore-houses, of the village matchmaker extorting his twenty per cent from the dowry, of the little girls and the adolescent boys facing each other for the first time across the bewildering nightmare of the marriage bed (for the first night only, it was usually conceded, they had it to themselves, with the old women fretting impatiently in the doorway); you thought of all these things and legalized free will did not seem so bad at all.

With all that, of course, went politics—the suffrage, the Committees, the dialectics. It meant the transition of women, in one bound, from the mother-in-law's scullery to the immutable tables of Marxist-Leninist education. It meant the All-China Women's Democratic Federation—

and it was no time before I was in the thick of *that*, sitting in one of Peking's uncountable and identical reception rooms (the pink wallpaper, the vast and threatening chandelier, the electric-blue upholstery, the endless procession of teacups; except for the reflective portrait of Chairman Mao, it could have been a woman's guild anywhere in South London). The All-China Women's Democratic Federation is what its name suggests; in the extraordinary extension of fantasy that permeates all contemporary Chinese life this completely Communist organization has contrived to affiliate with the national branches of both the Women's Christian Temperance Union *and* the Y.W.C.A., whose political flexibility in this matter, I felt, could scarcely enjoy the fullest approval of their headquarters.

"We Chinese women had to start from nothing—nothing at all," said the Madame Secretary, "and now look at us." I did; there were half a dozen of them in the regulation blue uniforms, very earnest and dedicated and less than lovely. How is it, I wondered, that feminist organizations all over the world must be built around a nucleus of characters so outstandingly un-feminine? There is a feminist face, somehow universally designed with recognizably militant teeth; an especial form of feminist smile, both arch and challenging at once; the ladies of the All-China Women's Democratic Federation were physically at one with the suffragettes from the word go. The blue boiler suits did not help.

But their facts were fluent and useful. "The women have reached a high level of patriotism," said the Madame Secretary. "The textile industry is mostly run by women. In 1949, a Chinese woman could tend twelve looms; now she can handle twenty-five. Of course there's equal pay. A woman worker gets fifty-six days of maternity leave with pay. Land Reform gave women just the same share-

out of land as men. A husband can't tell his wife 'I feed
you' any more, because all she's got to say is, 'My work is
entered in the Labor Book too.' " The Madame Secretary
said this with enthusiasm, and there was a general flutter
of applause. "As a matter of fact, women are now about
thirty per cent of the country's working power. And what
is more," said the Madame Secretary, snapping her fingers for the eleventh cup of tea, "they *go to school.*
Thirty-four per cent of the pupils in primary classes are
girls. In the high schools, it's a quarter. How many girls
went to school in the feudal days? Not one in twenty. Now
even the old women in the *Hsiangs* go to adult classes;
they want to know how to *read.* Unheard of."

Then, inevitably, the facts faded into the textbook
maxims; the lesson which could only be admirable in its
own right became a bore when touched up and colored
with the inescapable phrases. "The vital need to make
contact with the Masses . . . A state of emancipation
unknown in the Capitalist-dominated countries . . .
Thanks to the selfless leadership of Chairman Mao. . . ."
It could have been wholly and precisely true, but how
swiftly the jargon stultified the good ideas, fossilized the
excitement of the experiment. The women were always
the worst, unable to let a stimulating story tell itself, always forcing one, as they forced themselves, into overemphatic attitudes. I kept nudging the Madame Secretary's
rhetoric back to facts, then it was better; when she got
back to figures, she was glad and you could see she was
glad; she was one of the world's busy virgins who rock statistics in their arms like infants.

"Of course women are encouraged in industry.
There's legislation to see that they get eight weeks'
leave on full pay if they have a baby. Miscarriages are
well looked after, too—fifteen days if you have one in

the first two months, thirty days if it's after that. For working mothers there is a statutory thirty minutes off every four hours for suckling babies. The insurance laws let women retire at fifty—sometimes forty-five, if they're in a heavy job—on about fifty-five per cent of their pay. That is a *great* deal better than men; they don't retire till sixty.

"Of course we have the vote. Article Eighty-six of the Constitution gives women *all* rights. It has been only five years, and what have they done?"

They had done a great deal. There was Soong Ching-Ling, who is Madame Sun Yat-Sen, widow of the First Revolutionary; she is also Vice Chairman of the Standing Committee of the State Council and sits on the right hand of Mao (while her sister, Madame Chiang Kai-Shek—if one really seeks a paradox—sits across the water on Formosa at the right hand of the man whom all China officially execrates as a condemned traitor). There is Shuh Liang, who is Minister of Justice. There is Li Teh-Chuan, Minister of Public Health. There is Chieh Ying, Minister of Supervision. There is Ho Hsing-Ning, Minister for Overseas Chinese Affairs. There is Chang Chin-Chiu, Minister for the Textile Industry. They are all women, and where would they have been ten years ago?

"Doubtless washing dishes," said the Secretary crisply, "as quite probably so should I."

Down in the quarter where I lived, in the Tung Tan district of Peking, the narrow *hut-ungs* threaded in and out between gray faceless walls, the small streets and alleys that net themselves into difficult patterns behind the main avenues, each with its low undulating horizon of roofs tiled in unglazed green, its façade on either side unbroken by windows, only at intervals the heavy courtyard

doors of dark, dull red timber; each with its street blackboard. The street blackboard was a large rectangle of the
plaster wall painted black and covered daily with new
columns of chalked characters: items of news, new municipal regulations, directives and suggestions from the
neighborhood political center, lowest unit in the chain
of party control—the Street Committee.

The Street Leader of my district was Mrs. Chao
Ching. I went along with Wei to see her. The alleys
ducked and turned inexplicably; they were gray and drab
but completely clean; on almost every corner a vegetable
peddler stood gently wailing his wares, and the children
played their solemn personal Chinese games. Mrs. Chao
Ching lived not far away, through a doorway into the
usual square courtyard, inhabited on four sides, with an
ash tree in the middle. Her room was bare and bleak;
brick walls and a stone floor. Like all Chinese other than
the wealthy she seemed to have the minimum of *posses-
sions*; however long and full the life, there seldom seems
to be anything to show for it. Mrs. Chao had a bed, one
tall chest, a table and three chairs. Chairman Mao hung
on the main wall between a photograph of congressmen
(Mrs. Chao had been elected a deputy for the district)
and the bright red silk pennant that is awarded to Labor
Heroes or Model Mothers or anyone similarly distinguished
in good works. It was a room where clearly no one had
ever relaxed; there was nowhere to relax in. Mrs. Chao
didn't mind; you could see that she had never had an idle
or contemplative moment in her life; she bustled around
pinching out the strands of green tea that looked like sage
and smelt of flowers, talking and smiling and stepping
over the cat.

She was a woman of fifty, and her husband was a
teacher in a primary school. Everyone had told me that

Mrs. Chao was a fine example of the Chinese woman of middle circumstances to whom emancipation had come in middle age, who had shown an admirable sense of adaptation and political consciousness; she was a very public-spirited person, everyone said. I don't know quite what I had expected—something like the Secretary, I suppose, keen-eyed and masterful; certainly not this restless and rather embarrassed little housewife fiddling with the kettle and the enameled teapot. She talked in jerks, with long pauses, until—very soon the inevitable denouement, with the textbook words taking control.

She had lived around here always. She came from a handicraft family that got some sort of living making paper flowers for old-fashioned weddings. "I was never good at it, but I was allowed to make the leaf part. It was a long time ago, of course. I got married in the usual way —you must know about that; I never saw my husband before the wedding day. I didn't even know his name. It was all arranged by the others; there was nothing strange in that. Marriages were mainly a matter of mothers-in-law getting a new servant; that was all it amounted to. When you got married, you just went to work. It was worse here in Peking than in other parts, they tell me. All I knew was that I couldn't ever leave the house, and I was *hungry*. I got two bowls of noodles a day, and worked—oh, yes, I worked. It wasn't allowed for me to go to the door of the courtyard without permission. My husband—naturally he was loyal to his mother only; that was the way everywhere. There were so many of us like that. Once a month I was allowed out to the temple, and I used to burn a joss in front of the Buddha just because it was the only thing I ever saw that had a smile. . . . That went on for twenty years."

I asked: "Where did all this happen?" Mrs. Chao

looked around in a vague surprise and said, "Why, here. This house. Where else could it be? How else does a man get a house except as his parents die?" She passed her eyes about the stark empty room; the glass-windowed door into the courtyard with the thin, stalking chickens.

"It was hardest during the Japanese occupation. We were very poor. I had three children by then, and an orphan nephew. I used to go out peddling steam-bread and tea to the mule drivers. I know now I should have been even sadder than I was, but what did you do in those days?"

I became suddenly aware that Mrs. Chao was suffering from a deeply strangled emotion; her eyes continued to look brightly about the room, but she was crying. It was tremendously awkward and painful; it is an impossible thing to pass off a *crise-de-nerfs* through an interpreter. It introduced a bewildering new dimension into an impossible situation: you heard the stumbling pain in Mrs. Chao's voice and saw her furiously flick away a tear, and the words filtered solidly and with gray impassive accuracy through the unemotional voice of Wei, the translating machine. It was like reading "Hamlet" in Morse code. I muttered something about the time and half rose to go, but Mrs. Chao would not hear of it; the very suggestion restored her instantly to composure. One could see how the baffled bride of twenty years ago had been reincarnated into the Street Leader of today.

"Well, you see how things are now. I suppose in my mind I was waiting for the Revolution all along. Anyhow, I was forty-five when the Liberation came, and I thought I had better do something about it before it was too late. I'm Chairman of the Woman's Group, too; the local Congress meets once a month to discuss our affairs. . . . The Government gave me this task, and of course it meant

I had to learn things I didn't know and do things I'd never done. Don't think everything changed in a day; you can liberate the women but what about the men? My own daughter—her father was all against letting her go to school. 'What use is education to a girl?' he said, and of course he hadn't wanted her anyway."

But the husband now? I wondered. There was something Chekhovian in this strange household; this was the home to which Chao Ching had come to an unknown husband, to a dominating mother-in-law, to an accepted but nevertheless dreadful condition of helotry that had lasted twenty years, with the husband always and inevitably on the side of the enemy—and now this: a state that proposed to reverse all these bitter relationships overnight in the name of the law; for the first time in a life full of frustrated resentments and persecution the woman was legislated into equality; what happened to the twenty years of hatred?

"But your husband now accepts the new system—approves it?"

Mrs. Chao smiled; the last tear had long since gone. "There is no opportunity now for anyone *not* to accept it. My husband could not take up the old attitudes now. . . . The basis of female enslavement was economic dependence; that was all. It is well known. I'm not exactly independent economically, but I can be any time I like. I could go back to making paper flowers." She laughed. "It is no longer necessary for unhappy women to hang themselves, or jump in the rivers, or eat opium to escape from their troubles. Certainly there were difficulties with husbands at the transition time, and more still with mothers-in-law. But now the road is made clear, the new society offers to all a future of prosperity and peace-loving harmony, through the example and teaching of our great leaders. . . ."

And there it was again; the spontaneity fled before the thud of the maxims; the words harnessed together in drilled and practiced teams, like circus horses. Mrs. Chao the middle-aged housewife had stumbled over her phrases and had knotted her fingers; Chao Ching, the Chairman of the Women's Unit, reached out with easy accomplishment for the clichés of revolution and the texts of the new faith. It proved nothing against her. It proved nothing at all. The only thing it did was arouse once more the usual uneasy doubts of which one tried not to be ashamed. They had introduced me to Mrs. Chao—the two Mrs. Chaos; which one was the real one? Had the first Mrs. Chao, troubled into tears by a memory difficult to endure, been so splendidly schooled that she spoke the Party Book as though she had written it? Or— a dismal thought—had the painful moment of emotion been part of the act, the brilliant improvisation to give the moral weight? One thing was sure: *I* should never know.

She saw me off at the courtyard door that still had the threshold board to keep the devils out, a keen and likable woman who should have been wearing a cretonne apron instead of blue dungarees. Outside in the alley a blind man shuffled along beside the street blackboard, beating a pair of little gongs and trailing a board painted with red characters—a fortuneteller and caster of horoscopes; they still practice, even now. But he was wasting his time outside the house of Mrs. Chao; she knew where *she* was going.

Nevertheless the timekeeper at the Manchurian pithead was a girl; the weigh-clerk at the airfield was a girl;

a girl was sculling a cargo sampan across the Kialang River. Girls did everything—except play the female parts on the stage; they were always played by men. *Madchen in uniform* everywhere. Their hair revealed their sex—the modern pigtail, or the "Yenan bob," the square-cut fringe that used to mark the women of the People's Army—nothing else did. "The clothes are not attractive," said Madame Kwung Peng, of the Foreign Office—herself a woman of serene and intellectual beauty—"but then, they are not meant to be." The grim blue cotton suits, padded for winter, were the product of necessity—cloth shortage, the need for mass production; only later did the very drabness become ideologically modish—but they gave every woman the pneumatic, sexually meaningless form of a roughly stuffed doll. For anyone who had formed his ideas of Chinese feminity from the svelte and pencil-slender elegance of the girls in Singapore or Hong Kong—for myself, let us admit it, who had fallen esthetically for almost every Chinese taxi-dancer in the regrettably capitalist atmospheres of Saigon, of Djakarta, of Bangkok—this rigidly neuter façade was disappointing, though probably salutary. The Chinese girl is, or was, made anatomically in proportions generally, though not entirely, approaching the Western design—unlike the Japanese girl, who has short legs and who, knowing that she can achieve grace only when enveloped below the waist, took care to invent the kimono. Nature, while equipping the Chinese girl with delightful legs, did not provide her with breasts, a deficiency which in Hong Kong and Singapore is more than made good architecturally, but which is clearly regarded in Peking as a providential matter in the best interests of democracy. A display of corsetry and brassieres in a Peking shop would be unthinkable, both psychologically undesirable and politically unsound—a curious modesty in a city where, in the main street, exists a large medical store exhibiting in its window the most realistic and upsetting life-size waxen models of the female pelvis, representations of the reproductive process most faithfully limned, a stillborn fetus in a bottle, a series of posters of hygienic instruction that would find a ready sale in the shadier back streets of Cairo. Beside all this vivid socialist realism, studied earnestly at all times by young and old, the refusal to admit the simple values of the bosom seemed strangely puritanical.

In some ways it seemed characteristic of the great new Communist reaction of austerity so striking throughout the country. It had many manifestations: the new honesty, the new cleanliness, the new efficiency, and the cult of sexual virtue. Prostitution was abolished in Peking, almost overnight, by a clean-up operation of such Draconian vigor that several Party deviationists have not forgotten it yet. It was an incident which conferred distinction on all concerned: a powerful documentary film was made on the subject, and the girls, accommodated in a new Reform and Educational Academy, were provided with a special badge, of which they were inordinately proud. Together with the Marriage Reform Law and the emancipation of women generally came a tremendous tightening up in the morality regulations—"love" is now encouraged, in the sense of bringing together two souls "integrated in a common political ideal," but any romantic attachment that goes this distance, outside the marriage bed, is actually a statutory offense, worth six months in jail for the overeager young man to teach him to keep his mind on his Marx.

How lacking in this moral zeal and scrupulous dedication, one reflected, were the Chinese girls of Hong Kong, in the split skirts of their *ching-sum* gowns, their lipstick; one thought of them with disapproval, with reproach, with regret—still, one thought of them, repeatedly.

I had wanted to visit a divorce court. This, after all, was something new and progressive; for the first time in the history of China a woman could not only choose her own husband, but dispose of him by divorce; an astonishing advance.

This I would like to see, I said; at first they agreed and then after a day or two they began to hedge. "There isn't a case on," they said, or "The Court chances not to be sitting. There are not many divorces now," they said —torn, I felt, between the desire to demonstrate the new process of emancipation and a reluctance to exhibit something that might turn out to be somehow discreditable.

I found out later that this was perfectly true. (It was almost invariably the case; I do not think anyone ever lied to me—they were obscurantist and occasionally evasive, but facts, when stated, were facts.) There were not, it seemed, many divorces now for the reason that there had been so many before. The new Marriage Law had had such an immediate and liberating effect that the courts were speedily jammed with women anxious to avail themselves of its provisions before it, like everything in the old days, slipped out of reach and vanished. There was a great rush for divorce by women forced for one reason or another into unhappy or unsatisfactory marriages; in some areas marriage disputes took up to ninety per cent of the Law Courts' time in the first year of the new system. As more and more women in the rural areas came to hear of the law, they too took advantage of it; others waited until the Land Reform had given them their own patch of land

and assured their independence. By now the courts had
disposed of the backlog, and were getting a little peace.

One day, however, there arrived the customary polite
message: there was a divorce case being held that morning
if I should care to watch it.

The court was a small austere room, not much bigger
than a large drawing room—the bench, a clerk's desk, a
few hard cane seats in rows; that was all. The judge sat
with two assessors, a man and a woman, under the picture of Mao. They came bustling in, all in their blue suits,
bowed, and immediately called for the couple. It seemed
that Liu Su-Ling, the nineteen-year-old bride of Wang
Wang-Yu, who was twenty, had once before asked for a
divorce; her suit had been refused, but the law permitted
her an appeal. They came in together—in *their* blue
crumpled cotton suits they looked like a young brother
and sister leaving school—and sat in chairs facing the
Bench, ostentatiously at each end of the row. The girl
tossed her pigtail petulantly over her shoulder. She was
very pink in the face; there had obviously been another
row in the corridor outside.

The judge snapped into business at once, naming
himself and his two colleagues and saying that if either
side had any personal objection to them they could make
it now. He, too, looked like a little boy; his voice of authority sounded like part of a game. The whole pro-
ceeding—with the plaintiff's pigtail tied in a red ribbon,
the husband playing with a piece of string, the little fresh-
faced judge pretendng to be severe, everyone dressed exactly alike—the whole thing looked exactly like a handful
of children playing Law Courts. There were the three on
the Bench, the boy and girl, and a scribbling clerk; that
was all. No lawyers practice in the Divorce Court.

It seemed that Liu Su-Ling was appealing for divorce on three grounds, which sounded to me remarkably slender: firstly, that her husband did not give her enough money; secondly, that when she was in hospital he did not visit her often enough; thirdly, and rather sweepingly, that she couldn't get on with him. She restated her case in a piping voice, darting little sharp looks at the boy three chairs away.

For a case that anywhere else, one felt, would have been treated summarily as the bickerings of adolescents, this was treated with lengthy care and attention. The little judge did most of the talking, addressing first the girl, then the boy. "He didn't give you enough money—how much does he have? How much do *you* earn?" he asked the girl. "You support your mother?" From time to time the young man would bob up and make what appeared to be a spirited defense, shrugging his shoulders and raising his eyes, while the girl sat pouting and scuffling her feet. "Why don't you two *pool* your earnings?" demanded the judge. "You'd have plenty then—as much as I get, anyway."

The matter of the hospital visits was disposed of—yes, perhaps the young man had been a little slack. "I was trying to earn more money to pay for it," protested Wang, and the little judge nodded and said, "Quite right, but you know what women are when they are unwell."

And this third ground—they couldn't get on; what did that mean?

Liu Su-Ling broke into a long explanation. "He doesn't approve of my going to school. He says I ought to look after the baby." "I did not; I said she should *or* her mother should." "And then he doesn't like my working for production." The young man shrugged again, he looked across at his wife as though he would have enjoyed spanking her. It all seemed grotesquely trivial and overemphatic; here was the heart of the world's greatest Communist State, and we were sitting applying the majesty of People's Law to a silly tiff between a pair of youngsters.

This consideration seemed also to have occurred to the judge. He began talking very fast, leaning over the Bench, addressing first Liu and then Wang, waving his fingers at them, his treble voice rising and falling.

Then he sent them both out of the room to talk it over. "See how you feel when you come back," he said, and adjourned for half an hour.

The Secretary of the Courts, a thin courteous man of middle age, came over and brought me a cup of tea. This, he told me, was the routine procedure in actions: a couple stated their case, the judge would analyze it for them, and give them a chance to make it up.

"They are by themselves now?" I asked, thinking with some sympathy of Wang Wang-Yu, exposed without protection to that petulant whine. "Yes, quite alone." "Can't they ask for some legal advice to help the argument?" The secretary looked puzzled. "Why, certainly, if they need it, but I can't see why they should. There's nothing very intricate legally about this, surely?" I said no; indeed the whole thing seemed excessively simple and frivolous and in my country would never have come to court at all. What lawyer would advise a suit on such grounds?

But of course the situation here was very different, explained the secretary. He didn't think much of a legal system that hinged on how much money you could pay a lawyer. As we had seen, there was no interposition of purely legal argument here between the disputing parties and the judge. "But," I asked, "if anyone can come to court to ventilate any sort of idiotic difference of opinion, doesn't it waste a tremendous lot of time that could," I said ingratiatingly, "be better used for production?"

"Indeed, yes," said the secretary rather ruefully, "though much less than it used to. You must make allowances for women rushing to experiment with a privilege they've never had in history before. Once you concede the privilege, you can't tangle it up in too much formula. Though," he said, confidentially, "I can tell you that there is some talk of imposing a small charge—something nominal, but a *bit* discouraging—to filter off the really nonsensical appeals."

"Are all the grounds for divorce like these?" I asked him, and he shook his head. They were mostly, he said, something like this—money questions, mother-in-law disputes, and the like. Adultery—hardly. He reminded me that adultery is a punishable offense; an errant husband could be put in prison, and *that* would make an excellent ground for divorce. Article Nineteen of the Marriage Law says that if a soldier, man or woman, does not write a letter to his or her spouse for two years, that spouse can have a divorce on request. The whole principle of divorce, the secretary explained, is that if both parties simultaneously request it, it is automatic; they just go to the *Chu* or the *Hsiang* offices and de-register their marriage. A man cannot divorce a pregnant wife until the baby is a year old.

"If it's a one-sided appeal, then it is heard by the Court, which considers it the judge's job first to try to effect a reconciliation—as you've seen. If he can't do it, he makes a decision. The children? They belong to both parties after a divorce; the Court decides on who gets custody. Then there is Article Twenty-five of the Law which says that after a divorce, if there's no remarriage and *either* party has difficulties in maintenance, the other party has to come to his or her assistance. It is based on the assumption of complete economic equality between men and women."

Then the judge and his colleagues came back, and sent the clerk out for Liu and Wang, who returned looking furious, and sat down if possible even farther apart than before. It seemed fairly clear that the tête-à-tête had been far from successful; no two people ever looked less reconciled. Again the judge talked to them, and put the question. The young man raised his eyes to the ceiling; the girl shook her head until her pigtail whipped from side to side.

"He hasn't finished with them yet," whispered the secretary; "he will tell them they haven't been putting enough effort into it."

And sure enough the judge entered on another five minutes of what seemed like impatient reproof mingled with a sort of fretful regret, and when that was over Liu and Wang were once again outside. As the young man walked out of the courtroom, with a baffled and apprehensive expression, it seemed to me that he was at some pains to interpose the woman soldier, who acted as usher, between himself and the lowering figure of his bride. Whatever Wang's defections as a husband, as a provider, as a visitor to hospital beds, this seemed a punishment bordering on the inhuman.

"After this, I am afraid," said the secretary, "the judge will have to make a decision. It is not for me to say, but I *doubt* whether the young woman will win her case."

Somehow, I thought, strolling in the corridor—it was half filled by a ping-pong table—this was part of the Revolution, this was another aspect of the strange, persuasive Chinese approach to all problems, the small ones as well as the great ones; whatever big stick had in the past been used, and could be used again, at the moment the weapon was induction, suasion, advocacy and exhortation, the process of perpetual prompting and nudging applied everywhere at all times. The peasants must be *induced* to join co-operatives; the industrialists must be *convinced* of the productive necessities; the political criminals must somehow be *redeemed*—and Liu Su-Ling and Wang Wang-Yu must be argued into making up their stupid juvenile quarrels, even if it took a People's Judge all day. I didn't see it. What sort of domestic row, however childish, could ever be healed by shutting the pair up in a courthouse room? What could this angry little pair have to say to each other here that they had not said (the small wounds growing deeper every time) so often before, among the congested frustrations of their home?

Then the woman policeman herded them back into court; they both looked a little numb and shattered. When the judge put the question to the wife again— the small grown-up boy looking stern and minatory—she began to say something very long and explanatory, then stopped and nodded her head.

"Very satisfactory," murmured the secretary; "it took a little time, but it was quite a good reconciliation. Now the judge reads a transcript back to them, and off they go."

And so they did, trailing uncertainly one behind the other. It could doubtless be accounted a success for the system, but somehow I felt relieved that I was not Wang Wang-Yu.

(6)

The Stone Walls

It is possible that, if anyone had told me, a week or two earlier, that I should shortly find myself behind the walls of a Chinese political prison, I might have found the thought improbable, not to say pessimistic. However, so it came to pass; and the fact that I did not emerge from bondage already under contract for my horrifying reminiscences is due only to the fact that I spent most of the time taking tea and small cakes with the governor.

It was possibly an odd way of dallying with hell-fire, but I found it instructive, strange and sad.

It so happened that, in making my official requests for sight-seeing facilities, I included, as a forlorn and rather ironic postcript, such unlikely expeditions as Lhasa, the border province of Sinkiang, and the nearest political prison. I shall doubtless go to my grave without seeing either Lhasa or Sinkiang, but it is fair to say that I was in the jail in next to no time. This was in its way characteristic of the obscure workings of the Chinese official machine, which could be unbearably slow over matters that seemed of little importance, and almost preposterously prompt when least expected. I recall once casually asking one of the Information staff what the postage rate was between Peking and Paris. After profound self-examination he said that he would refer the matter to the Ministry of Communications. (I cleared the point up myself in five minutes by merely going to the post office.) Yet the high authority produced the prison overnight. It was a simple question of approach. After some time in China I learned the secret of keeping abreast of affairs, which was: never in any circumstances to make an enquiry at that office, called "Information," of which I have already had too much to say. Casual questions in the street were occasionally useful; direct demands to the Foreign Office were almost invariably met; at a pinch one could retire to one's bedroom and dream up the answers for oneself. All these methods were more rewarding than asking information from Information. Approached at the proper level the Government never, to my knowledge, let me down. At the Information level all was mystification and obscurity.

So one day we drove to the prison.

It lay outside the walls of Peking, in the complicated maze of suburbs that sprang up and multiplied almost while you watched; a huddle of buildings set up forty years ago by a local war lord for the convenient disposal of his opposition. It had been inherited by the Kuomintang, who maintained it in business, while allowing such infinitesimal amenities as the war lord had installed to decay, so that when the People's Republic took it over, in the ordinary course of events, as part of the fittings of feudal China, it was not a place even to put a landlord in. The Communists retained its purpose, which was not substantially different from that of the war lord, but they spruced up its accommodation and drastically modified its methods.

At the best, however, I am no fanatical lover of jails.

In this dispiriting establishment—where, as everywhere else in the New China, man and woman met on equal, if depressing, terms—the regime claimed to "treat" its dissidents and "reform" the unreliable. To hear the governor, a sprightly angular man called Liu Hsiang-Chun, speak in chiding terms of his counter-revolutionaries and criminals, while the armed guards manned the observation towers outside, it seemed a system somehow born of Heinrich Himmler out of Hans Andersen.

We arrived through a gate like all prison gates, for even under communism they had not yet got around to growing roses round the door. There was a moment's colloquy between my escorts and the turnkeys, while a few searching glances were cast around the interior of the car. In a little while we were walking through alleys of production graphs and Model Workers' attestations and demands for the liberation of Taiwan, exactly as in every factory throughout the nation, though perhaps a trace more touching in this context.

For anyone who, like myself, had always thought of revolutionary jails as uniquely situated among the icebound salt mines of Siberia, this was in some sense a shock: the prison was, quite simply, a great textile factory. It is true to say that there was a massive wall, and on top of that an electrically charged wire barrier, and armed men stood at the door.

"But please note," said the governor, "that they're all outside. Security, you know. Inside, we run affairs our own way."

I wandered around the place quite openly, though with the rather shamed embarrassment one must feel, as a free man, in zoos and prisons. No one gave me more than the one brief guarded glance that is the prisoner's acknowledgment of a stranger.

At first glance the jail seemed to be dedicated much more to production than to reform. To begin with I could see little but weaving sheds, an uproar of looms through a thin cloud of dust; dyeing sheds; long rooms filled with knitting machines. Everyone appeared to be desperately hard at work.

"And that is the manner of their redemption," said the officer who was with me; "the policy is reform through production" . . . in the clattering weaving sheds, the knitting benches; men and women making striped socks eight hours a day; they had tried to oppose the irresistible, now they were working their passage back to orthodoxy among the thudding looms.

There were two thousand convicts in the Prison of the People's Court of Peking. A hundred and thirty of them were women. Two thirds of the total were classified as "counter-revolutionaries," which technically included four categories. There were straightforward Kuomintang agents. There were committeemen of counter-revolutionary leagues and associations. There were "bandits," or saboteurs of State property. There were "counter-revolutionary landlords and despots." They were serving sentences up to life, though I was assured that the average was something under ten years. Almost every one of them had been sentenced for crimes committed "before the Liberation."

Outside in the courtyard the off-duty shift was occupied in the desperate sort of leisure of captive people —playing basketball with a wild zeal, leaping and clapping and making overemphatic gestures; reading in corners; doing physical jerks in solitary corners. At one side a thirteen-piece orchestra—under a young conductor who, they told me, was serving life for sabotage—was rehearsing for the weekend concert. They played moderately well, stealing glances over their shoulders. It all seemed so fortunate—the band was there, the basketball team was there, the P.T. zealots were there, and I was there. I felt it was inhuman to stay; while I was standing by how *could* they relax?

The governor said, "There are four stages of re-education. First, there is the explanation of their crime. That is not always easy for people whose standards of behavior are improperly adjusted. Then there is labor education. After all, few of them ever had jobs of any kind. Then there is production technique—merely how to use the machines. Then there is the current events class, the classes for correct ideological thinking and the simpler Marxist-Leninist principles. For the illiterates, there is culture. We aim to teach them at least two thousand characters."

"Do they all respond?" I asked.

"Most of them. Some take longer than others. They get remission of sentence for productivity and improvement in ideology. They can see their relatives once a fortnight for half an hour. They can be fairly comfortable on the whole if they seriously try to reform their backward political ideas."

"And if they are obstinate about that?"

"There are, of course, penalties," said the governor. "The most serious punishment here is social rebuke. That is to say, the critical attitude taken up towards the offender by the more progressive comrades, which manifests itself in an atmosphere of disapproval." He sounded, for one curious moment, like the solemn principal of some progressive school.

"And if they are stubborn enough to be unmoved by that?"

"Very few are," said the governor. "However, there are privileges which can be removed—supplementary gifts from their families, and so on. Or their sentence may be reviewed—that is to say, increased. There is no form of physical punishment here; it is considered to be useless ideologically."

"But people are executed from time to time?"

"That is as may be," said the governor. "It is certainly not in *my* province. We have no capital punishment here. I do not know where it is done, if it is done."

The separate men's and women's living blocks radiated out in spoke fashion from a central hub, or lobby; the war lord had employed modern ideas in prison architecture. Most of the cells slept twelve people, ranged tightly together on trestle beds. The usual slogans and portraits of Mao Tse-Tung were on the lime-washed corridor walls, and a huge communal mosquito net hung overhead, sagging here and there under little accumulations of bird droppings. Apart from that everything was starkly and almost aseptically clean, though palpably in need of repair. At one end of the corridor was a notice advising the prisoners that winter was approaching, and to be sure to put on enough blankets at night.

As I left an empty cell, I saw the edge of a piece of paper protruding from under a pile of mattresses. I picked it up to see what this twilight counter-revolutionary wrote in the long nights, but it was only a little obscene drawing.

The officer said, "We don't ever lock the cells." Sure enough, the hasp of the door was broken off. "They can't get out, anyway. They might as well circulate and talk."

The food, he said, was enough. "By no means too much, but enough. Every day a pound of vegetables, a third of an ounce of oil, half an ounce of salt, a variable ration of rice and flour, with four ounces of meat once a week."

Back in the factory the machines clattered and thumped; some men plunged hanks of yarn into vats filled with scarlet dye, like blood. The expressionless men and women fed the knitting machines, churning out socks of violent candy-stripe—you saw those socks all over China; the factory's norm was reckoned, alarmingly, at four thousand dozen pairs a week. Men and women worked together; the gaudy socks piled up all around them with a strangely frivolous effect. Nobody spoke.

"We've had no escapes, ever," said the governor, "no physical punishment, and no escapes. Deaths? Maybe four or five a year. . . . When a prisoner is re-educated, and freed, the Labor Bureau tries to get him a job outside. As a matter of fact," said the governor, suddenly and fantastically, "some don't want to leave. They ask to stay on when their time's up. In that case, we just keep them at work, and pay them the standard union rate. Yes, we have about a hundred and fifty men here who could go any time they liked. They have separate quarters. I suppose they *like* it."

I was about to suggest that the gunmen on the towers, the electric fence around the walls must be as much to keep people out of this idyllic scene as to keep them in, but I didn't. The Chinese officials were kindness itself, and psychologically as elastic as a rubber band, but they do not joke with the Book.

So we had more cups of tea, and all the blue-suited cadres came to see me off, just as the factory stopped and the unknown political prisoners moved across the yard. They wore shirts and vests and colored kerchiefs and patches. It was odd, I thought, driving back through the gray tiled streets, that the people in jail are the only ones in China not in uniform.

I could now say "thank you" in Chinese, and "good-bye," and "Long Live Peace" and "more yellow wine, please." I could also recognize the middle character of my name, which is *mah*, but I dared not say it because, without the correct tone, it could mean "horse," "mother," "hemp," or "curse." I am all for ambiguity, but that went too far. It would be some time before I could read Confucius in the original.

It would also be some time before I could learn my way through the formulas. In new China the language trouble went a lot deeper than the total values.

This, I risked the feeling, was a delightful country, an enthusiastic and zealous country, almost inevitably a successful country. To anyone who knew the general standards of the East it was a living miracle. For this it owed nothing to the West. And now the Asian elusiveness overlaid by the more familiar double-think had made English the hardest tongue of all.

In these circumstances old phrases assumed a new meaning, the very words of which they were composed had buried implications, accepted by the devout. There was a glossary. Today one did not casually speak of "communism" but of "democracy"; for "progressive" one read "revolutionary"; by the word "feudal" was meant "before 1949." "Landlord" implied "robber baron"; for "Soviet" read "infallible," for "Mao" read "God." A "hero" was a worker who has exceeded his norm; a "saboteur" was someone who hadn't. For the real outsiders were saved terms like "individualist," "bourgeois" or "liberal." They were all highly original and new on our side twenty years ago; it was interesting to see the pattern absorbed here as readily as a new bicycle.

In Chinese, which is a beautiful language, full of complex imagery, much of the curse was taken off these time-worn adages. In any case they were not particularly sillier than the opposing jargon of the other side, which spoke of "Chinese expansionism" (as though these people did not appear to have their work cut out to fix up their own mammoth countryside), tagged a secondary meaning onto "progressive," and produced "fellow traveler" as the final kiss of death. It was no sillier, but it was exasperating to find *anything* silly in this ancient land which is possibly the unsilliest in the world. They didn't mean it; they just said it. They were carving an utterly new and extraordinary thing out of the groping wilderness of China, and they were defining it in the banal old terms of Union Square—of people who still had someone on the ground to fight.

The affairs of the world's largest Communist republic, the greatest human community on earth, were run by numbers of likable, able, often brilliant, noncommital men of a certain age, who all looked like schoolboys, who dressed to a man in well-tailored dungarees, and who looked upon me with much the same guarded astonishment as I did on them. It was like working on both sides of the zoo bars at once. The inquisitive stranger, then, spent many a long hour among these powerful, young-old, skilfully ingenuous veterans of the Revolution, sitting amongst the most dispiriting Tottenham Court Road fittings (in midst of which might well be a reproduction of a Tang horse), drinking endless cups of fragrant tea and smoking Chinese cigarettes (which were excellent). They gave me every courtesy, showed every wish to help me in what they considered a doubtless respectable and wholly incomprehensible job. They presented me with assessments and figures, which were usually percentages of a non-available base, but statistically expressed to the square root of zero. When that happened I was usually fairly glad; if I wanted to see China's new prosperity, I could walk in the streets, or look from the train windows, or visit the markets, or spend a morning in one of the multitude of nursery schools among the most enchanting children alive. If I wanted to see where new China *fails*, then I could wait long enough; if the demonstration existed, I should not see it. So it was no good the Vice Minister for this or for that wrapping me up in graphs and lining his periods, like a cook spicing a cake, with "Under the glorious leadership of Chairman Mao," or "With the inspiring example of the Soviet Union," or "Since we emerged from the imperialist yoke." Those matters I was prepared to take for granted; I did not have to be sold on the vicious system the Communists replaced; everyone knew it. I did not have to be told, when I was asking for a definition of "rich peasants," that the proletariat is well fed; I could see it wherever I went. I did not need to be told how grateful People's China is for the Soviet industrialization contribution; I could read it in any of the millions of dedicated handouts that seemed to constitute the entire product of the People's Democratic presses. I had come so seriously to admire the Chinese over the last few weeks that I could occasionally have hit them for the imbecile way their leaders sometimes talked.

The times came fairly soon, on a job of this kind, when one balanced the awkwardness of being denounced elsewhere for the heresy of liking the new Chinese, with the longer-term risk of compromising with the facts, as apparently revealed. A lot of troublesome reflection was thereby wasted before you were compelled to say that the Revolution in China had produced a nation more united and, as far as one could see, happier than ever before, and that by every recognizable evidence they were, as they endlessly claimed, peace loving. At the same time it was manifest that no individual had the least control over the broad policy and performance of their leaders, and that the leaders in their turn knew as little about the language of international persuasion as the Russians, which is to say very little indeed. There were even surrealist moments when one had the lunatic impulse to say, "Just let me run your propaganda for a while and I will present you as you are: industrious, anxious, well-meaning, friendly people— but by no means immortal, *nor* the only ones on earth. One occasional hint of fallibility could do you more good than a million words of jargon from the arid files of the Comintern."

It was vain and pointless to talk wholly in terms of personal experience, but there it was—the suspicion that mellowed the moment one's companion realized it was not mutual; the resentment born of frustrations that were still more Oriental than Marxist. And then one saw the simple peasant, chosen at random, and he was so palpably well rehearsed, one's questions faded away; one asked for a village, and one found oneself in a place so immaculate that its roads were tramped smooth by the feet of the endless delegations that had gone before.

"How did these people *live?*" one asked, and the answer seemed always to be: "In answering silly questions from nosy foreigners and telling them how well off we now are." Would they *all* give that answer? Perhaps. Six million questions would be a lot to ask.

Perhaps the enduring memory of China would always be this curious alternation of hope and despair. The splendid and admirable things you found out for yourself, the bad somehow always exposed by your guides and mentors. The delight came from the columns of well-clad and clearly beloved children, the evident devotion to babies, the impulsive friendship for strangers, the simple fact that everyone *looked* redeemed. The weariness came from the emphasis on all the peripheral aspects of communism—the badges on people's tunics, the deism of Mao and Malenkov and the other immortals, the evasiveness—no official ever knew the name of the street in case it was reactionary; no one knew the day of the week; to find out what was the price of a phone call you were referred to the Minister of Communications. You knew they were good, and they forced bits of paper on you saying they were perfect. You wanted to cry out, "Just be happy and well shod and love your babies as you clearly do, and your country as you clearly do, and not only shout all day long about peace but do something about it, and I am on your side. But just keep on telling me about the glorious leadership, etc., and that we shall have peace even if we have to lick the world for it, and my mind slowly closes down."

This was probably the greenhorn's reaction. Soon, I thought, I should have this petulance killed or cured. In the meantime—this was a totalitarian state; I was using their wires and mails. I cabled these observations, word for word, *en clair*, through the Chinese Posts and Telegraphs. They arrived, swiftly, and untouched. Later I did worse. No one moved a comma. That was not an inconsiderable fact.

(7)
Several Temples

THE prayer flags stood in spinneys like the masts of invisible ships, sails half furled, slender bamboos with fifteen feet of stripcloth, restless and swaying. Every flutter a prayer, every stirring in the wind a propitiation and a duty fulfilled. Some were tattered—would that then be only half a prayer, or a prayer halfheartedly said? You heard them overhead, purring. Nobody knew for whom the prayers were said; there was nobody there.

The Lama Temple was bright and spotless; it stood —the most immaculate Lama Temple, surely, in all Asia —among the pedicabs at the corner of the Tartar City of Peking. Business may be poor since Liberation, but prosperity met you at the door. The under-lama who acted as guardian of the Seven Buddhas and the Thirty-nine Manifestations of Power was a civil servant now; he showed me round his gaudy cloisters with an air that held a curious shifting blend of professional reverence and contempt. I have been in many lamaist *gompas* before, but never one so glossy, so gay, so much a product of the feather duster and the permanganate of potash. The joss sticks smoldered away gently in their jars of sand, leaving no ash.

The temples ranged back in courtyards, one behind another; on their curling golden roofs the little ceramic monsters grimaced at the gray sky, and the bells donged mournfully in the breeze. We stood before the First Buddha, the Laughing Buddha—potbellied and jocose, like a fat comedian in a Turkish bath. All around hung the great *thang-ka* paintings of the Four Directions and the Wheel of Life, which must say the same thing whichever way it is read. Here, at least, can be no improvising—the designs must embody the Eight Lucky Signs: the Umbrella, the Shell of Victory, the Vase, the Lotus, the Golden Fish, the Lucky Diagram, the Banner and the Wheel. On the other wall, the Glorious Offerings—the White Turnip, the Mirror, the Intestinal Concretions, the Dharwa Grass, the Curds—or the Seven Personal Gems, the Five Sensuous Delights. . . . Somehow it hardly seemed like the capital of Communist China. "If this is dialectical materialism," I said to the man, "then I am a Parsee."

"The Temple was built," said the lama imperturbably, "at the time of Yung Chan of the Ch'in Dynasty, in the eighteenth century. Nobody bothered much about it. Naturally the Kuomintang clique let it fall to bits; they would. When the People's Government took it over, they repaired it. In 1952, they spent eight thousand four hundred million *yuan* on it, and look at it now."

Look at it now, indeed; no paint was redder, no godlings' masks more lovingly enameled in the proper expressions of violence and horror, on each outstretched arm a new votive cloth of muslin, signifying gifts. The old believers had let the Temple decay; the Kuomintang had sacked it; it was left to the atheists of the new regime to spend eight thousand four hundred million People's *Yuan* on the elaborate monument to intricate and wholly reactionary worship. Why?

The Chinese Communists are flexible and accommodating, but they do nothing without political reason.

When they liberated Tibet, they drove straight for its heart, which is religion: Lamaism, the amplified and distorted Buddhism. Communist China owns six million Buddhists, and another seven million in Tibet, Sinkiang and Inner Mongolia. From the very start it began to woo them with Buddhism itself. Peking does not export Marxism to the minority areas, not yet. The Communists impose no land reform on Tibet, no legal reform, no marriage reform. As for religion, Mao Tse-Tung repeatedly shrugged his shoulders and said, "If it does not interfere with the operations of the People's Republic, the People's Republic will not interfere with it." The enormous implicit reservations in that were not emphasized, at least to the Buddhists.

The State made haste to create the All-China Buddhist Association for "the unity of all Buddhists to support the Motherland and world peace." They made the Dalai Lama and the Panchen Lama patrons; for President they chose Yuang Ying, the seventy-one-year-old Chinese abbot of a seminary in Shanghai.

Thus one of the first effects of the Revolution was the customary paradox: an immediate and officially sponsored revival of Buddhism. Monasteries were organized and brought into political prominence; the Abbot Hsijai-chiasto was extricated from the Chinghai Monastery and made Vice-Chairman of his provincial government. A really excellent stroke of luck caused the sudden discovery of the hundred and fifty-seven caves in Kansu Province filled with sculptures and murals of the classic period of Buddhist art.

And the Lama Temple of Peking was turned into the smartest place of worship ever to be used as a demonstration of the adaptability of the Communist faith.

Again, why? It was not a question of tolerating a

Chinese religion: was there ever a Chinese religion? Every authority is agreed that in no sense have the Chinese ever been a devout people; throughout their enormous history they have attached themselves to no deism, no especial priesthood, no scripture. At the very best the Chinese had, instead of religion, philosophies, shot through with wild and erratic superstition. Long ago the West "discovered" the Chinese metaphysical system with a sense of revelation—here was a remarkable principle of ethics unspoiled by any spirituality; a religion without penalties or rewards, without prayer, without resurrections, without heaven or hell: the morality of reasonableness. Confucius, inscribing his immortal cynicisms and sentimentalities a century before Socrates, was a teacher all the more consoling to the skeptics because he was in no sense divine. And a good reliable Tory, what was more. All will be well, said Confucius, if the upper classes remain upright and conscious of their responsibilities. It all depends on the Civil Service, mused Confucius, that old Civil Servant; govern by moral influence and not by force, and put authority only into the hands of cultivated men of elevated character.

But religion? Five centuries before Christ the philosopher had his answer. "You must revere the Gods," said Confucius gravely, "just as though they existed."

If the Confucians were positive ("Do good, so that you do not do wrong"), the Taoists produced a philosophy of inaction that was remarkable even by the languid standards of the Orient. The *Tao* was the great reality which created and governed the Universe, to conform with the *Tao* entailed a masterly control of doing, as far as possible, nothing whatever. Men should *behave*, said the Taoists, not *perform*, lest by unconsidered action they be led into error. Reduce society to its simplest, they said; abolish the value of money (which would thus automatically abolish covetousness and avarice). The Taoists conceived the perfect conception: a village whose inhabitants would be aware of the existence of other villages because of the sound of far away roosters crowing, but who would have no ambition whatever to know who lived in them. The ideal society—without communications, trade, correspondence, or integrated government. Anarchy *plus* apathy; what could be more agreeable?

Such Taoists as still exist (and there are some) can be taken as having a thin time under the new regime. Yet by the very virtue of their own principles they can scarcely care. Nobody could call Taoism a religion any more than Confucianism, or the School of Law, or Buddhism, or ancestor worship, or the cult of burning little boats to propitiate the river-gods. Or for that matter the faiths that have accreted here and there, minority corners in the great empty room: Christianity and Islam. The Chinese remained, and remain, what they always were: philosophical and tolerant and cynical, agnostic and eclectic. To this day the architect who has passed his compulsory dialectic-materialistic course at Tsin Hua University will still allow space on his rooftrees for the seven little heraldic monsters who have stood sentry against evil for three thousand years: he will still build a board across every threshold to discourage the penetration of devils (who, as every Marxist knows, can travel only in straight lines, and are thus baffled by any impediment).

Indeed this accommodating stupidity is the chief quality of most Chinese gods, and anti-gods. Place a high step across your doorway and you are safe from the crawling demons. Should they attempt to besiege you from the roof, you curve your eaves upwards and the sliding spirits tumble to earth at least six feet away. ("Respect the Gods by all means," said Confucius, "but keep them at a proper distance.") By the grace of God, the gods were easily fooled. If the sailor's boat was endangered by storm, it was necessary only to throw a paper reproduction over the side and the gods would sink it, and spare the other. If the gods demanded a sacrifice at a funeral or a wedding, then a specially made, worthless paper money was ostentatiously burned. Anything was good enough to deceive the gods, so long as the gesture was made. For the rest, formulas were formulas; a patient man could be Confucian, Taoist, Buddhist, animist or rationalist, alternatively or all at once; he could believe in complex ritual and austerity, zeal and sloth, metaphysics and common sense—he was a flexible and tolerant man; he was Chinese.

Now, of course, he is something else again: he is Communist. Or some of him is, the part that matters. Yet here in Peking, a mile from the unidentified dwelling of Chairman Mao himself, the joss sticks still burned—only today, of course, nationalized.

The temple bells swung and disputed gently in the cold breeze; somewhere across the Seventh Courtyard an acolyte cleared his throat with a thunderous rattle, remembered himself in time, and disposed of it in a spittoon decorated with the Endless Dragon. In the shadows beyond could be seen the shape of the demon, carrying in each of his sixteen hands a different instrument of violence, demonstrating thereby the many opportunities man is offered for his own destruction.

"And finally," said the under-lama, emerging from a dream, "the Great Room, dedicated to the Lamaist faith two hundred and fifty years ago. You will observe . . ."

But there was nothing to observe in the vast gaunt chamber but the image itself, the upright standing representation of the Ruling Buddha—a towering thing ninety feet tall, black and forbidding, the white-painted ferocious eyes glaring across to some unseeable horizon, a minatory hand as big as a billiard table. For one terrible moment he looked, standing there with his gigantic head in the shadows of the roof, almost bigger than the portrait of Chairman Mao.

Outside in the street a dreich wind stirred up the ashen dust, the pedicab drivers huddled together like sheep, wrangling among themselves to keep warm. A hundred yards away was a turn to the right. I walked for two minutes between the windowless walls: another gate, another door, another temple. The vestiges of paint flaked away from the planks, the wicket swung on one hinge. This was the Temple of Confucius.

The comment was too obvious to be avoided: the prophet had no honors *here*. Confucius was a discredited soothsayer in the People's China; Confucius had been invoked too often by the old regime, he was inextricably tied up with Chiang Kai-Shek. In China today they say, "What were the moral precepts of the old paternalism but something that allowed the emperors and the mandarins to force obedience to these gentlemen-scholars? Were the gentlemen-scholars of Confucius a privileged class, or weren't they? This classical-traditional-formalistic idea is the perfect dogma for opposing democracy. What did 'filial piety' ever do except discourage national consciousness and encourage nepotism? Who said 'Courtesy is not served to commoners and punishment is not served to lords'?"

Doubtless he said better things too, I murmured; but it made no difference. There was no room in the Revolution for Confucius and his hierarchical system, his pattern of loyalties (son to the father, wife to the husband, tenant to the landlord, servant to the master, fool to the sage), his insistence on individual quality, the implications of docility. No eight thousand four hundred million People's *Yuan* for Confucius—but his Temple remains. I looked through the shabby old door and saw it at work, even then—for even then in that shadowy courtyard the disciples were gathered, some two dozen of them, seated blue-suited under the bending tree, deep in their books. Religion was free in China today, but accommodation was scarce. The Temple of Confucius had become a study room of the Peking department of the Marxist-Leninist Institute of China.

"Revere the Gods," said the disenchanted voice, two and a half thousand years ago, "just as though they existed."

The first Sunday in Peking I walked down the end of Former Morrison Street, and there on the right was a church—apparently active, clearly Roman Catholic. It was built in a rather painful European-Russian style; on its façade it had the lowering date "1905"; its tower carried a cross and, above that, a red star. It was clearly a church, active in its fashion; and not a sacked or abandoned or commandeered church. I went in; one can always learn something from churches.

The front door was locked. When I tried it, some Chinese appeared—you can do nothing in China but someone appears, instantly, usually *en famille*—and with great courtesy led me round to the open door at the back. The church was empty. Yet a sacristan was arranging fresh flowers, and the altar light was burning. It was a church —not an eight-thousand-four-hundred-million *yuan* museum, nor yet a decayed and transmuted temple. It was certainly "reformed"—in the political sense; it was one of the churches that accept the leadership of the new Government, that make no tedious insistences on un-equivocal speech, that send the "reformed" nuns to show their redemption by walking in the National Day pro-cessions. But it was a church.

"Do people still come here?" I asked the attendant.

"Yes," he said, "sometimes."

And then one day I took a turning I rarely used, that led from Hata Men to the Market, past a tall, gray, anony-mous building of which I had taken care not to enquire too much. Very high up, almost invisible, was a stone Christ in a niche, the windows were always shuttered; I had heard some stories about its being a school now.

This day a little group of porters and pedicab drivers had gathered round the gates. I looked into the yard and saw a group of nuns in white habits, half a dozen of them standing in a silent row down the steps from the big front door. I had never seen it opened before; now it was, and four men came out carrying a coffin. Without much difficulty they manhandled it onto a wheelbarrow, and tied it down with ropes, grunting and chattering and straining on the knots, while the silent nuns looked on, their faces shielded by their hoods, their hands folded over their long rosaries.

Then someone opened the creaking iron gate and two men pushed the wheelbarrow out into the street. I saw it had two white ribbons tied over it to form a cross. There was no cortège, no flower, no words; only a coffin in a wheelbarrow jolting alone through the streets. It turned the corner among the traffic, and when I looked back the nuns were gone and the door was shut again.

One convent, then, remained in Peking. I found out about it very soon. It was allowed to remain because the

sisters were teaching, and the convent was a school—
the only school—for children of the diplomatic and con-
sular colony in Peking. Many times thereafter I used to see
them—small Europeans and Indians and Pakistanis—arriving in cars with the large red character that meant "C.D."
in China, and vanishing into the shuttered building.

Only six nuns were left. They were, it was said, increasingly unhappy and in difficulties because the priest
had gone, and could not be replaced. Before long, everyone said, they will try to go away themselves, if they can.
They were Franciscans, of many nationalities; no one
knew just what. . . . When anyone asked them they
merely said, "We are nuns." They did not leave the
building. It seemed a gray and nearly hopeless life.

For a long time I did not go near the convent because
my own position was ambiguous, and I felt that any effort of mine to make contact with the nuns might be
unhelpful to them; at the least embarrassing. But one
day I heard—somehow, in the curious way one hears
things in such a place—that they were not afraid, that
they would welcome a visit.

When I rang the bell there was no sound; I waited for
five minutes and was on the point of leaving when the
door was opened by a Chinese nun. I went in—empty,
echoing; a blank unused waiting room with a sacred picture and a vase of paper flowers. I was unexpected, I had
timed my call badly, I was foolish to have come. I waited
another ten minutes before the Mother and a sister entered, their pale, waxen, gentle faces uncreased by faint
smiles. They spoke French, but I stumbled and hesitated;
I did not know what to say. They would not know me,
clearly, for friend or enemy. I was not even *croyant*; I had
not that much excuse. I said I was only enquiring after
their well-being—a fatuous remark. They said, "We must

not complain." I was torn by the anxiety to learn something of this extraordinary half-life behind the convent walls, with Red China surging all around, and an even greater anxiety not to appear to lure them into any remark even faintly compromising. But everything seemed either futile or dangerous. The nuns sat patiently; they said, "We have our work—the school. We are busy. We do not have much contact with the city. . . . You have come a long distance?" they asked politely, and I spoke a little about Europe. I think they were relieved, in their gentle way, when I took my leave.

I had only put my foot on the step when the door was shut behind me. I went out through the yard and the gate, where the coffin had gone, strapped on its wheelbarrow, bumping alone to the Chinese grave past the gray walls and the red flags and the demons on the eaves.

(8)

The Sound Barrier

THE proprietor of the restaurant called "That Which Is Richly Endowed," of which there are few more agreeable in all Peking, appeared at the courtyard door and bowed, and expressed himself in a few brief words of execration. "May you, your sons, and your sons' sons," he seemed to say, "burn forever in the pit." He smiled with gentle courtesy, and ushered us in with a gesture of welcome, murmuring, one felt, "Let me formally state my loathing of yourself, your company, and your custom. . . ." His quiet voice behind the kindly smile tailed away on a querulous note of regret.

Thus the sound. What in fact he had said—he, the most genial restaurateur who ever sliced a lacquered duck—was the traditional greeting of host to guest, used still today as it was in the days of the Empress: "Your presence," he had said, "illumines the walls of my room. May the poor food that awaits grace the appetite your generosity deserves."

How, one thought for the five hundredth time, can one *ever* learn Chinese? How can one ever divine, not its meaning, which is beyond all ambition, but even its *purpose?* A man may be ignorant of Russian, or Spanish, or English, or Bulgarian, or French, but at least there are narrow limits within which he can detect at least their *mood*—the speech has phrases, the phrases have rhythm; at least one knows when a sentence has come to an end. Without knowing Italian, or Hebrew, or Greek it is possible to infer from the intonation some sense of its general intention; a phrase will end on a note of interrogation, or anger, or amusement, or threat. But to the Chinese tones are not mood, they are meaning itself; only by investing his few monosyllables with a great variety of sounds and playing tunes on his words can he express himself at all. Chinese has no enquiring note of interrogation, or flat tone of conviction, or if it has, it is only to distinguish the *mah* that means "mother" from the *mah* that means "horse," or the *mah* that means "curse," or "hemp." Thus the most endearing phrase can, by the unalterable necessity of its word-tones, sound like an imprecation. There are no clues.

The Mandarin language demands an instinctive and supple ear and a wholly certain grasp of the Four Tones —*ping*, the equal tone; *shang*, the equal high tone; *chu*, the rising tone; *ju*, the falling tone. (The Cantonese, elaborating the mystery, insist on *nine* tones.)

So the Chinese can have no interrogative sound, no positive or negative intonations, no aggressive, no affectionate, no cajoling or ironic; no nuances can be imposed on a language that has no spelling, *only* sounds. Depending on whether he sings his syllable in *do* major or *re* minor, the Chinese alters it from a noun to a verb, from a "knife" to a "boot," from "honorable" to "devilish," from wisdom to nonsense. To know Chinese you must *know*; you can never guess.

This is strange, and sometimes frightening. That skillful French interpreter of the Oriental mood, Claude Roy, recalled that when Jean Cocteau, in his *Sang d'un Poète*, thrust his hero into nightmare, he sought just one incident that would establish forever the sense of the fearful and the bizarre: Listening at the closed door of a hotel room, he heard someone inside talking Chinese. . . .

It is not, they always told me, that the words are intricate or mysterious; on the contrary, it is the simplicity and indeed poverty of vocabulary that makes necessary its impossible tonality; Chinese is a language of monosyllables and few at that. Chinese babies learn to *talk* when other babies are cooing. A Chinese word is a brick; a Chinese sentence .is a wall. Other nations may use their language as a palette, a reservoir of assorted meanings capable of infinite variation; to the Chinese words have a function precise and arbitrary, at no man's mercy. Shakespeare and Racine and Dostoevsky could mold sentences by an immense process of modulation, inference, subjectivity. ("When *I* use a word," said Humpty-Dumpty, "it means just what I choose it to mean; neither more nor less.") To a Chinese such flexibility is incomprehensible. If a European sentence is a painting, a Chinese sentence is a mosaic. A Chinese rose is a rose—without genders or cases, without prepositions or articles, declensions or conjugations, prefixes or suffixes, without an alphabet, without (as we know the term) grammar of any kind. Rich, no doubt, in verbs; verbs must stand in for adjectives. A Chinese river is not yellow; instead "the river yellowfies." There is not such a thing as an angry cat; "the cat angers."

Chinese is untranslatable; there is no English shorthand capable of rendering the succinct simplicity of the language; it is like reproducing the austere economy of a Picasso drawing by embroidering it with thread. There is the example that has become classic in the new regime, from Mao Tse-Tung's "Revolutionary Strategy" which, it is hardly necessary to add, is to be found in many translations in the International Bookshop of Peking. "The rudimentary yet fundamental guerilla principle," wrote Mao, "can be expressed in six key words. . . ."

What follows must have been a matter of serious awkwardness to the translator, since one does not monkey about with the holy words of Chairman Mao, and at the same time one must hesitate before denying the truth of what he says. It goes on: "The enemy advances; we retire fighting; the enemy entrenches, we harass him; the enemy tires, we attack; the enemy retires fighting, we pursue." The six key words become twenty-three. Mao did it in half a dozen; Chairman Mao's command of the language is outstanding, everyone says.

All this I learned, over the weeks, from the industrious and sedulous companions whose strange task it was to do, for hours a day, exactly that which is so nearly impossible to do—the interpreters, the two or three young men who became, in the end, a sort of extension of myself. They were good, very good. On the whole they were also kind. It was not long before they—being Chinese, and therefore intensely individual—emerged from the rather businesslike impersonality of State servants and became people, with very considerable human variations of temper and mood. I got to like them very much, even the ones who sometimes did not like me.

It might serve no good purpose too closely to distinguish between them by their real names. I sometimes had the impression that we walked a tightrope between friendship and suspicion; once or twice, after a period of increasing familiarity with one or another of them, ending in some wholly social and delightful carouse, I would lose sight of him; for many days he would just not appear and would be replaced by another. This was always explained at second hand by the pressure of other work, and could well have been true; not infrequently I was misled by the rather tense atmosphere of the times into imagining contrived situations that were probably genuinely accidental.

In the end the company was reduced to a steady handful. I came to think of them as Young Li, who looked like a promising prefect in an English school and was at least always as eager to learn about me as I about him; and Quiet Hsi, who had a face like a leathern mask and a nature, curiously, most sensitive to rebuff. There was Big Wei, whose English was better than mine, never at a loss for a phrase, however recondite or technical, the most inflexibly Communist of them all who, perhaps symbolically, had been to college in Philadelphia and who sometimes murmured his most bitter maxims in the pure accents of the Delaware. There was the French professor, a wiry young-old pedagogue whose French had an odd and subtle charm, who knew all there was to know about silk paintings of the eighteenth century. . . .

There was the seminarist, the most peculiar of all. He was a studious and gangling youth of a physical awkwardness bordering on the grotesque; he wore enormous boots and his thin wrists protruded inches from the sleeves of his blue jacket; he knew just enough English to make conversation between us extravagantly difficult.

Somehow he had contrived to absorb all the most subsidiary and unnecessary words of the language, all the accessory phrases and conjunctional clauses, all the "howevers" and "neverthelesses." He would say, "By the way . . ." or "As matter fact . . ." or "Oh, I say . . ." and then taper off into perplexed and groping speechlessness.

He came to be known as the seminarist because

in some curious Oriental way that was exactly what he looked like; his social graces were nonexistent and he had a heart of gold. When he ate with us, he would sometimes affect a cosmopolitan air and try to use knife and fork, but it was clear they both mystified and embarrassed him, and soon he would be reduced to putting his face down to table level and shoveling the noodles two-handed into his mouth, with tremendous eructations and belchings and anxious unhappy smiles.

He was made use of by the other interpreters as a kind of servant, looking after baggage, knocking on doors at mealtimes with the call, "Ah, yes, as it were . . ." and then a long pause. "For all that . . . Feeding present now."

Whenever one needed assistance of any kind the seminarist would come shambling along with pleased and willing awkwardness, ready at any time with his convoluted thought to turn a difficult situation into an impossible one. At the end it was he whom I missed as much as anyone; alone among my interpreters, watchdogs, analysts and friends did the seminarist *not* fill me with a sense of my own aimlessness.

It was Young Li and Big Wei, however, who fostered my interest in the Chinese language. One took no risks with that; it was like taking an interest in the Quantum Theory, one could be superficially beguiled without running into any danger of involvement. The Old China Hands, after all, rarely had the inclination or the ability to learn the language; when it defeated them, they despised it. From the unsatisfactory union of the two disparate cultures and purposes was born a bastard, deformed and retarded: Pidgin English. This corrupted both English and Chinese in a double sense, removing the music of the Chinese words and the grammatical symmetry of the English; it strung isolated English words in the Chinese pattern, without grace or syntax. It compromised with the Eastern inability to disentangle the sounds of L and R, and gave a horrible sanction to the school of *vellee muchee*. (This particular aberration has always puzzled me deeply; there is *some* justification for it; throughout the Far East one seldom finds anyone capable instinctively of sorting out these consonants. Both the L and the R can readily be pronounced, but somehow only in reverse order. In Tokyo it had always struck me as extremely odd that the only way of verbally identifying the Press Club was to refer to it as the Pless Crub. Mysterious.)

To begin with I tried, in a rather hopeless way, to learn what anywhere else might have been called "a few handy phrases"; very soon I abandoned this as not only impractical but positively dangerous, since the smallest defect of intonation could not merely blur the meaning but actually invert the whole sense. The foreigner says, "Where is the office?" but the startled doorman only hears, "I abominate your mother."

I am, nevertheless, an amateur and indeed enthusiastic collector of phrase books, less for their practical value (which in my view is nil; either you cannot express a phrase or you express it so effectively that it elicits a long and effusive reply in the same tongue, with subsequent humiliation) than for the manner in which they seem to reveal the worst aspects both of the compiler's mind and of the language he is explaining.

Anyone who has ever had to conduct a conversation through, for example, an "Old Traveller's Hindustani" will know how firmly and masterfully it avoids all expressions other than barks of command, peremptory complaint, and abuse. It is an ineradicable belief in the minds of those who write phrase books that no one could conceivably find himself in a foreign land without instantly wanting his laundry done, his servants denounced, his food taken away, and his bills questioned.

Of the two Chinese phrase books I had, both erred at opposite extremes.

One was a very old paper-backed pamphlet of many pre-revolutionary years ago. I had bought it long before in Singapore, I fancy, against some improbable emergency. It was called "Sentences English," and it had clearly been created for the cultivation of small talk, and rather unusually futile small talk at that. One felt that its anonymous author could have gleaned his material only by eavesdropping at some burlesque garden party in the suburbs. There were pages of: "Lovely morning, isn't it?" "Fine day, isn't it?" "Rotten weather, isn't it?" "Looks like going rain (snow, wind)." "Cold (hot, wet, dry), isn't it?" "Getting cooler (hotter, wetter, drier), isn't it?" They were followed by more pages of equally unrewarding detail: "How do you do?" "I am do fine!" "How of family?" "All well too!" One might have thought it some mad Oriental satire on how the English are supposed to talk, with curious local adaptations and nonsequiturs: "You see, Dr. Chang!" "Yes, Professor Li!" "Much spending, Doctor!" "Fifty dollar a gallon, Professor!"

But it had one even greater and enveloping disadvantage; the Chinese part of the work was written in Chinese characters, which reduced its already dubious value to zero as far as I was concerned.

Infinitesimally more useful, though far more awkward, was a Chinese phrase book which had been issued by the United States Army. (I regretted having bought it, since I felt obliquely compromised by it; I would have gladly disposed of it had it not been for the extraordinary practical difficulty, which I have already explained, of *ever* throwing anything away.) This work, however, gave an English version of the Chinese characters, full of elaborate typographical devices to indicate inflective changes, which produced an oddly alarming effect.

"Obey or I fire!" it said: *RUH! sher BOO! TING! war DUH MING! LING!* "Are you hungry?" asked the book, with a clipped emphasis: *UH! boo UH!* In its glossary a private soldier was, rather evocatively: *UHR! dung BING.* But a staff sergeant was, as one could well imagine: *SHAUNG! SHER!* There was a brief enquiry: "Where is a restaurant? I want to buy food," interpreted in terms suggestive of a man ravening with famine: *SH-UM-muh DEE! faung yo FAHN! gwahn DZ! waw YOW! ma-ee CHER duh.*

Some words almost explained themselves; a howitzer was *YOO DAHN! POW!* and a husband, with a dying fall: *shy shun.*

And, perhaps best of all, a stimulant—*SHING! FUN! YOW!*

But times had changed. Here was I in Peking among the Puritans, and there was not much Shing, very little Fun, and absolutely no Yow at all.

"Since you are interested," said Young Li one morning, with what may have been a gentle undertone of irony, "we could take a morning off from politics, economics and industrial reconstruction, and go and see Wei Chueh. Words!—he knows them all. He can get *most* exasperated by them. Wei Chueh is Vice-Chairman of the Committee for the Reform of the Chinese Written Language. One of our major reforms. When it comes off, that is."

Wei Chueh turned out to be a scholarly gentleman

of a somewhat distrait courtesy, clearly harassed by the magnitude of his enormous job, which had already been some years under study and looked like being many more. It would indeed be quite difficult to devise any philological proposition more staggeringly difficult than to reform a script that has no letters, no sequence, an arbitrary storehouse of tens of thousands of separate individual drawings, any one of which may well have up to half a dozen separate individual meanings. Yet clearly it had somehow, and some time, to be done.

"It is no good saying that we know just how," said the scholar, "because we don't, although we have some ideas. It is *very* troublesome. In fact, it is a troublesome language. It is far from easy even for us. A ten-year-old schoolboy should know about two thousand characters. With about seven thousand he can read the *People's Daily*, though I imagine they have anything up to thirty-five thousand or more in their composing room. But what a fuss! Every character requiring a separate effort of memory! Every character requiring to be drawn like a portrait! No alphabet, so no way of keeping the characters in order—so no type-setting machines, no satisfactory way of indexing anything. And the telegraph! Why, every time a Chinese sends a wire it has to be broken up into numbers. Most picturesque, of course, and nothing like it for literature, but think how it impedes the progress of education among our illiterates. It just isn't *democratic*, that is its trouble. But how to change it?"

The overwhelming difficulty has always been that what the Chinese *hears* has no relation whatever to what he *sees*. Writing began, they say, when the legendary Tsang Chieh devised the notion of writing by observing the processes of "natural" writing—the footprints of men in sand, the skeletons of leaves, the rings of tree trunks.

Today still the little drawings that represent the fact, or the concept, begin purely pictographically: "home" is a roof sheltering a pig; "man," a simple pair of legs; "rain," a series of drops; "dawn," the sun on the horizon; "to think" is the twin symbols of brain and heart.

In time the representational ideograph gradually became as muted visually as the Greek roots in English. To distinguish the especial meaning of a character its ideographic sign would be united with a phonetic indicator. As life became more complex and men expanded their intellectual sphere, ideas could be represented only by associations of characters, families of drawings, each one of which could have a separate *or* a group-life. Thus the character *hsueh* alone means "study"; when mingled with the character *wen*, or "writing" it becomes *wen hsueh*, or "literature." Combine it with the characters *sheng wu*, or "living objects," it produces *sheng wu hsueh*—"biology." The marriage of words breeds new words, often delightful. When or if you ever get the hang of it, my interpreter friends would tell me with a genuine reflective pleasure, it becomes both semantically satisfying and artistically right—and sure enough, as I had suspected, even the arid phrases of contemporary politics achieved a sort of primitive coziness when broken down into basic ideas. "Capitalism" is *money-root-policy*. "Communism" is *together-production-system*. "Democracy" is *many-at-once-peace*, and "parliament" is *talk-govern-meeting*. To me, somewhat numbed over the years by the variegated impact of international jargon, this seemed to me a system almost miraculously valuable in restoring, at least to one people, some fundamental idea of what these corrupted and punch-drunk words actually *mean*.

"Doubtless, doubtless," said Wei Chueh with a certain rather sad impatience, "but we have to be practical.

We don't want our political concepts to be comprehensible only to a crowd of professors. By all means let us keep the pleasant associations, but we have to *simplify.* Let me show you what we are getting at." And he went to a blackboard and began to stab at it with short, controlled movements of the chalk.

"There are, of course, only a few basic strokes. You can have characters with as few as two, but most of them are horribly complex, and to know the precise order in which to draw the strokes takes a lot of doing. Up to a point we have simplified already; many literate people use a sort of shorthand which we call 'running script.' It is fairly new, not more than a thousand years old.

"But it is nothing like enough—there it is; I am sorry, but the old characters will have to go, however decorative they may look to people who don't have to waste years learning what they mean. We have to complete the change-over to a phonetic alphabet—in the proper way, and under the proper leadership, of course," he said, apparently abruptly conscious that the discussion had been drifting into undesirable shallows.

"In the Dictionary of the Emperor Kang Hsi, three hundred years ago," he said, "there were forty-five thousand characters, for what? Little verses extolling the glory of the palaces and accepting the squalor of the villages. The delicate description of a leaf alighting on a lake. A stanza on the echo of a mountain stream. Surely we can do better?

"And again, why *should* we invent an alphabet?" he suddenly demanded, almost crossly. "I know, it is necessary. But we must not forget that the Chinese written language is national just because it is *not* phonetic. A man from the North will have difficulty understanding what a Cantonese says, or a man from Fukien—but no trouble understanding what he writes. Nothing to do with the sound, you see. Like mathematical symbols in your part of the world. I believe all Europeans understand the meaning of the *plus* and *minus* symbols, however they may say them? That is the analogy. We have some very peculiar dialects, I may tell you, largely because of the poor communications in the past, but they are all *written* the same way. A phonetic alphabet will be a difficulty there, no?"

I said that I supposed they would just have to have several phonetic languages.

"I should hope *not*," said the professor grimly. "*That* would not be progressive in the least. One of our great problems in the New China has been abolishing these regional and class differences. You know there has always been a literary distinction between the so-called 'spoken' language and the written tongue. It was supposed to have been abolished in the big May Fourth Movement of nineteen nineteen, but the Kuomintang crowd still insisted on writing Government ordinances and things in the classical form, which hardly anyone could understand. Now, over the years we've managed to develop this *lingua franca*—the *pai hua*, the common tongue. Less elaborate than Mandarin, which we call *Kuo-yu*. The Constitution was written in it. It is used in Congress, and ninety per cent of them understand it. Except the National Minorities, of course. . . .

"Oh, there's another problem, indeed. My dear sir, we have more than forty million people belonging to the Minorities—and the tongues they talk! Kam-Thai, Miao-Yao, Tibeto-Burman, Mon-Khmer, Uighur, Mongol, Tungusic . . . all of them subdivided and mutated and mixed up all ways. Our Minority Institute here in Peking teaches fourteen separate languages and twenty-five dialects. Some of them have accents and no tones, some have tones and no accents. In the Altai family they have 'vocalic harmony'—the phrase has got to *rhyme*, can you imagine? Some of them have scripts of their own, too—we don't stop them; our Government lets the Minorities pretty much alone, as you know. But there are still five hundred and fifty millions of us, the Han people. . . .

"No, we have not yet decided on an alphabet. However, this is sure: Chinese is certainly going to be written horizontally, and it is certainly going from left to right. It is unlikely we shall invent a wholly new script—*that* would be complicating chaos, surely. We don't know whether we shall use the Latin script or the alphabet used by our Soviet allies.

"Whatever it is, it will be gradual. Our Chinese writing has been in existence for thousands of years. We want to spread our education, but we don't want to change everything overnight and turn all our present educated people into illiterates, do we? Imagine the vacuum that would form! Slowly, slowly. We are not *abolishing* things. There will—in the future—be nothing to prevent interested people and experts from studying the old Chinese script just as other dead languages are studied elsewhere. We are only trying to *help*. . . .

"Dictionaries! How do you have a dictionary without an alphabet? What did Chairman Mao say, in nineteen forty?" He looked at Young Li, who took the cue like a well-judged pass: ". . . our written language must be reformed on certain conditions and brought close to the people. We must know that the people are the inexhaustibly rich source of our revolutionary culture. . . ."

"Now," said the professor, "let me show you some

of the difficulties of writing an ordinary character of multiple strokes; the simple word *li*, meaning 'beautiful. . . .' "

Young Li and I went down to the Chinese City and into a shop where they sold all manner of things that were very old and very beautiful, and some that were less old than they appeared but not necessarily the less imposing for all that. At the back of the shop—behind the rows of jade snuff bottles and porcelain bowls and long scroll paintings stacked on shelves and the old seals of anonymous personages, signatures fossilized in silver and jasper and porphyry (and doubtless bakelite and pre-stressed perspex too)—an old man with filigree whiskers sat at a table below a single staring bulb and wrote things on a piece of silk.

At his hand was his little tablet of ink—a tablet, because the ink was solid, tiny sable tombstones inscribed with characters of gold, a small rectangular palette moistened into a medium wholly dense, opaque, fuliginous, a black that was *black* beyond qualification. In his hand a brush charged with this splendid solidity, a brush with a fine point, held vertically against the surface of the silk like a spear. And then without haste yet without hesitation—the small gestures, the little arabesques, the controlled compositions of strokes that melted into the characters, one below the other, that meant—I had no idea what they meant, it seemed a matter of small importance; an expert writing Chinese can be appreciated by anyone. Yet there is the extra magic of the Chinese language: such is the intrinsic virtue of good calligraphy that it is lovely in its own right. A poem, therefore, achieves this double virtue, simultaneously it holds the heart *and* the eye: it is beautiful in two dimensions at once.

"No," said Young Li, "three; you forget the material. Beauty of phrase; beauty of line; and beauty of the silk itself.

"Or I might even add . . ." he said, as we walked back over the broken paving stones, past the swinging tripes at the butchers' doors, past the scented barrels of the chestnut roasters, past the dealers in fur hats and the merchants of dried fish, ". . . a fourth dimension of *value.* You have been here long enough to know. At least you recognize this phrase," said he, pointing to the banner one sees at every turn and hears quoted every day —and of course I did; at least fifty times it had been defined for me: the curious pattern of lines and squares that says, *Ho Ping Wan Tsei*—"No-war-a-thousand-years," or, as we might say, "Long Live Peace."

"Here," said I, surrendering, "endeth the first lesson." But Young Li merely nodded; clearly he was no Christian.

(9)
Man of Letters

THE day I met Tsao Yu was memorable for several
things; first in importance to me was that I had recov-
ered from a week-old headache, at least momentarily. It
gave a lightness to the morning that was not too far
from gaiety; I started the day feeling almost like someone else. I remember chiding Zig on his choice of tie—
he wore the R.A.F. colors, to which he was fully and hon-
orably entitled, and I somehow found that a cause for
humorous complaint; I shall never remember why. I
think I assailed Doctor Globo again on his open windows, his all-night typewritings, his obsession with fish
—everything, with the warmest good humor. I was
probably, in that astringent Peking atmosphere, quite
insufferable. But I was fairly happy; an odd condition,
productive of extremes.

Long ago, in some circumstances far removed from
these, I recalled a conversation—it may have been in
Hong Kong, or Viet Nam; somewhere on the periphery
of China—in which I first heard the name of Tsao Yu.
A dramatist, a man of letters—he had been known in the
old China for his work; somehow he had contrived to
remain known, and accepted, and indeed fully occupied,
in the new. He wrote, I seemed to remember, plays of
vigor and character; if he was not the Racine of Tartary,

nor the Ibsen, he was at any rate the Somerset Maugham.
I heard all this I cannot remember when, and at once
stored it for pending oblivion.

Quite soon after my arrival in China I had applied
(my long list of applications: everything from a talk
with Mao Tse-Tung to a trip to Lhasa) for an informal
meeting with *someone* who could speak personally of
the contemporary arts. It was obvious that many such
people existed, at least in some form; plays were being
performed, books rolled off the press, the Establishment
of Prosperous Harmony (a State concern) continued
to issue tons of engravings of unquestionable beauty. I
could not believe that so many generations of literary
excellence had reached its summit in the editorials of the
People's Daily. Who was writing now, and what? There
was clearly an implicit impertinence in the request (as
though I could even attempt a comparative assessment;
I can only know Chinese writing at a remote second
hand; could a Zulu appraise John Donne *versus* Ilya
Ehrenburg?). But I guessed, rightly, that this was the
sort of enquiry that would be considered proper, and
even praiseworthy. The ineluctable characteristic of the
Chinese is the value they put upon matters of reflection,
however bumbling.

After the usual decent interval the message came:
Comrade Tsao Yu would be delighted to give me tea
the next morning, at the International Club.

He struck me as being at least twenty years younger
than I had expected. There was nothing unusual in that;
in China there seems to be no intermediate age-group
between the juvenile and the veteran; I was forever meeting slight, smooth-faced young men in their late fifties
who controlled one or another facet of administration
involving several million people. I sat down with Tsao

Yu in one of the starkly depressing drawing rooms for which the International Club is justly renowned; the tea came, the cigarettes came, and I asked (since one had to ask something): How is the drama today?

The great dramatist endeared himself to me right away by very clearly not knowing how to tackle a gambit of such portmanteau character. Moreover, he was most evidently conscious of Wei, the interpreter. One of the international constants, in my experience, is that the more intelligent and articulate a man is, the more uneasy is he in the presence of an intermediary translator; he *knows* how nuances can be modified, how inflections can be ironed out; conversing through the best interpreter in the world is like making love through Malthus. Furthermore, official interpreters have not only ears, but memories.

I tried to prime the pump. "Are you busy now yourself?" He jumped at it: yes, he was indeed; he was at that moment rehearsing a new play. Had he known I was interested, he would have asked me round yesterday for the final reading. It was called "Bright Day," and its theme—well, said Tsao Yu, fingering the air, it was, naturally, the question of world peace. Was there any subject of more immediate importance? It was the story of a doctor. This young man had been trained in the United States, and returned to his homeland with many difficult and dangerous habits of mind. He did not, for example, believe in the terrible fact that the United States had made use of germ warfare during the Korean campaign. When he takes up his duties in the People's Hospital, he comes into conflict with his compatriots, already schooled in democratic principles. . . . He is not wholly unsympathetic, you understand, said Tsao Yu, only his thinking has been seriously distorted. Obviously the situation is dramatically provocative. The development takes the young doctor through his education to his eventual redemption. That is the "Bright Day."

"It has been extremely interesting and educative for me, too," said the playwright. "I myself learned a great deal from the hospital. You understand our modern principles and methods? You write plays about factories *in* factories, you dramatize hospitals *in* hospitals. There we advance over our predecessors. In the past the Chinese creative writing suffered from the defects of abstract generalization, the subjective method of creation. Our authors took ideas as their point of departure, not life itself. I myself was guilty of bourgeois imaginative thinking. We did not, in fact, get perception through personal experience, through observation and study of the people. . . ."

Once he had begun, the playwright spoke with a practiced, even an alarming fluency; he was a very handsome man with humorous eyes and most gracefully expressive hands; he drew his phrases from the air for all the world as though he himself had that moment conceived them. I liked him so much I very soon began to feel sad again. The trouble was, I had just read his source material, as will shortly become clear.

"You see," he said, with a smile, "the old writers—and among them I must include myself—portrayed life not according to the development of life as it is, but subjectively, according to some preconceived formula. What writers do *now*—as you must know—is establish *personal* contact with the masses. A writer will go to a factory, for instance, not just as an aloof observer, you understand; he will for the purposes of his study become one of the workers. Or, perhaps, to a village. In my case, to a hospital. One has come to understand that life must be observed and studied from the Marxist-Leninist standpoint on the spot, as well as from the standpoint based on Party and Government policies, so that one is not overwhelmed by the complexities of human nature."

"And you yourself spent some time in the hospital to absorb the atmosphere?"

"Of course. Many months. Not just for the technicalities of procedure—though I must say," said Tsao Yu in a kind of absent-minded parenthesis, "these things are remarkably useful, mechanically—but for the spirit that animates the workers whose life we are going to portray. We have to oppose abstract generalization, formulism, and anti-realistic tendencies, or we'll never make any progress."

"But had any situation roughly parallel to your American trained doctor ever arisen in your hospital?"

"Certainly not. A degree of imaginative construction was necessary, but obviously it had to be subjected to the test of realism. No? That is probably a new conception to you, too. When the author's work—play, novel, verse, whatever it is—is drafted, he must submit it to the workers in the factory or village for their approval or otherwise. Frequently they suggest amendments in its spirit."

"You mean, they tell you if you've got a technical fact wrong?"

"Not just that. They express their attitude"—Tsao Yu began to look rather desperately at me; his torment was that he understood English, though he could not or would not speak it—"they criticize its dramatic approach, as workers. They examine its theme. After all, they *are* workers. Unless they consider the play has the correct ideological position, how can one pretend it presents a realistic picture?"

"But how do you know you are going to meet in your factory, or your hospital, people with the precise characteristics you require for your theme? Can't you invent them?"

"You certainly *can't*," said the playwright, with some force. "I am sure someone would jump on you for that. That is to say—the worker in the new democracy is very conscious of his standpoint—there are such things as principles, you know. We are not writing for pleasure, but to advance the social system. After all, I am only a professional author; who am I to know better about the spiritual processes of workers than the workers themselves?"

It was a dispiriting business, watching this excellent man fighting the phrases, endeavoring to rationalize a theory of such numbing foolishness. It was high time, I thought, that he should be rescued from what looked like an endless dilemma. I returned to technicalities; did he expect a long run for his new play?

"As to that," said Tsao Yu with what seemed to be relief, "the object today is not so much to get long runs, as such, as to build up a repertory of plays which can be drawn upon all over the country. Don't forget that the Chinese theater has a history of only about fifty years. I'm talking about the theater, you understand, not the opera; *that* goes back to goodness knows when. But there aren't, in fact, very many Chinese plays at all. We are still groping for a technique."

I said, "But you have inferred, haven't you, that in the circumstances of today technique is less important than content? Isn't it a question of *what* you say—the moral values—rather than how you say it?"

Tsao Yu looked pained and uneasy, fluttering his elegant hands. "Well, perhaps. That isn't to say that

there's *no* question of artistry, though—surely? I try to
be a craftsman, an artist. The difference between now
and the old days is that once I could get away with spin-
ning words round an unimportant theme, whereas now
. . . Yes, the Chinese people definitely seek content in
their plays, not just manners. Surely that is the same in
your country?"

I risked an emphasis I did not wholly feel and said
no, I thought otherwise. I suggested that many a silly
play had succeeded in Britain because of something
quite irrelevant, like the performance of a big name. Was
there no sort of star system in China?

"In opera, yes. A name like Mei Lan-Fang will still
fill any opera house anywhere, for anything. But as I say,
we've only had fifty years of nonmusical drama; there has
been no time to develop big personalities. In fact," said
Tsao Yu, glancing over his spectacles, "our actors aren't
very *good*. So don't imagine that an unsuitable play
could succeed through technique, even assuming an unsuitable play got itself put on."

"You would have a job," I said, "selling that idea
to London or New York." Nor, I suggested, had it ever
been part of our theater. "Shakespeare," I said, "—isn't
he *only* technique? Examine him from your point of
view. His themes wouldn't arouse much enthusiasm in
your people. Shakespeare wrote mostly about the personal conflicts of exceptional individuals, most of whom
by the standards you speak of would be considered
aristocratic and worthless. I don't think Shakespeare
produced many ideological messages. Yet his writing
technique was so unsurpassed and his artistry so con-
summately achieved that his plays remain as fresh as ever
—*only* through technique. Where's the 'message' in 'Ham-

let'? The tale of a Scandinavian prince with an Oedipus complex—is that a subject to excite four centuries of democracy?"

"Ah, now!" said Tsao Yu, delighted. "Here you have me at your mercy, at a hopeless disadvantage." It seemed to give him the greatest possible pleasure to be so cornered; at last he was sidetracked from the grim realities of formula to a matter of simple theory. I had at once the feeling that Tsao Yu's interest in the drama had wider boundaries than industrial realism. "How can a poor Chinese discuss Shakespeare with one of the great man's countrymen?" he asked. "I know practically nothing of that great artist"—but it was clear he knew plenty. "It is all a question of historical context. I would venture to say that Shakespeare was quite progressive *at the time*. Perhaps his themes did largely ignore the great mass of workers, but without doubt he was making use of his princes and people symbolically. What was the social situation of England in the time of Shakespeare?" asked Tsao Yu, beaming. "A dispersed collection of localized authorities, dukes and barons and war lords, did you have? Perhaps not exactly. But plenty of petty rivalries, anyway. As I see it, Shakespeare advocated the centralization of power and government instead of all these conflicting affairs. As we know now it was a bad idea, as things turned out, but *at the time* it seemed a good thing, because"—he reached out two fingers and extricated a reason from the air—"it would help production!"

It was a sincere pleasure to observe the dramatist's relief and satisfaction; to have allowed himself this bourgeois discussion *and* to have rounded off the indulgence with a good political moral was a feat both rewarding and stimulating. Gaining confidence, Tsao Yu became more and more human; the debate that had begun so creakingly grew warmer.

"That is it, good for production," he said. He caught my eye and smiled in spite of himself. "Take 'Romeo and Juliet,' a beautiful play. Its theme may seem pretty stupid now— I beg your pardon, I am of course no authority—but at the time I feel sure it had quite a valuable message."

"Such as advocating a Marriage Reform Law?" I asked.

"Oh, very good!" cried Tsao Yu, slapping his knee. "Oh, excellent! I should have thought of that. Naturally that is what it *does* do. But what I *did* have in mind was the play's exposure of feudalism, the uneconomic effects of these rivalries between politically important families."

I said I was uncertain whether every playgoer in England derived that message. Perhaps, I suggested, the poetry had something to do with the play's enduring qualities.

"Of course—such an artist. As far as I am able to judge, that is. I am sure no Chinese translation is satisfactory. Still, I remain persuaded that Shakespeare was too sincere an artist not to have been politically impelled. As you say, what is 'Hamlet'? I say: Shakespeare wrote 'Hamlet' to expose the neurotic tendencies in royal households; a good anti-monarchist theme." He gave me the smile of one who has trumped the ace.

"But," I protested, "doesn't every principle of Shakespeare's methods—or indeed *any* artist's methods —conflict with *your* system of simply recording life faithfully, and submitting the result to the criticisms of the workers?"

"Shakespeare submitted *his* work to the criticism of

the workers. I am sure that the theater was a proletarian entertainment in those days."

"Only *after* he had produced them."

"Well," said Tsao Yu, "never mind. Times have changed. Our job is to reflect life as we write."

I said I had heard much criticism in China that the contemporary drama lacked romance, and humor. "And a very proper observation," said Tsao Yu. "It does. We are conscious of it. Especially does our work lack humor —and that is a serious fault, since the Chinese people are full of humor, and any theater that ignores that fact is not faithfully portraying life." He shook his head with a proper regret. "This is an acknowledged shortcoming, which we are trying to cure. We are having many committee meetings to find a fashion of introducing humor into our plays."

"I have also heard that no one writes light comedies, only heavy drama."

"Again true," said Tsao Yu. "And with reason. But please remember that China is not only unaccustomed to the theater, but also to democracy. When a person is hungry, he needs solid food first of all. The little piquant dishes can follow. Already, in our serious plays, you can observe the first buddings of a lighter spirit. But another thing is, of course, that there never *has* been a light-comedy tradition in China—not in anything, opera, verse, or plays. There is certainly farce, but that is different. In China there is no school of—who?—Oscar Wilde. Maybe it will come."

"Does the new China encourage young men to enter the theater?"

"By all means," he said; "in several ways. The *Theatre Monthly*, an official journal that circulates about a hundred and thirty thousand, helps the new writers by distributing their work, advising them, and so on. If they appear to have a special talent, and they live far away, the journal brings them to Peking and sponsors them while their work is being circulated. We have a very well-known case, young Kao Yu-Pao—he was born into a poor peasant family, but somehow or other he wrote a great autobiographical novel without even really knowing how to write anything. He had such an indifferent knowledge of the written characters that when he had to express something beyond that knowledge he used to draw little pictures. He was sponsored, and in the end became almost famous. The Writers' Association does the same sort of thing—brings the new authors up from the country, and pays them whatever wages they were earning while they follow a course of study in the Chinese classics. Foreign ones, too—Tolstoy, Shakespeare, Molière."

I said the picture it produced for me was most intriguing: all the new writers being transferred from the factories to the study, while all the professional authors were being driven out of their studies into the factories.

"Very good!" laughed Tsao Yu. He was full of small enthusiasms; as a playwright I had no means to judge him, but as an audience he was most rewarding. "Exactly! What a facile observation! But not really such a paradox. The young man must learn his craft, and the old must learn to apply it."

"In the end, it is a paying proposition? What about" —I hesitated, but I could not think of another word— "royalties?"

Tsao Yu shrugged again. "The author gets three per cent of the theater takings, after tax. If the play goes all over the country, as it usually does, that is not a bad sum at all. He also gets fifteen per cent of the published book sales. At present most authors are supported by the

State in some way or other; so far there is no Chinese tradition of writers maintaining themselves solely by their pens. For example, Lao Tze is Chairman of The Writers' Association, and works for the Peking Department of Artistic Associations, which is a Government affair. I myself am a Director of the People's Theater. But the Government is planning now to raise our royalty rates so that we can be properly independent. Even so, we're not bad off. We get our three per cent, our fifteen per cent, and our salaries. We get a hundred and fifty thousand *yuan* per thousand words for whatever we publish in the magazines. It *can* be very profitable. As a matter of fact," said Tsao Yu, glancing quizzically from me to the interpreter, "if there *is* a privileged class in our great democracy, we're it."

Tsao Yu was one thing; his textbooks were another. All visitors to China who evinced the slightest interest in matters of culture and the written word were referred at once to the standard work of guidance for authors, poets and playwrights under the new system. It was called *China's New Literature and Art*, and those who introduced it to the enquiring stranger did their country a disservice of an almost irremediable nature. Quotations do it less than justice; to obtain the correctly analgesic effect, it should be read at a sitting, preferably on a blue plush settee under a naked bulb while the tea grows cold at hand.

"For More and Better Literary and Artistic Creations!" says the opening chapter. It begins unexceptionally: China, it says, is now steadily launched upon the great task of socialist transformation; the working people have already seen the improvement in their material circumstances, and are now in need of a new spiritual life, which can be born of the written word. It then sets forth an argument, a literary footpath, the strange quality of which can just be hinted at:

"The most important and valuable results of our revolution are the heightened political consciousness and labor enthusiasm among our people. These are the things which our literature and art must primarily reflect. . . .

"Taking the labor enthusiasm of our industrial workers and the class struggle as their themes, our writers must depict the character of Model Workers and leading cadres in industry. . . .

"We have reformed and developed the various forms of national art which still survive . . . but this heritage can meet the needs of the people only after it has been reassessed and evaluated from our new ideological standpoint. . . .

"Though the bourgeoisie of our country has not made any contributions to, nor does it occupy any position in, our literature and art, this does not mean that our literature and art are not constantly in danger of being influenced by bourgeois ideology; particularly at present, when the working class is co-operating with the bourgeoisie, we should be more vigilantly aware of the danger of such influence. . . .

"Our literature must give expression to the thoughts and emotions of the workers, especially to those of their most advanced elements. That is to say, we must stress their resolute fighting will, their selfless labor enthusiasm, their unbounded loyalty to the well-being of the collective whole. The literature of the bourgeoisie is diametrically opposed to such a goal; it expresses invariably only the bourgeois world, in that it propagates individualism, the worship of individuals and self-admiration. The film 'The Life of Wu Hsun' was extremely harmful. . . ."

This was an interesting piece of *autocritique*. 'The

Life of Wu Hsun,' made by the Communists, told the story of a beggar who lived in Shantung province in the middle of last century, under the Ch'ing dynasty, and who founded schools with the money he had begged. The film portrayed Wu as a precursor of the Revolution, but . . . "The film subtly advocated an ideology of submission to the reactionary feudalistic rule and tried to spread the bourgeois doctrine of 'reformism.' The stoicism which the film extolled was only an abnormal and disguised form of individualism. The film put these pernicious ideas into an artistic garb, thereby confusing many artists and writers, even certain Communist Party members among them. . . . The timely criticism on 'The Life of Wu Hsun' initiated by the Party and Chairman Mao Tse-Tung in 1951 gave an unforgettable lesson to our writers and artists. . . .

"Literature and art should of course express the policies of the Party. In observing and describing life, our writers must be guided by Party and Government policies. They must appraise social phenomena from the standpoint of Party and Government policies, and give expression to the great influence these policies have on the life of the people. To mirror policies through artistic creations means therefore fundamentally mirroring the close kinship between the Communist Party and the people, mirroring the leadership given to the people by the Party, mirroring the struggle between advanced and backward elements among the people, mirroring the exemplary role played by Party Members as vanguards of the people. . . . Faithfulness in describing life is the highest principle of realistic art."

Then it said: "The Soviet Union's great achievements in the literature and art of socialist realism give us the best examples to follow. . . . The conclusion: 'Fol-

low the path of the Russians' is applicable to literature
and art as well as to the realm of politics."

There was a deep and chilling sincerity about this
work, so manifestly produced a million miles from the
seat of any creative impulse; its solemn and patient
insistence upon the impossible went in places to such bizarre lengths that it is hard to stop quoting it. There are
sad and puzzled moments when facts are faced, when
with worried hands the honest hack who wrote the book
scratches out a glimpse of the obvious:

"Creation is a difficult task. A writer not only has
to understand the objective world correctly, but must
also be able to express his images through the use of
language. . . ." Thus does the ideological literary arbiter
stumble on the terrible truth that troubled Confucius
and Shakespeare, that made difficult the task of my friend
Tsao Yu, and that unquestionably upset himself: that
the only problem about writing is the use of words.

But there was one elixir, one imperial yardstick by
which all authorship might be assayed: "Through Soviet
literature we see a social order such as never existed before and one that means the fulfilment of all human happiness. . . ." Whatever doubts arise are there to be
crushed: "Although some of the heroes in the Russian
classics," says the critic guardedly, "did not always have
the strength to act, nevertheless they never *reconciled*
themselves to the ugly reality around them. . . ."

How does one reconcile *oneself*? Tsao Yu, the dramatist, had squared his particular personal circle; he had
carried fame and, one supposed, a certain fortune over
from the old times to the new, from the days of feudal
freedom to those of ideological correctitude. By dint, it
seemed, of an adaptability that permitted him to say that
Shakespeare wrote the Tragedies in order to boost pro-

duction. Yet I had liked him so much; that was the trouble.

There is just one more quotation. I was given before I left a poem, much admired as representative of much that was powerful and vivid and correct in contemporary verse. It handicapped itself by what is possibly the most unpromising title ever to cover an ode like a leaden lid— in a land with an unmatched lyrical tradition it had to be called: "The Seventh All-China Congress of Trade Unions."

It went on for two hundred and thirty-seven lines in thirty stanzas, of which almost any one would serve as ghastly material for some ironic conservative parodist. In essence it catalogues the delegates to the Congress in a verse as blank as a factory door:

"A slip of a lass
from Wuhan; head erect,
looking over the packed benches,
tells of that other day;
of the long hours,
and the swollen feet. . . .

"A Government Worker reports
how this year new construction
is commencing; how
strength must go into
Basic Industry. . . .

"I was a girl worker
despised by everyone in the old society
today, Deputy Director of a Clothing Factory,
elected Member of the Tientsin Municipal Council,
delegate to Berlin for a World Textile Workers'
Conference; ninety per cent of
the working women of Tientsin
have taken up educational courses. . . .

"A Negro worker from Dakar
is grateful for Marx and the Paris Commune
and tells how the name of Mao Tse-Tung
now resounds through the forests of Africa. . . .

" 'I came from Factory 724'
A worker's dependent,
she organized other worker
dependents, to support workers;
her husband was backward, now he
understands. . . .

"The figures are brought from
the Northeast, of wages raised
quality of production improved;
production costs reduced; completion
of plans; emulation drives. . . ."

And so on, a terrible dish of mock-Mayakovsky (or maybe not so mock) which is the final objective, apotheosis and end of everything recommended in the Book of Words.

I claim to be no judge. But it takes a good democrat to make China seem *dull*.

(10)
To the Wall

THE next day fulfilled an ambition of many years.

The chance came to go to the Great Wall of China; it was permissible to forget the eternal political truths for a moment, and go momentarily tourist.

The thing about the Great Wall of China is, of course, simple enough: it is one of the wonders of the world. It is the greatest fortification ever built by the hand of man. Everyone is told as a child that it is the only man-made structure on earth that could be visible to an astronomer in Mars. Uncounted thousands of men died making it, untold fortunes were spent on it; it was put up an appreciable time before the birth of Christ, and it never did the slightest good to anyone. As soon as I could, I took time off from communism and drove out of Peking to see what on earth such a prodigy could be.

One of the unexpected things about the People's Republic of China was that they were dying for one to see the Great Wall. They liked you to see the Ming tombs, too, and the Temple of Jade and the Summer Palace and all the objects that were so patently and manifestly part of the decadent and tyrannical past that they were so vigorously trying to discredit. Nor did they represent them as horrible examples; they merely said, being sensitive and appreciative people: "Aren't they lovely?" Even when

they remembered to talk about the reactionary despotism
and the feudal exploitation, they were rather absently ad-
miring the glaze of the tiles and the admirable pitch of
the curling roofs.

This part of China was so markedly lovely that even
veterans of the Eighth Route Army could not say a word
aesthetically against it, though they went through plenty
of personal difficulties in the neighborhood, and for a
long time. As they would readily admit, the only people
who ever introduced second-rate architecture into Peking
are they themselves—by a sort of necessity; the place
was bursting at the seams. The trouble was that the classic Chinese architecture is horizontal; they wanted to
build skyscrapers. They were still trying to find a formula
that pleased both the Fine Arts Commission and the
Housing Authority.

While they fretted at that problem I went to the
Wall. It was some way off, so there was a certain amount
of the administration that provides foreigners with visas
to leave the city. We drove towards the Western Hills,
threading through endless caravans of mule carts; every
one an identical model: an antique basketwork wagon—
but on rubber tires. The Chinese had been shrewd about
that; they spent no capital on new mechanics where there
was something existing, traditional and local that would
serve. They had not wasted their substance on prestige
air lines, like almost everyone else in Asia; they would not
even buy Russian lorries and trucks—the thousands of
carts were there; what they *did* do was fit them up with
new wheels. Today at least eighty per cent of China's industrial traffic was carried on these carts. Individually they
did not carry much, but there were uncountable crowds
of them—long caravans, with the silence of the rubber

tires compensated for by the strident squealing of every other moving part.

We got to the Wall at last, at the Green Dragon gate, and—well, there it was—a wall. It was so well worth waiting forty-three years to see that for a while I forgot the zealous uniformed men back in town, forgot Formosa. . . . All one had to do was observe this ineffable piece of masonry snaking over the mountains—thirteen hundred miles of it, five yards wide, castellated and embrasured, climbing the ridges, rising and falling, a simple wall, as long as from London to Sicily.

Reality crept up, however, when I asked my guide the usual idiotic tourist questions. At once he began to hedge: the Great Wall was, naturally, a military fortification; it would be necessary to get official sanction to reveal the facts that were printed in every guidebook in every library in the world. Or else, of course, he did not know.

So I, at least, could tell him that it was the Emperor She Hwang-Ti of the Chin dynasty who started the project as a measure of discouragement to the Mongols on the other side. One is amazed, now, at the strange pretentiousness of it, the consideration that it could have worried any invader for any time; enormous as it is in total, at any point a competent scaling party could broach it. The true surprise is somehow not the immensity of the Wall, but the tremendous size of the garrison it must have demanded.

Well, what did it matter? There was a party of off-duty workers there, too; they had arrived in a phenomenally antique charcoal-burning bus, and together we plodded up and down the ramparts till we wearied of it, and went back to the gate.

By and by someone appeared with an accordion, and

someone else appeared with a measure of authority, and in no time we had set up a sort of *palais-de-danse* just under this enormous vast residue of two-thousand-year-old stonework. They made me dance, too, murmuring "Ying Kuo"—English; someone had told them—and off we went in the sort of routine I was so often to see in China: a kind of Morris dance, or square dance, with simple repetitive steps; successions of very small partners in the uncomely blue overalls, about as feminine as wheelbarrows; little peasant hands hard as teak; tut-tutting when you missed an unfamiliar step. I finished up with a welterweight lady corporal in the Chinese army who could, I felt sure, have broken my arm with her teeth. My childhood reveries had included no proposition so bizarre.

Then an odd thing happened. Bill had a camera. Halfway through the dance a caravan of tinkers—even here they looked like gypsies—had passed up the road, leading a troop of monkeys, and Bill had pursued them a hundred yards for a photograph. That hundred yards had taken him through the Wall gate—and there, it seemed, was a railway, the line to Inner Mongolia. It was supposed he might have photographed it.

Into this innocent *fête-champêtre* appeared quite unexpected Security Officers. Tremendous discussions took place. There was an ugly suggestion that the camera should be confiscated. Someone got on the telephone to Peking, while Bill waited around disconsolately and rather apprehensively. How the matter was finally resolved I never quite learned, having no overwhelming wish to involve myself in matters of such delicacy. The camera was not taken, but the incident thoroughly broke up the party. The man in charge blew a sharp blast on a whistle and in two minutes everyone had vanished. They reappeared later in the decaying old gazogene bus, grunting through the Green Dragon gate with the accordionist playing, as a final touch of fantasy, "Home on the Range." It would have been a great day, one felt, for the late Emperor She Hwang-Ti.

In a long gray shed in an even longer and grayer street of Peking was a man who, it seemed, had the keys to all knowledge at the ends of his hands. They lay there before him in vast banks and rows, small square leaden things a quarter of an inch across; there were many thousands of them and the man (a shaved head, a blue cotton suit, a pair of silver spectacles mended with insulating tape) had merely to choose the right ones, and there he had the incontrovertible gospels of Marx, the eloquent certainties of Confucius, and the beguiling flippancies of Sun Yat-Sen at his command. He could be said to have been composing pictures, or demonstrating the indefatigable urge of man to complicate life in symbols. He was, in fact, setting a stick of type.

His *vis-à-vis* in Europe, painting thus, had before him a keyboard of arbitrary and familiar shapes: the letter A and the letter B, and their two dozen alphabetical associates. The blue man in Peking had before him no such a rationalization, but perhaps fifty thousand small and intricate drawings, each one imprisoning an idea. His choice did not lie at the end of ten fingers, but at the end of four thousand years of invention so intricate that, to reproduce last night's speech by Chou En-Lai he must rush around the room selecting characters with a practically inconceivable effort of memory. It was for all the world as though some inhabitant of the Louvre should tap-tap his message through the selection of canvases, at the rate of twenty-five a minute.

This was the office of the *Jen Min Jih Pao*, the Peo-

ple's Daily. Hitherto I had known nothing of this famous newspaper except as the source of occasional very acid comments on the behavior of the capitalist world in general, and Mr. John Foster Dulles in particular, which would shoot out of Peking Radio at moments of international stress like small and accurately aimed drops of vinegar. I had asked if I might call on the editor and see something of his office, partly because I have an enduring interest in newspapers that many years in journalism have not altogether managed to undermine, and partly because of the illusion, still flowering after many setbacks, that local writers welcome impromptu calls from their foreign counterparts.

However, any idea I might have entertained of a comradely reunion among Peking's equivalent of newspapermen was very smartly dispelled when I received a rather stiff communication from the Board, informing me that if I submitted a list of questions, an appointment to receive the answers would in due course be made. This was scarcely as warm as I had hoped, but it was something. I wondered how the editor of *The Times* would have reacted to a similarly social gambit on the part of a traveling Tass man; probably in a fashion not a great deal more friendly, I decided. So I ran up a list of questions of purely professional interest, and in due course presented myself rather pessimistically at the office.

To this day I have never discovered who precisely it was that received me, but they were very agreeable in a fashion that could scarcely have been more stately. To one accustomed to the somewhat less formal occasions of El Vino's, or the Crillon Bar, or even the Mucky Duck, this fraternal encounter struck me as being supernaturally decorous. We all sat in a prim row on pink sateen chairs sipping scented tea and enquiring after each other's health (a lengthy and irksome process through interpreters). At last the senior host said, "We shall answer your questions as follows: Number one . . ." Most of the information was of a strictly technical and ephemeral interest. Having delivered his replies, the editorial executive (if such indeed he was) looked at his watch and said, "You may add to your questions if you wish."

Now the *People's Daily*, which is the organ of the Communist Party of China and by far and away the most important national publication, was, of course, one hundred per cent unintelligible to me, but I had it fairly thoroughly translated on days when I felt especially robust. I formed the impression that, like so many journals considered ideologically reliable, it was excruciatingly dull. It had a way of presenting subjects, themselves intrinsically prosy and recondite, in a fashion that skillfully concealed any lurking germ of interest; the process of disinfecting the printed word of any hint of drama or urgency was carried out with consummate skill. It dealt at great length with matters involving production and the exceeding of norms; its ideal was a story in which the statistics outnumbered the narrative by eighty per cent. When it got its hands on a subject that fulfilled every critical standard of somberness and lack of novelty, it would harp on it for days. Since the highest qualification for literary success appeared to be a sound grasp of the half-dozen indispensable political clichés, it was sometimes extremely difficult to distinguish the current issue from that of a month ago. Finally, in practically no circumstances was reference ever made to anything that had happened elsewhere than in China—or, if so, in the most minimal and disparaging terms, and always five days late to the tick.

It occurred to me to ask them, then, why a paper of world importance such as theirs considered it unnecessary to print international news. The question was received with indignation. They sent for the files and pointed out a succession of items with foreign datelines. "Bulgarian Minister Pays Tribute to Chairman Mao," the headline would run, and below it would be printed that tribute, verbatim. "Roumanian President Sends Good-will Message to Chinese Republic." "Czechoslovak Delegate Offers Greetings to Peking Workers"—and there they would be, the message and the greetings, unabridged, in identical terms.

"How can you say that we do not print foreign news?" demanded the official. "We have items like that almost every *day*."

Certainly they had correspondents abroad, he said. Where? Why, in other countries. Which countries? *Other* countries. Such as——? Well—Moscow. Anywhere else? Certainly. Where? In Prague. . . . No, that was all. They considered Moscow and Prague ample coverage for the world scene. There was also Hsinhua, the Chinese News Agency. It also had correspondents—in Prague and Moscow. And now, said the official pleasantly, if there are no more questions . . . ?

The *People's Daily* printed in Peking, flew mats to Mukden and Chungking and printed there, too. Its circulation was eight hundred thousand—two hundred thousand in Peking. Two hundred thousand in a city of three million people—one person in fifteen read the *People's Daily*.

And that, I said to myself, is the sort of false logic into which one must *not* tumble. On almost every street is a board, covered against the weather, in which the four pages of that day's paper are displayed. I never once passed such a board that was not being earnestly studied by anything up to a dozen people. They would stand there, patiently waiting their turn to browse through the Monthly Report of the Ministry of Textiles, the appreciative musings of the Albanian Cultural Delegate, to read once again of the satanic machinations of the Traitorous Chiang Kai-Shek Clique. They were there, day after day. The circulation of the *People's Daily* is not large; its readership is immense.

The *People's Daily* does for China what *Pravda* does for the Soviet Union: no one ever hears of anything else. China has in fact a hundred and seventy seven newspapers, and many periodicals. (Two newspapers, one in Shanghai and one in Tientsin, are still under private management.) The bookshops and newsstands are fuller than any I ever saw anywhere in the world. Those who do not buy stand about and read. There is, in Peking, a Children's Bookshop with very small counters and low stools, and a profusion of juvenile literature that is, page for page, rather better and more effective than that for adults. Everything had a highly educative flavor, with moral undertones: the hero was the boy who kept the streets clean, who swatted flies, who grew up to exceed his norm, who became first a Pioneer and then a Democratic Leaguer, who understood the Facts. There were some slightly bloodthirsty picture books from the Korean war. Shelves of books were in "strip" form. It was novel and salutary to see in these the traditional American strip technique, as it were, reversed—the Baddies here were not sinister Orientals but sinister Occidentals with unmistakably Caucasian long noses and the well-known dangerous round eyes.

To satisfy a personal curiosity about an aspect of the New China that nobody appeared to have bothered about hitherto, I made an analysis of what is available to read—a brief list most easily to be skipped by those who, no doubt properly, do not care a damn.

In Peking there are, beside the *People's Daily*, three other dailies—*Peh Kin Jih Pao* (the *Peking Daily*), which looks after the local city news within the usual framework of norms and statements; *Kuang Ming Jih Pao* (the *Bright Daily*), a cultural and educational review; *Kung Jen Jih Pao* (the *Daily Worker*), circulating largely among the factories. One thing they all had in common; a striking reliance upon readers' letters, almost entirely full of complaints. When I once remarked that newspaper readers the world over appear to become articulate only when infuriated, I was told that this was intensively encouraged as a means of keeping officialdom in touch with the people. Citizens were urged to write letters denouncing this or that example of bureaucratic inefficiency or discourtesy, this or that neglect of duty. The paper would then dispatch a spare minion from the reporters' room to investigate the allegation and, if necessary, reinforce the private grumble with an editorial broadside. In this respect, as in others, the newspapers obviously regarded their function only as an extension of the administration. Desirable as one felt this needling of the functionaries to be, it left a dubious forecast of the public informer.

The specialist periodicals were endless, and with a truly accomplished method of handling the most unconnected and disparate subjects in precisely the same way. The *Current Affairs Magazine* led with an ample story on "why the Chinese Constitution is good, and how those of the capitalist states are hypocritical." The *Women's Magazine*, on the other hand, dealt in detail with "how the Chinese Constitution is beneficial to women, and the subject place of women in the capitalist economy."

World Culture analyzed the reasons why Formosa must be liberated; *Women of New China* indicated that you cannot copyright a good idea, and explained why the liberation of Formosa was desirable. Some radical irrelevancies turned up in *Science Pictorial*: an article on the dehydration of vegetables, instructions on the growing of chrysanthemums, a speculative article on space ships, and a thoughtful argument for the liberation of Formosa. There was *Films for the Masses,* with one abrupt surprise, a review of "a progressive Italian film"—it was "The Bicycle Thief"; the article was subtitled: "Reflections on the Struggles and Sufferings of the Italian People."

Not much, one felt, was left to chance.

But there were imponderables, too.

In the journal *China Youth,* which is the organ of the Democratic Youth League, appeared a piece of counsel addressed to a public that rang unusually: "The Bourgeois Youth." It contained advice to the right-minded revolutionary youth from bourgeois families, who wondered if they were behaving inconsistently in continuing to live with their well-to-do parents. Its message was direct and fatherly: terrifying.

These puzzled young men were told that their bourgeois background need not necessarily be a handicap "so long as they comply with the revolutionary obligation of re-educating their families, and acting on behalf of the State as a corrective influence." They need not be afraid to take money from their parents as long as it was spent for their living and education, and not for ostentation. . . . "It cannot be denied that birth in such surroundings influences one's ideological outlook." But it need not be fatal. "When you discover any act involving tax evasion, speculation or manipulation, you must not keep quiet; you must take steps to expose these wrong acts, and help the People's Government to apply the necessary criticism." At the same time the bourgeois youth should strive to educate their families to make their commercial enterprises successful for the benefit of the community, and to take their due share of profit in accordance with the law. . . .

One saw in imagination this doomed family, this grim, well-to-do home shadowed by the course of bourgeoisie, by the right-thinking youth who remains in a patriotic ecstasy among the speculating, fiddling parents, waiting to re-educate, to act as "a corrective influence"; this dreadful Bourgeois Youth with the final sanction of denunciation behind his back.

I do not know what *China Youth* does to the bourgeois enemy, but by God it frightened me.

(11)
Manchuria

AFTER the charm and grace of Peking, Mukden was a
city of such grim and chilling ugliness that the heart momentarily sank. I have had the same impression of visual
emptiness elsewhere, but never before in China. If you can
imagine the most lowering industrial town of the Ruhr,
double it, subtract any casual amenities, scatter it with
gray dust and plant it deep in the cold of Manchuria, you
have an approximation of the charmlessness of Mukden.
It made Essen look like Florence; it made Clydebank
look like Monte Carlo. It looked exactly what it was, a
vast urban no man's land which had been wrangled over
so often for reasons unconnected with itself, which had
changed masters so often that it had lost all individual
living spontaneity, like a disputed child in a divorce
court. Or, like Glasgow or Pittsburgh, it was content to look
like a pile of iron and coke, because that is precisely what
it was proud to be.

Nevertheless today it was, very properly, the pride
and show place of resurgent China.

The old was very old. Around the tombs of the
Manchu Emperors still clung an enclave of dusty nature; there were ancient trees and patches of durable turf;
groups of people wandered along the avenues bordered

with antique heraldic beasts carved of stone and took photographs of the graceful mossy mausoleum. All around surged the three million inhabitants of this great industrial colony dedicated wholly to the thick end of the Five Year Plan. The new had quite overwhelmed the old: miles and miles of vast workers' blocks, identically square, identically stark, equally spaced over the acres, each gaunt unit of human habitation identified by an enormous white figure painted on its blank wall: 301—303—305. . . . It was like something out of some dispiriting old prophetic German film; the principle of home reduced to the hive. Somehow it did not seem like China at all. And, of course, it was not.

This was the already huge and still growing industrial complex of Manchuria that had now to be called North East China—the "Manchukuo" that the Japanese seized, developed and lost; that the Russians freed, held and relinquished; that the Chinese absorbed, rebuilt, and . . . no one knew quite what, except that it was held to be the heart and sinew of their reconstruction, of the machine age which had replaced almost everything in the Chinese official heart. They were intensely proud of it, and with reason.

We reached Mukden in the morning, and went at once to the hotel. This alone merits a moment's digression.

Sometimes I feel obliged to apologize for what, to others, seems an almost obsessive interest in hotels and places of lodging; it is an occupational disorder due, I suppose, to having to live in such places for a substantial proportion of my life. Like everyone who moves from country to country even fairly frequently, I like to consider myself an authority on hotels. I admit to being a hotel snob in an inverted, perhaps even perverse way; I consider that after several erratic circuits of the globe I am familiar with more wretched and abominable hotels than any contender of my weight, that I am in my way an expert on all the refinements of expensive discomfort, every variation of obtuse inefficiency. I have frequently debated this claim with travelers nearly as well versed as I in the global science of bad innkeeping, and I have usually been able to secure the decision by the detailed recollection of some little-known but incontestably terrible hotel, almost invariably, I am bound to say, within the British Colonial Empire.

After Manchuria, however, I consider myself in a wholly unchallengeable position.

All hotels in the new China of my acquaintance shared one characteristic, which should not be surprising in a Communist economy: they have ceased to be hotels. They have become, as befits their function where people circulate only on specific instructions, a form of institution. The word "guest," to a Chinese hotel, means exactly what it says. One was allocated accommodation in this or that establishment; only one person in a thousand was ever required to pay a bill; there were no kicks or comebacks. There was consequently none of the ancillary nonsense required by Western hotels—a reception clerk to receive you, a hall-porter to indulge or insult you, as takes his mood; a bellboy to escort you to your room, a *femme-de-chambre* to burst in upon you with an armful of sheets at the most inconvenient possible moment. There was, quite simply, a large building, an elevator, a series of corridors, and a room. One could very easily pass a week in such a place without, in fact, having human contact with a living soul.

I had no complaints whatever about my lodging in Peking, in Canton and Hankow and Shanghai; indeed, almost everywhere I was cared for with a technique of dispassionate adequacy; bearing in mind that the personal factor was in no way involved one could say that one was treated handsomely. The food was always excellent, the accommodation Spartan. It was in Mukden that, for the first time, I began, very slightly, to pine.

The hotel in Mukden was a large gray building which, given a slightly more festive and convivial atmosphere, could well have been a metallurgical institute or an unusually severe reform school. Its name, I was told, was the "North East Hotel," but I suspect this of being an improvisation; its original name had almost certainly been something even more inappropriately floral and Japanese. It had been built by the Japanese during the occupation, and the Japanese, as everyone knows, are the unapproachable architectural masters of the summerhouse, or bungalow chalet. When faced with the proposition of a five-storied establishment in a heavily industrialized city, however, they had decided in favor of a ruthless concrete cube with strong interior domestic affiliations to Sing Sing. It is only just to say that its rooms, or cells, were fitted with a form of lavabo accommodation (a great improvement on what was to come), but the fittings therein had clearly been built not just for Japanese, who are by no means the tallest of races, but for dwarf Japanese, for pygmies; it was doll's-house plumbing. To wash one's face one had to kneel on the floor before a miniature basin some two feet from the ground; to shave necessitated an attitude like that of an Eskimo entering his igloo. Other functions involved acrobatic performances even more difficult to describe. One struck one's head twelve times an hour on the hanging lampshade; there was no wardrobe, no cupboard, and no drawer. The beds, in the best Asian manner, were constructed of especially hardened ferro-concrete slabs. The windows gave onto a back street of forbidding somberness, relieved by no activity whatever except the relentless industry of a laborer who spent his time hammering on resounding pieces of tin. All in all, it was not a resort in which one would willingly have spent the evening of one's days.

Still, it became home for a while; by and by one forgot the concrete starkness of its corridors, the Lilliputian difficulties of its sanitary arrangements, the flinty bed. If one walked down two flights of stairs, there was a bathroom, tended by an unquenchably jovial Chinese clad in a curious assortment of what appeared to be other people's garments; this bathroom was unique in my experience in that it contained three tubs in the one room, possibly for the convenience of Japanese business acquaintances unwilling to break off negotiations halfway through the evening. After a while one went to bed, and sometimes to sleep.

One morning I drove out to Fu-Chun. It was vastly and even alarmingly impressive—for miles the most imposing and dreadful skyline: smoke and steam and chimneys, rigs and domes and cooling-towers, laced and netted with power lines and railway tracks; blackness over all; indeed it was the industrial scene to end all industrial scenes, ringed by a wilderness of company homes, factories of flesh to feed the factories of steel. One might be forgiven for being simultaneously sentimental, bewildered and aghast.

This year (it was 1954) China was spending 113,-227,000 million *yuan*—a wholly impossible figure, roughly translatable into four and a half billion dollars, or half of the total budget expenditure—on economic reconstruction, and half of that on capital projects of heavy industry, coal and power. The Soviet Union was underwriting, so they said, at least half of *that*. Here was the shop window. I arrived at Fu-Chun, feeling like a man from Mars.

I can never make very much detailed sense of industrial facts; to me factories roar, chimneys belch, engines throb, rolling mills roll; I have not the wit to enjoy them for their own sake. An hour of closely reasoned production statistics induces in me a kind of desperation, swiftly followed by torpor. In this condition I can listen practically indefinitely, nodding shrewdly here and there, and absorbing absolutely nothing at all.

This was such a period, a weekend of numbing education in the management offices of vast thudding workshops, hours of norms and percentages, of Marx and tonnages, under the portraits of Mao and Malenkov—frankness and friendliness, with one eye on the interpreter. I will not attempt to reproduce in the reader the anesthetic trance it produced in me. The high lights were otherwise.

For example I came upon this: the place where, one day in 1913, a Manchurian walking over his fields had stumbled on a little outcrop of coal. He had dug around, and worked about it—and that was the beginning of the Lung Fung mine, the prodigious open-cast working that the Japanese took over in 1931. Now it was a hole in the ground nearly four miles across by half a mile wide, six hundred feet deep . . . I am ready to say the biggest scoop out of the earth I ever saw. The coal seams were each as thick as an ordinary department store, producing twelve hundred easy tons a day, apart from the yield of shale for the synthetic petroleum factory that stood on the rim of the canyon, producing—so they told me—seventy tons of gasoline a day, or thirty per cent more than the Japanese got out of the plant.

Of the fifteen hundred workers down this great cavern I picked, or had picked for me, a man called Chang Chan-Ken—a most likable and forthcoming person; one knew by looking at him that elsewhere he would have had some influential appointment with the Boy Scouts; he was an articulate person by nature. He wore on the bridge of his nose the little blue tattooed scars that trademark miners over the world; I have had to work a good deal among miners and I like them, if that is not an impertinent statement. Chang Chan-Ken had been in this pit for just twenty years: under the Japanese, under the Kuomintang, and under the Communists. He worked an eight-hour day; he earned three hundred and one units a month. All industrial pay in China is reckoned in these units: there is an All-China rate for the job, with the unit itself varying in value according to local commodity prices. Chang's unit was worth two hundred and thirty *yuan* (say about ten cents), so he earned some nine dollars a week. The translation of currencies gives a wholly false comparison of values, of course; I cannot imagine why one does it except that one is expected to do so. Chang's two-thirty units was considered rather good money in the district, with cheap canteen facilities and sickness benefits and labor insurance, and working clothes provided by the State. With a family of a wife and four children he said—while a great Russian mechanical grab tore away at the coal stratum below our feet—he could save up to three units a month. Yes, he was a cadre, a Party member—which made him exceptional (in workers' circles there are about one per cent members) and was not impossibly the reason why he had been the one who had so readily come forward. When we stopped talking, Chang Chan-Ken saluted and went back to work; I felt as though I had been talking to a brochure. It often happened that way.

The town of Fu-Chun was characteristic of this great gray growing neighborhood—a city of seven hundred thousand that had quadrupled itself since 1949, since the "Liberation." What this means in China's new productivity is hard, perhaps impossible, to say. It had three underground pits, besides this monstrous open cut; another three synthetic patrol plants on the way. The Secretary of the Municipal Government was a young woman called Hsu Lan, strict and efficient in her no-nonsense blue patrols; we sat around the inevitable cups of green tea while she fired off statistics. Nineteen new clinics, ninety cooperatives, eleven more schools, five more cultural centers —you knew she had said it so often before, to so many nodding delegates with badges in their lapels. Yet she meant it, every word. When she spoke of Educational Units, her eyes even smiled a bit.

The next day we drove on even deeper into Manchuria.

The train ride to An-Shan was fantastic: a lunar landscape of new bricks and drifting smoke, heavily guarded bridges, great gangs and communities of people laying immense girders over river beds—duplicating, as it seemed, existing bridges; perhaps as some farsighted measure of precaution. Over every scene of construction floated a red banner or two; one sensed again the presence of uncountable multitudes, a man power inexhaustible. Goods trains of vast length passed by frequently—all the rail traffic from Korea passed by here, was reinforced and redistributed. Port Arthur lay down the line; all the station names were duplicated in Russian.

It was curious in North China that while all the hotels looked like railway stations, all the stations looked like exhibitions. They were generally covered with elegantly painted political slogans, decorated with portraits of the Governmental hierarchy; usually they were crowned with a large relief reproduction of the Picasso dove. It would be hard to find anywhere in the world stations more immaculately clean, more scrupulously organized. Here and there companies of soldiers filled the platforms, round and tubby in their padded uniforms and fur hats, struggling under huge packs and bundles of extraordinary shapes; one man carried a frying pan and a two-stringed violin.

At last we reached An-Shan. There I stayed in a municipal guest house which had just been newly and expensively erected. It had a foyer like an austere super-cinema, public rooms decorated with elaborate hanging chandeliers and plush draperies of startling colors. It did not, however, contain a single bathroom. Immense trouble had been taken to see to it that no corner of this imposing place was without its candelabra, its inlaid flooring—but when you wanted to wash, you stood in the corridor with an enameled bowl of water. It was an intricate way of living the simple life.

There was only one thing that mattered in An-Shan: the great An-Shan Steel Company (now, obviously, a State concern). In 1949 it had been in ruins; destroyed by the Japanese, they said, sabotaged by the Kuomintang. Now there were seventy-five thousand workers in a plant capable of producing three million tons. The figures rolled on and on, while more people in gauze masks brought in more tea; when the phone rang, the manager would just knock it off the hook. Yet it *was* extraordinary; so much energy and so much litter and scrap and decay, things rusting here and other things gleaming there. How much was a legacy from the industrious and resourceful Japanese; what did it all *mean?* And always behind everything the big question: What *had* happened between 1945, when the Russians had marched in at the war's end, and 1949, when they had handed over to the People's Republic? No official ever knew; they weren't local, they had been drafted in from somewhere else. Once I got a foreman to admit that he had been there all his life, including the Russian occupation. Did he know? "No," he said. "In those days I wasn't politically educated; I didn't pay any attention."

But the great place, the steel-rolling mill—that was there all right; it was as new as it could be, finished only two months before after fourteen hectic months of construction. The Russians had built it, out of equipment made in 1952. And now, they insisted, there were only two Soviet technicians left, and twelve hundred Chinese workers who had only to push knobs to produce fifteen hundred tons of steel rails a day. So why was it, one wondered, that the Prime Minister, Chou En-Lai, had had to complain publicly to Congress that the emphasis on speed was causing mismanagement and waste? He had quoted the example of the Tai-yuan Power Plant, where twenty-three billion five hundred million *yuan* had been wasted through bad management. He demanded that State industries cut down costs and raise efficiency. He inferred that too many State enterprises were being run by good reliable Party cadres, and not by experienced managers.

The forty-one-year-old Li Wen was the friendly director of the rolling plant. His training, he said, sipping his tea, had been as a publisher. Perhaps by now, I thought, you would find all the non-cadre steel men running bookshops in Peking.

But the steel came out; never again, they said, would China need to buy steel rails from the West—not even from Russia. Never before in history had China manufactured her own steel sheeting; she was doing it now—probably not efficiently, probably not as well as she said, but it had surely begun. This was as much China as the legions of bare-legged peasants treading waterwheels in the southern paddies; as much as those new railroads crawling to the North; as much as the millions who daily cried "Long Live Mao!" and "Long Live Peace!" without knowing exactly which was which; as much as the hordes of babies who now did *not* die in the endless human hives dedicated to the production of their kind. Perhaps even publishers knew something, after all.

"And tell me," said the director of the biggest mill in Manchuria, "what is the production of rolled plate and seamless steel tube in *your* country?"

There, I was ashamed to say, he had me; but he didn't mind. He was a man of thirty-four who looked about nineteen; his name was Wang Cheng-Teng, and not long before he had been a millhand himself. He spoke like a graduate of the Marxist-Leninist College, which as a matter of fact he was.

"You can see ours," he said, and there it was, smoking and banging and shooting off sparks. "I can assure you it is effective. Russian, certainly—one of the hundred and forty-one industrial projects they are doing for China. But they have now largely gone; the routine is now almost wholly automatic. We are, however, working at eighty per cent of our planned capacity. We still have technical shortcomings."

High in the air a great traveling conveyor swept over like a bomber, driven by a serious-looking little girl in pigtails. She picked up a ton or two of steel on an electromagnet and roared away. A great poster on the wall said,

"Long Live the Selfless Generosity of the Soviet Union."
Possibly it sounded different in Chinese. Everything
clanged, thudded, hissed. People who looked like school
children stood around at switchboards pushing and pulling inch-long levers; enormous strips of white-hot metal
heaved themselves about and went clattering down run-
ways, while mandibles of steel chewed them and elon-
gated them and sent them rolling noisily down the line.
Wherever they paused, there was a plump and serious female adolescent to divert them somewhere else.

Roughly one in every ten factory workers in China
is a woman. For a Chinese who recalled the wholly in-
valid and feudal state of women a few years ago this
was the really memorable transformation. They did the
work of men and got the pay of men. Everything about
them testified to their self-conscious asexuality; it was
possible that below those uniform boiler suits the female
bottom was mathematically broader, but only mathematically.

In this steel industry, I learned, there were eight
groups of wages—paid, like industrial wages, in units.
Here the lowest was one hundred and forty units and the
highest four hundred and ten. The unit was worth, in
this instance, two thousand three hundred People's *Yuan*
—about eight cents, by an arbitrary calculation. An en-
gineer who got the standard two hundred and seventy-
five units a month was earning about seven dollars and
forty cents a week; the director, who made six hundred
units, was making about fifteen dollars.

But the productive workers got many concessions;
most of them lived in company dormitories or company
apartments, paying about six units a month for their rent
and the services. The canteens where they fed were very

cheap, selling a pound of steam-bread for about sixty per cent of the outside price—say five cents. They worked an eight-hour day, with seven days' holiday a year—but not all together: there were three days for the Spring Festival, two for the National Day in October, one for May Day, and one for themselves. These may not sound like idyllic conditions for heavy industrial workers; the answer is that, compared with what they used to be, they are.

When one came to the trade union side of the deal, everything took on a rather off-center look not altogether unexpected in the case of an industrial organization within a Workers' State. It is possibly fair to say that such circumstances result inevitably in union officials becoming in effect Government nominees, used for the simple purpose of putting official directives into effect. That has been held by authorities on industrial negotiation to be a very bad thing, and doubtless it is.

I talked it over at some length with Tsao Ting, who was President of the local Trade Union Committee, representative of all grades of workers. There are, strictly, no "trade" or "craft" unions, only "factory unions," each of which acts as what might be very loosely called a "joint production council," which sponsors socialist emulation drives, organizes the wall newspaper, and so on. The Company Union was part of the Municipal Committee, which again came under the All-China Union Committee, which in effect was an extension of State planning.

"But how do you elect officers?" I asked Tsao Ting. He said, "So far, we haven't. This was an entirely new plant, without any serious establishment. The committee was drafted from outside factories by the next echelon up. You could call the whole organization nominated; if you did, it would sound worse than it is. Go ahead and do so, however. Nevertheless, I do not know how otherwise you would create a trade union movement out of a vacuum."

"Is it possible," I asked, "to opt out of the union?"

The rather surprising answer was, "Yes. Though the works have a ninety per cent membership." (I suspect the loose ten per cent to have been new employees, not yet registered.) "Non-members of the union get only fifty per cent of the union insurance benefits, but they can readily join in the cultural activities . . ." (the political ideology course, et cetera). "Full members pay one per cent of their wages in union dues, which go to pay the officers, and the union's share of the State Labor Insurance scheme. If a worker is injured on the job, he gets a hundred per cent of his wages made up from the fund. If he— or of course she—is merely ill, then an agreed portion of the wages. The whole affair is governed by the code of what we call 'Labor Discipline.' It's a double-handed agreement, exacting from the worker so many hours a day, and from the management certain concessions— like letting the nursing mothers off to suckle their babies, and so on. It works admirably. There has, in fact, been no cause for a wage dispute yet. If there were, it would have to be a national matter, because of this All-China unit system."

"But does there, within the union constitution, exist —for example—the right to strike?"

"Why—yes. Yes, there does. In practice, however," said Tsao Ting, "it has never happened; the necessary combination of circumstances has never come about. In effect, we don't strike."

I said it did not surprise me. I said that by certain standards, adhered to in the West for possibly sentimental reasons, deriving from a general Labor tradition of independent and particular organization, this would be considered a very unsatisfactory situation. They said, "Doubtless, by those standards," and left it at that. What I should do, they said, was discuss the whole matter with a Model Worker. There were several, immediately accessible.

A Model Worker is not quite so high as a Labor Hero, but nevertheless good enough to get his photograph on the wall newspaper, and to be very well thought of all round. (There were also Model Peasants, Model Mothers and Model Sanitary Behaviors, forever busy with ominous containers of galvanized iron.) They gave one to me: a plump and supernaturally arch twenty-three-year-old poppet called Wang Chia-Cheng. She was a duty foreman at the tubing mill and, like everyone else one seemed to come across in industrial China, she was fluent and persuasive, manifestly from long practice. I cannot say I liked her, but I admired her with all my heart, in an empty sort of way.

Miss Wang had left school two years before, since which time her only ambition had been to dedicate herself, she said, to increasing production for the sake of the people's welfare, because Chairman Mao had this very much at heart and therefore, she felt, so should she. It was her duty to be an example to all workers, and for that she must learn first the processes of correct thinking, so that . . . It was a very trying *tour de force*; I had forgotten such astonishing smugness existed. It was not Miss Wang's fault. Once again I waited, with glazing eyes, thinking: Why *this* approach? Here am I, bending over backwards to give honor to the triumphs of the Revolution; I am determined to see the best through a smoke screen of hokum; I *like* these people and their country. Why had they to produce for me this terrible unreal prig who talked like Samuel Smiles? I think this deadening moral process is possibly necessary to the Communist development, but it brings out some sad features in the human personality.

"I have to be good," she said brightly, "so that I may show my appreciation to Chairman Mao and the selfless generosity of the Soviet Union."

No, she did not think that marriage and children could compete with the production of seamless steel tubes. There was really no conflict; if she got married, there would be the factory nursery for her children, and nursing mothers were allowed time off to feed them. Could one ask more?

What did she do with her spare time? Well—she was Vice-Chairman of the local branch of the New Democratic Youth League; there was much studying to be done in order to learn to work better. . . . It was all a terrible shame, especially for me; I so much wished they had not done it. Thank goodness they were not all like that pious swot, that saboteur of the People's League for Democratic Fun and Laughter, Wang Chia-Cheng. Ironclad and rectangular though she was, invulnerable between her twin defenses of righteousness and unattractiveness, I wished I could have rolled her over once or twice in a scented haystack, just to see what would have happened. I think I know: it would have been terrible.

But even in Manchuria, Saturday night was Saturday night. That evening I eluded the perfectionists and went to the Workers' Club. "They will be glad to see you," I was told. The odd thing was that they *were*, or seemed to be; at least they stared and smiled and giggled and offered glasses of tea. They even clapped in a desultory way (though I grew weary of this formal "delegate applause," *i.e.*, all strangers are obviously guests of the Government).

There was, however, a most convenient ruse for dealing with this; if you did not clap yourself, they stopped.

It was indeed a bleak place. What grim conditions must have been endured, one thought, before *this* could seem good! It was stark and dim—a library of thick revolutionary tomes among the portraits of the Leaders, as impersonal as idols; a room for chess and checkers, like a cellar. But the workers were there in their hundreds, and by their very multitudes infected the dismal ambiance with a sort of corporate charm, since they were themselves so eager to smile, so very pleased with so very little.

There was a big dance floor; even there everyone wore the working blue cotton working clothes. It was fun, in an intensely formal and constricted way; rather the feeling of a welfare institute in one of the more dispiriting English provincial towns. The men danced mostly with men, the girls with girls. Was five years too short a time in which to break down the sexual inhibitions of centuries? The band played loud and indeterminate tunes, neither Eastern nor Western; the floor was dotted with somber blue uniforms; only too often it was hard to tell whether a Chinese girl *was* a girl. Mostly they danced the new popular Chinese square dances, which entailed the absolute minimum of physical contact. I had learned one of them during my day at the Great Wall, and I joined in. But everybody stared so hard and the crowds surged around, abandoning their own dance, gathering in dense rows to watch the Big Nose blundering through a succession of prim little female charge-hands. Soon I gave up. It was really bitterly un-gay.

Then I started to leave, and suddenly people came swarming out of the gloom, trying to shake hands and

saying things one could not understand but that seemed
eager and kind, and it did not seem false at all, but generous and full of lost laughter, and I was glad I had left
Miss Wang to her Marx and come to see the people
who, even here, were happier than they had ever been
before.

(12)
The Land

THE peasant Chao Heng-Yu was old and dignified and doubtless simple enough to have stepped straight out of *The Good Earth*. He wore a sparse wisp of beard on a face apparently made of crumpled brown shoe leather; his teeth were huge, a dark mahogany color, and looked as firm as rocks. He had seen many years come and go over the village of Kao Kan, of which the brightest and best, he would tell you, was that of the People's Revolution. He would tell you that because he had been telling it for some time—to fraternal delegates and cultural missionaries and dedicated investigators and me. Everyone went to Kao Kan, the most co-operative Co-operative in China.

Kao Kan was held to be a prototype of one stage in China's great socialization of the land, which is by many times the biggest ever attempted in history. It always fulfilled its norm, it was well populated by Model Peasants, and was clearly regarded none the worse for that. "If everywhere were like Kao Kan," they used to say with a sigh, "China's agricultural problems would be solved."

I remembered at one stage becoming querulous at being presented always with the show place, the model. I had asked to see contemporary village life, I said, why must I be always given these exhibition places? Their reaction was a genuine surprise, a sort of touching logic. "But obviously, if you want to see villages," they said reasonably, "you would not expect us to pick out some unsuccessful or disagreeable example to show you? Surely it would be scarcely sensible *not* to take you to the best one we can find?" I found this uncontrovertible; it was also honest—no unreal claims that the best was the average. I stuck to my point, however: I would also like to see some ordinary places, somewhere not on the delegate route. By all means, they said, though they seemed to infer that it was a long way to have come from Europe just to see commonplace things; it was clearly only courteous to admire the things they were proud of. But as time went on it always worked out at one extreme or the other; it seemed almost impossibly difficult to see a controversial country otherwise—either you went as a devotee, to worship at the Model Villages, or you trailed around with one eye always cocked for the hidden failure, the back-street horror they didn't want you to see. In the end you came to believe that there was no such thing as an average anything.

When we drove out to Kao Kan from Mukden there was no pretense that this was a casual encounter; they had been talking about Kao Kan for days. It was very clean, they said, just you wait. They wished I could have seen it in the old feudal days. Now . . . there had been an article about it in one of the illustrated papers.

In the house of Chao Heng-Yu, however, all this excellence was not obtrusive. There was not much room in it for anything but the big *kang*—the great communal bed made of brick, with a fire built underneath it for warmth—a few cooking pots, a duck or two, a sack of kaoliang grain, and the inevitable icon of Chairman Mao. When you added the family—Chao and his wife,

the son and daughter-in-law and four grandchildren—
the room had, to say the least, a lived-in look.

I will not say that I had the final analysis of China's
land reform from Chao Heng-Yu. I had talked it over
previously at some length with the Minister of Agriculture, Liao Liu-Yen, who had, I calculated, caused more
real estate to change hands in the past four years than
any other man on earth. Sixty-five million acres had been
reshuffled between four hundred million peasants. The
plan was characteristic of China's wary and persuasive
approach to a monstrous problem. The whole proposition of land redistribution and collectivization was tremendously complex, and not easily summarized into a
simple matter of sharing out. The old system was appalling; it was not necessarily Marxist propaganda to recall
the terrible exploitation of the peasants, the humiliation
of human dignity, the system that was not indeed, as the
Communists called it, "feudal tyranny," but only because the peculiarly private and family nature of Chinese
agriculture made feudalism difficult, but exploitation
easy.

Most Europeans have some difficulty in conceiving
the extraordinary intensity of effort necessary even for
subsistence in most of the overpopulated agricultural
areas of Asia, where the *average* peasant could be over-
balanced almost into starvation by the most marginal
circumstances—by a poor harvest, by capricious extra
tax levies from his local governor, even by the hazard of
a wedding, or a funeral, entailing another crippling load
of debt. China was always a land of small, indeed miniature, farms; in the wheat areas they averaged under five
acres, in the rice areas rather less than three. Chinese
agriculture was not farming, it was gardening. It was,
however, gardening of a kind so exhaustingly hard that

it left little energy to spill over into politics, and government had always been something inconceivably remote, without reference to daily life except insofar as it was a factor to avoid by every stratagem, especially at times of tax collecting and army recruitment. And, of course—the clue to the matter—a very few people owned almost all the land.

The obvious Revolutionary attack would have been the Russian one: a forcible collectivization, and the liquidation of the kulaks. The cautious Chinese one, which did not overlook the disastrous effects on production of several Eastern European experiments, was rather different— "Based on the readily admitted principle," said Liao Liu-Yen, the Minister, "that all peasants are cagey and reactionary, even liberated ones, and the Chinese perhaps more than most. We could have plunged them all abruptly into collectivization—which would have meant an immediate drop in production—the last thing China's economy could afford at this stage."

Moreover, even landlords had a pair of hands, and while they had to be jumped on and disfranchised and "re-educated"—about fifteen million of them—they could still in the process hoe a row of beans. The process, then, was the very Fabian one of a three-phased development. First the Mutual Aid Teams, on the basis of personal property—the land, shared out among the peasants, remained their property; they could grow what they liked and dispose of their yield as they thought fit, while spreading their own tools and efforts around the community. That—at the time of my arrival—absorbed sixty per cent of all Chinese village life.

Phase two was the Producers' Co-operative, in which the villagers retained their title to the land they were given, while handing over to a committee the decisions concerning the nature and disposal of crops. To-day there are about a hundred thousand of them. "Not nearly enough," said the Minister, "but the numbers increase, as the peasants get the hang of the idea. Instruction teams go out. . . . We want eight hundred thousand by the end of the Five Year Plan. I'd like to hurry it, but I can't."

The third phase was the straightforward Collective, where all land was held in common and results distributed according to the amount of personal effort put in. There were only a few hundred of these. "To a simple peasant," said the Minister, "who never had any sort of a deal before the Land Reform, the mere possession of a plot of his *own* is a tremendous thing; he has to enjoy the feel of it for a while before he can bring himself to submerge its identity in a Collective. It will come. We don't ask of a man more than we think he's got."

Outside this softly-softly process existed the two thousand official State Farms which—especially the sixty or so that are actually mechanized—were used mainly as glowing examples to tempt the dubious villagers along the path to complete socialization. "I fear that they are not yet a major factor in the country's grain supply," said the Minister; "there aren't enough of them, for a start. Nobody has *yet* thought of a satisfactory way of mechanizing the cultivation of paddy rice. We shall see. They show what can be done."

All this seemed to me to be a very intelligent process, and the fact that its flexibility and tolerance was grounded only on the rigid demands of expediency did not affect its superficially paternalistic appearance. Not long before, Teng Tzu-Hui, the great economic expert of the Government, had said, "Nothing must be done to hamper the peasant's activity as an individual economic unit." (The next week, however, the *People's Daily* announced the execution of a small farmer in Hunan province; he had been convicted of "spreading false rumors to the disadvantage of the socialist plan"— the grousing farmer, the discontented old man who saw no good in idle new-fangled notions; he had dreamed up a few lies; *that* had cost him a bullet in the brain.)

It did not often happen. Not now. There had been a time . . . nobody concealed or denied it; there had been grim and startling scenes throughout 1950 and 1951: the drumhead courts in the village squares, the desperate *ad hoc* tribunals with denunciation taking the place of evidence and the piled-up hate and bitterness of years overflowing, memories of oppression and over-taxation and rape assuaged by the sight of the kneeling landlords and the crisp smell of gunpowder. It must have been a terrible orgasm of revenge while it lasted; it was all over now. Many of the hated landlords still survived; there was even one in Kao Kan, living there like the tamed bully in the school story—less gloriously, even; he never showed himself at all. The landlords were still officially execrated as satanic despots (actually most of them had been not much more than petty squireens with a pocket of land) and were in fact rubbing along much the same as ever, although undoubtedly getting their hands a good deal dirtier than before. They had been given exactly the same share of redistributed land as every one else, but the law said they must thole their as-size for five years before they got their vote back.

Land Reform had created, or at least rationalized, three classes of villagers: the vast multitude, with less than half an acre each; the "middle peasants," with less than five acres; and the "rich peasants," a rather emphatic way of defining any villager who can afford to employ a few hired hands. Throughout the whole deal the accent was on Long Live Communism, but get the crops in anyhow.

The village of Kao Kan was in the halfway stage of socialization. The errant thought occurred that it might be maintained in this halfway stage for years, as a model show place rather convenient to Mukden and the columns of visiting firemen who plodded through the country taking notes. I was welcomed in the meeting room —the long tables, the scented tea, the hortatory posters; I felt I had been roosting in such places all over China. I heard all about it from Chang Chung-Hun, who was Chairman of the Village Executive, and from Mrs. Chao Kan, who was a member of the Women's Federation and an official Labor Hero. Labor Heros wore special badges, and a rather righteous expression. Kao Kan, they told me, had a hundred and sixty households, a population of seven hundred and seventy in about two thousand three hundred *mou*, which is some three hundred and eighty acres. They used to have eight landlord families—that is, eight per cent of the village owned ninety-one per cent of the land.

"We lived like beasts," said Mr. Chang. "A man who rented twenty *mou* (three and a half acres) produced perhaps four hundred pounds of grain a year. He had to give seventy-five per cent of that to the landlord. He had to give another ten per cent for taxes, another two per cent for local levies of one kind and another. Then he had to give a present to the landlord, in order to keep his tenancy. We were *hungry*. Why, we often were down to eating grass, or celery, to keep alive." He had automatically taken his place at the head of the table, his back to the poster of Mao. The harrowing story was only too true; it was only that the dramatic effect was too accomplished.

"We were liberated in 1948," said the Chairman; "we took the land for ourselves, and shared it out—as it happened, constitutionally. By 1951 we had organized our Mutual Aid teams. After that year's harvest we were able to buy three rubber-tired carts and five donkeys. . . . The next year we did away with the boundaries between the holdings. The yields went up. More stables, another forty-eight wells. . . . We built sixty-five new rooms with tiles, and thirty new rooms with thatch." (In China the unit of house-accommodation is the "room": a standard space between the ceiling beams—just as in Japan they assess houses by the *tatami*, the size of mat on the floor. It has actually little to do with "rooms" in the sense of enclosure; China does not understand privacy in the Western meaning of the term.) "We now have twenty-eight children at school; each of us has two suits . . ."

It could not be denied, it was a very political peasantry, sowing the doctrine and reaping the statistic. There was no groping for figures or seeking analogies; the Chairman knew it all.

"We get at least twenty meals each month of good rice or wheat, instead of the coarse kaoliang, which was all we ever got before. And culture . . . Mrs. Chao here could not read at all until two years ago; now she can read two thousand characters. That is so, Chao Kan?"

"I can read two thousand characters."

It was the recurring dilemma: how *right* they were, and how proper that they should know it; how admirable it was that these people should appreciate their new conditions in such detailed terms—if only it didn't come so trippingly off the tongue, filtered so smoothly through the interpreter's unchallengeable clichés. So I went off in illogical irritation and found old Chao Heng-Yu, and *he* said the same thing. Why not? one thought; after sixty years of hanging on to life by guess and by God (though there was not even God) why should this *not* be heaven? It is true to say that I was by now needling him; I said, "All right. Since you can now read, as you say, what does this mean?" And I seized the first piece of paper in sight. He peered at it mildly, and thought a while, and said, " 'Under the selfless leadership of Chairman Mao Tse-Tung we shall . . .' " It wasn't much of a test; what else does any piece of paper say? But he was a Chinese and therefore infallibly courteous and tolerant; he said gently, "I know some of the phrases, but mostly I know that we are neither cold nor hungry. I got this bit of land with the Reform, the first I ever owned in my life. They let me build this house. I am paid by the Co-operative half in grain and half in money—though of course I have to pay my taxes in grain."

"Are you a Communist?"

"Of the Party? Of course not; how can I be?" He smiled; it was as though I had asked him if he was a member of the Athenaeum.

"Will your grandchildren be?"

"I suppose so, if they learn enough. I believe it isn't easy. But I do not know much about it. As a rule the visitors see the Chairman of the Village Executive. You should talk to him; he is familiar with things."

I asked him about savings; it turned out that he had five hundred thousand *yuan* in State Bonds and three hundred thousand in the bank. (It was about twenty-four dollars and fifteen dollars respectively.) For taxation purposes the Government estimated their production per *mou*, and taxed them on that estimate, regardless of the actual production. The assessment was made by the villagers themselves, at the time of the redistribution, when it was clearly in the peasants' own interests to be accurate.

And the hated landlords? Well, they were still there; they had philosophically put up with the routine execration; they were content enough to be retained as horrible examples so long as they kept their necks, and there it was—they were just grubbing around the Co-operative like anyone else, reduced from the exalted status of despots to something rather grimly like pets. At least—one could see them thinking, remembering 1951—they had survived.

Then we drove out of Kao Kan, scattering the piglets and ducks, and back to Mukden; the little rural enclave disappeared in the vast extending suburbs of the industrial town, endless streets of little workshops reaching out like spiders' arms, people under the lamplight hammering and scratching away at pieces of tin through the night. The wind mourned down from Mongolia with a drift of snow in its teeth, sweeping the gray streets empty of people—a million and a half citizens of Mukden, and nobody afoot; where did everybody go? There wasn't anywhere to go, except to work, next day. I felt scared at the thought of facing that terrible hotel for the evening. I asked if there was a cinema one could visit, and they consulted with each other and said they would try to find out, so I lost interest. In the end I did go back to the hotel, and bought a bottle of *mao-tai*—it was grim stuff, but a good way out of Mukden for the time.

(13)
Elder Brothers

Now it seemed that the great Russian nation, which had retrospectively invented the radio, the airplane, the internal-combustion engine, the bagpipes, the works of William Shakespeare, and the wheel, had at last dallied with the effete and created the Oxford-bag pants. The evidence was before one's eyes. If one ever wondered what had become of that curious fashion of yesteryear, the answer was here. Every Soviet citizen in China—no mean multitude—was recognizable from afar by three things: his enormous shoulders, his brief case, and his bell-bottoms. They were *immense*. Two ordinary Chinese politicians could almost have secreted themselves inside, one in each leg. In a country where the great thing was for everyone to resemble everyone else the Russians maintained their own internal conformity; from Ambassador P. F. Yudin down to the silent strangers reading *Pravda* in the airport, they looked like rowing blues of the 'twenties from the waist down, and Bolsheviks from the waist up.

". . . and find out," someone had called out, as someone always will in the final desperate minutes at home before the dash to the aircraft, "what the Russians are up to in China."

Nothing was easier. They ate, they drank, they slept,

they went shopping; they sat in overheated offices filling in forms; they moved in fast black cars from unnoticed starting points to undisclosed destinations; they greeted each other at diplomatic cocktail parties with double hand clasps and staccato bursts of murmured conversation, doubtless of mysterious international significance. They went to cinema exhibitions celebrating the successive National Days of this or that People's Democracy. They disappeared, sometimes for months, into the gray, cold confusion of the industrial Northeast. They were forever seeing one another off from the airfield, always in tight groups assembled round one central figure whose shoulders were an inch broader, whose trilby hat was a fraction more solidly on the brow, whose trousers were more voluminous than the rest: he would be the delegate. They walked, they rode, they spent money: it seemed that they made love—one saw their women, stern and square and cinder-blonde, with the expression and costume of head warders in some old-world female penitentiary; yet there must have come about some stony monolithic coupling behind the padlocks, because from time to time children appeared, tumbling in gay unruly parties through the streets of the Legation Quarter, not yet petrified and chiseled into reliable rigidity.

But what the Russians were up to in China—that was less easy.

For five years the absorbing speculation about China had been that whole riddle of Soviet influence—whether it grew or diminished, whether the deadlock on Chinese economy had bred gratitude or resistance, to what extent the interesting and obvious Chinese deviations would be corrected or propagated, just how far the tail might learn to wag the dog . . . all inevitably leading to the sixty-four-rouble question: Was China the rock on which the

Communist wave might finally break? *That* would have been something to know. *Who* did?

The Chinese dependence on the Soviet Union was immense. Everything was done to emphasize the relationship—the insistence on Soviet leadership, the public fêting of Soviet institutions, the rediscovery of all the old phrases (so new, so realistic and gripping at the time!) that somehow seemed subtly malapropos in the courteously formal language of the Chinese. There was also, of course, the manifest fact that Russia had contributed hugely—though perhaps less hugely than some thought —to the tremendous upsurge of the Chinese standard of living. Every official pronouncement made that fact clear; every personal and private attitude avoided it.

There were many more Russian experts in China than there had been a year ago. Only the Soviet Consul knew how many, and he was unlikely to tell. The Chinese agreed to "many thousand more." The biggest concentration was, naturally, here in Peking—more than in Shanghai or Canton; even more, some said, than in the huge industrial core of Mukden. It was a close and privileged community, but its lot, I sometimes felt—perhaps unreasonably—was even less agreeable than my own.

In Peking the Soviet families were billeted all over the place. One of the brand-new 1954 hotels was reserved for them alone, and there were blocks of apartments earmarked for them in the others. They lived as Russians tend to do wherever outside the Union they are to be found: in close groups, not assimilating on principle. They had their own restaurants, clinics, schools, clubs. They maintained the absolute minimum of contact with other nationalities, including Chinese; it took a screw driver to extract a good morning from someone met every day.

This was far from being an intrinsically churlish mannerism; it was, one knew, a deeply considered and politically important attitude. The position of the Elder Brother (Big Brother? How unlucky, one felt, was the Chinese phrase) was not the easiest one to maintain.

Three categories of Soviet citizens were based in China: the military advisers, who were seldom seen and never identified; the technicians, advising at the industrial centers scattered all over the gigantic country; and the cultural, medical, educational and political cadres who, with the diplomatists, showed up pretty generally at the endless social functions with which Peking distracted its steady stream of delegations.

Since their historical beginnings—through generations of isolation followed by foreign domination of one kind or another—the Chinese had been what the Americans (had there been any available) would have called "allergic" to foreigners. The accepted epithet was "Big Nose," no doubt properly. They had so long been considered the privileged class, both financially and politically. The extraordinary position of the Legation City in Peking's and Shanghai's International Sector still inflamed emotional Chinese memories. At the beginning of this honeymoon the Russians had overlooked this important point; they were privileged, and looked it. They were well paid and at intervals were left with personal surpluses of local currency; disposing of this took the visiting comrades on sensational shopping sprees, to use up their non-convertible People's Money. This caused some offense, and was finally stopped. Now the Russians lived in the greatest possible non-ostentation. There were several shops in Peking that were somehow—I could never detect just how—reserved for Soviets; no one else ever seemed to go there; they were identifiable by the parties of broad-trousered men and cubical, solid women who seemed usually to be emerging with parcels of brocade.

The Chinese policy was, and remains, not to retain any Soviet citizen longer than necessary. Every new Russian technician brought to China was contracted for a specific period, with a clause that he must be replaced by a Chinese national *before* the expiry of his term. It was on this basis that the vast industrial enterprises in Manchuria were being gradually handed out. The Chinese would extol the generosity of the Soviets in equipping and training them, and then beam with pleasure as they said, "But they've all gone now. We are now on our own." In some cases, like the heavy steel-rolling mills in the Northeast, that was actually already the case.

Nevertheless, China's dependence on Soviet—or Czech or Polish—help was so huge that an entirely new definition of "face" had to be made. Under the existing Five Year Plan about six hundred industrial units of one kind or another were being built or developed, of which the real backbone were the hundred and forty-one Soviet-aided heavy industrial projects. Of these, seventeen were complete and operating. "There is not the slightest need to exaggerate," the Chinese told me over and over, "since on the contrary we consider the Plan unfulfilled. Thanks to the Soviets, we are really in business for keeps."

Far away in Sinkiang Province, where almost no stranger ever went, were the big oil and mineral projects operated on a fifty-fifty basis with Russia under the 1950 thirty-year agreement. Of that corner of the picture I did not imagine many people knew much more than I, which was just about nothing.

Here in Peking the two great Russian shopwindows were the Soviet Red Cross Hospital and the Exhibition. The hospital was possibly one of the best in Asia—two hundred beds, fifty-four doctors (all Russian) every sort of equipment from electro-surgery to nature cure, and all dedicated to the principles of Pavlov ("the Founder of Soviet medicine"). It did not have any general wards, only semiprivate rooms with two or three beds, and if you were not a Soviet citizen, they told me, or a high Party or Government official *in extremis*, the chances of getting in were slender indeed. But politically it was most highly thought of.

Then there was the Soviet Exhibition, the current essay in the supercolossal, the State opening of which very nearly undercut the National Day celebrations, so remarkably lavish was it. The ceremony was part of the intensive festivity of the time, and invitations to it, I was assured, were not lightly given. However, any grand ideas I might have entertained were swiftly dispelled when, on arriving within sight of the edifice, I found myself at the end of a column of guests, both distinguished and insignificant, which must have been all of a mile long. The opening, it was plain to see, was on the compulsory list of every delegation between Outer Mongolia and the China Sea. We stood in dense and practically immobile squadrons, marshaled by vigilant little policemen who prowled watchfully up and down the queue, shouting brusque commands through megaphones at anyone momentarily forced out of line. Almost everyone wore lapel badges denoting allegiance to this or that aspect of democratic thought; some, including myself, had been given a small and rather distasteful decoration merely denoting that we had, in fact, visited the Soviet Exhibition. By the time we reached even earshot of the dais the speeches were long over, which as far as I personally was concerned was no great loss, since those that were not in Chinese were, reasonably enough, in Russian.

I had therefore plenty of time, both then and for weeks thereafter, to study the intricate splendor of the Soviet Building, which I can compare to nothing ever seen elsewhere, unless it be one of the more costly and elaborate monuments of confectionery ordered by millionaire meat packers for the weddings of their favorite daughters. It was (and without doubt still is) an enormous white building in the form of an arc, surmounted by an even vaster spire, not at all without grace and charm were it not for the mad profusion of applied decoration—the porticoes and oriels, frescoes and crenellations and crests and structural flourishes that recalled nothing so much as the architectural heyday of Byzantium, or indeed Wembley. To the Chinese eye, trained in the placid school of unbroken vertical planes and flat surfaces, it must have suggested a building on the very point of boiling over.

Inside, the affair was much more businesslike, doing very effectively what it was intended to do: demonstrate every aspect of Soviet technique and culture. It did this faithfully. Everything utilitarian was tremendously impressive, and everything remotely connected with esthetics was matchlessly dreadful. There were galleries of paintings of celebrated revolutionaries in dedicated attitudes, and busts apparently made, by some skilful process, of blancmange. Each gallery was dominated by a presumably standard painting of the late J. V. Stalin and G. Malenkov engaged in what seemed to be a very strained and unfruitful session of autocriticism, each portrayed in that strange style that gives to its heroic figures the appearance of effigies in some hastily improvised wax museum. The *realisme sovietique*—how stunningly unreal it all was compared with the admirable tractors and cranes and complex agricultural machinery, the engines and the steel. The public, however, stood before these paintings entranced. Either the artistic and sensitive Chinese do not follow the principles of Western art, and think these works are quaint, or else, I decided, they just like looking at portraits of Malenkov—a taste explicable only in a people who also like hundred-year-old eggs.

Anyway, it turned out that there were queues outside the Exhibition until I left the country, and the Russian restaurant inside had every table booked solid for two months ahead.

Perhaps one has to go back to some ancestral memory for the answer, since human nature hardly filled the bill. Individual to individual, the Chinese would seem to have much greater psychological affinity for the humorous capitalist than for the flinty Elder Brother. Perhaps what goes on now is the negative reaction of a new and sensitive country which feels it has no friends whatever outside the Eastern Democracies, and must therefore go to them for what no one else in the world will give—help and confidence; something that is neither contempt nor fear.

But I had not come to China to see the Russians. Only once did my business lie directly with them—at the very end, when I went to the Soviet Consulate for the visa that would allow me to travel home through Siberia and Moscow. (For how many years had I waited vainly in London for such a visa? It was odd to think that here, in Peking, I could scarcely be refused. . . . Nor was I.)

The Soviet Consul was an athletic young man with curling hair, like an American college hero, wearing a suit seemingly designed by a blacksmith. He sat me down in an office that positively throbbed with the heat from a great tiled stove, gave me a cardboard cigarette and said, "You come here for vice?"

I was about to consider this remark in dubious taste, to say the least, when I realized that this was merely his pronunciation of "visa." I said yes, indeed, if he would be so good.

He thumbed casually through my passport and stopped, as though by some peculiar instinct, at the page that bore, of all things, a valid visa for the United States of America. He reflected for a moment, and then glanced up at me in a fashion that in anyone else, I swear, could only have been called roguish. He said, "You like your vice alone?"

With some difficulty I refrained from the obvious reply, though I still had no clear idea what he meant.

"Separate vice, eh?" said the Consul. "Piece of paper, no?" With a delicacy that made the gesture almost but not quite imperceptible he indicated the United States seal. The Consul had not been born yesterday; clearly he knew the difficulties attendant on those whose passports bear the double vice: US and USSR.

I said, "That is uncommonly considerate of you, and I greatly appreciate it." I did, too; I thought of the dreary and inescapable complications of the contemporary traveler's life, the snarling or satirical immigration officers reading motives into rubber stamps, the modern idiocies of people who must have two passports if they travel to Israel; all the boring exasperations of pretending not to care. I said, "Thank you very much for the idea. But if you look on the next pages—I have a Chinese visa, a Chinese exit visa, on which the red star is particularly prominent and which can scarcely be overlooked. I don't *think* a Soviet stamp can do *this* passport much more damage, from the point of view you have in mind."

He gave me my vice separate anyway. Several times I nearly lost it, and they took it from me altogether in Moscow. But Senator McCarthy might as well know I had it.

(14)
The Train

IN A less realist atmosphere this train would have been called the "Ricebowl Express," or the "Shantung Special," and Graham Greene would have written a film about it with a dispiriting ending. In People's China it was called the "Number Fifteen Train to Shanghai," and it seemed to have no ending at all.

We climbed aboard in the early morning and went to Tientsin, and from Tientsin we turned about and made for the South, crawling all day through the paddy fields of Hopeh, which looked flatter than any country *could* look; an endless dun-colored checkerboard of fields sometimes only a few yards square, dotted with the little nipples of grave mounds. It has always been the Chinese convention to bury their dead in barrows on the surface; the hummocks protrude everywhere. They said that something like three per cent of the cultivable land is wasted, out of respect for the lumpish memorials all around. The little tumuli are the only relief to the flatness. In this vast empty plain how did a great guerilla army operate for so long, without a hill or a hole for shelter or ambush? Yet this was one of the famous regions of the Fourth Route Army. Somehow vast numbers of men existed, hid, rose and attacked, vanished—it must have been worse than concealing an army corps on a Dutch polder.

All day long, all day long—sometimes a group of willow trees beside a ditch, a river overflowing at too sharp a curve, like the water meadows of Sussex. Then there would be a buffalo drowsing in the shallows, resting his gray-black muzzle of world-weariness and melancholy boredom on the surface of a pool, with a little boy asleep on his back. An entire family would come floating by in tiny circular coracles scarcely bigger than buckets, as though the inundation had swept them from their kitchen in whatever utensils came to hand. They drifted along, paddling idly with things like wooden ladles, coming from nothing and going nowhere; there was not a house to be seen for miles.

When a village appeared it was surrounded by mud bricks drying in the sun—the villages that grow out of the land, that are made from the land, that crumble back again into the land to make more bricks for more villages: the interminable processes of China. The villages of Anhwei were as though the flat earth had wearied of eventlessness and had spontaneously humped itself into little hollow rectangles. Why did people live *there*, rather than anywhere else? Could it be possible, one thought, that the Administration had contrived to establish its cadres in such a place, so far from anything? And then there would be a glimpse of a wall washed black and covered with characters, a red star, a stenciled dove—*ho ping wan-tsei:* Long Live Peace, even here: had they ever known anything else?

But each bridge, each station, each crossing had its little concrete strongpoint, its machine-gun fort. You couldn't escape anything anywhere.

Certainly you could not escape efficiency—technology—fuss—all the things that made Chinese railway travel both a sort of entertainment and an ordeal. Every

time it seemed highly revealing of the Chinese character, of the curious intensity and aberrations of the new
regime.

Once you were in a Chinese train you were *in*, usually for days. Like everything else in the country, where
paradox was the norm, it was built on contradiction.
The rolling stock was old and awkward, of the school
of architecture that never completely made up its mind
between heavy varnished paneling and bulkheads of steel
network, but it contrived to move with a stately smooth-
ness far more solidly than many of the *grands express*
of Europe. It was lavishly equipped with handles and
devices of Edwardian opulence—none of them worked,
nevertheless the train was so impeccably clean that it
became a considerable embarrassment. The corridors
were decorated with posters exhorting one to tidiness
("Keep *Your* Train as Clean as Your Home!")—but you
could never find the ash tray; whenever some daring or
ill-informed fly appeared, it was pursued with a bitter
relentlessness by an official fly-demolisher with a swat-
ter, and more often than not its carcass was sent spin-
ning into one's tea. At every halt men rushed up and
down swabbing and polishing the outside of the train
—but inside the taps didn't work; there was no water;
and the other toilet arrangements involved acrobatics
distressing to the Western frame. On the trains the mode
of surgical masks reached an especially enthusiastic level
of craziness; all the moppers-up and brushers-down wore
them, removing them momentarily only for the tremendous ear-shattering hawkings and spittings for which
China has always been so justly famous.

There was, however, a sort of splendidly chaotic order. The terrible old days of overcrowding and privilege
and squeeze had gone; every seat in the two classes

(Hard and Soft) was reserved and numbered. There was a special coach for mothers—or indeed fathers—accompanied by babies; a magnificent scene of groping, crawling deportment, for even in infancy the Chinese is manifestly a believer in personal discipline. Another coach hired out books and games. More masked men drifted perpetually around refilling the glasses of green tea—of a variety so green, so very vegetable in appearance that one's glass soon resembled a small aquarium. Only one cachet of tea was provided, but there were countless replenishments of water from a vast zinc watercan. (The next morning I was, for want of an alternative, obliged to shave in mine.)

The one truly purgatorial factor was, as usual, the noise. For the rest of my life I shall remember China as the place where the quietest and most restrained of people seem tranquil and at ease only in the midst of ferocious discord and din. Through all the daylight hours and well into the darkness the loud-speakers in each coach roared out their advice and admonition ("Don't crowd, comrades. . . . Help the children off first. . . . Don't drop chicken bones on the floor, it's your train now. . . . Long Live Peace. . . . Have you got your tickets?"). These inhuman instruments—and I am afraid that this cry of despair will become tediously familiar—were without either pity or fatigue; between the shrill announcements of the *speakerine* they emitted snatches of Chinese opera, high pentatonic cries among the gongs and cymbals. Then, at one station, a man got aboard with a cricket in a little bamboo cage; it chirped and twittered in a thin demanding tone. The man said that he kept it with him because he liked the sound. . . .

There was a moment of fantasy halfway through the night. The radio had stopped at last; the arguments

on either side had stopped; even the cricket had relapsed
into whatever is the cricket's equivalent of sleep. At three
in the morning the door was swept open, the lights were
snapped on; in the doorway appeared a stern man who
stared around seeking, one despairingly felt, for some
impotent guilty character out of Kafka. And then he
entered, and from his steaming water-can once again refilled the empty glasses of tea. Thus ended the only successful hour of sleep. . . .

Then in the morning they did a remarkable thing:
they picked the whole train up and put it on a ferry and
floated it across the Yangtse Kiang. It was the sort of
thing that for some time has been getting knighthoods
for European engineers. These people had been doing
it for years with the help of a tank-engine and a crowd
of people in straw hats. The railway stops. Ahead lies
nothing but a mile of flowing water, spotted with the
dowager shapes of the high-stemmed junks from the sea,
of the slender shapes of the sampans from the far Southwest, drifting down or crawling up the stream of the
third greatest river in the world. The train was instantly
overwhelmed by a multitude of random people, who appeared to have some fifty separate and distinct purposes;
very soon the train was sliced into three separate and
parallel lengths and loaded on the ferry. "*Wei-ho,
wei-ho,*" they cried, as though they were handling sacks
of rice or railway-sleepers; in about half the time it takes
the Dunkirk Ferry to disengage itself from the dreary
land our Number Fifteen was lying trebled-up on a flat
deck and sliding crabwise over the porridge-colored waters of the river. It was a moment of exhilaration: the
division of the train had somehow amputated the loud-
speakers from their source of power: there was no sound
but the slap-slap of the little wavelets on the hull, and

the faint singing cries from the drifting junks, loaded with silk from Szechuan.

To Nanking—it had once been the Kuomintang capital; now it was nothing: a pattern of tiled roofs scattered at random; every variety of plane and attitude, like a handful of dominoes thrown casually down, miles and miles of houses all facing inwards, in the Chinese way; a million people with their backs to the world, staring inwards at each other.

But the train was running; it was on time; it was there. Five years ago that could not have been. The Mao Tse-Tung Government had taken over a railway system reduced to ruin by the Civil War, and the Japanese War. Lines had been pulled up, signal systems destroyed, sleepers burned for firewood, roadbeds ploughed up. When the guerillas eliminated a stretch of line they *eliminated* it—for miles there would be no sign of rail or nut or bolt or foundation: the steel was buried, the sleepers were ash. Where they had lain was a newly dug and planted field. . . . When you have enough *people* you can do anything. Along the Peking-Canton line, for instance, every bridge was down for fifteen hundred miles. The tale of the restoration of the railways is one of the genuine triumphs of fabulous teamwork, determination and, indeed, skill. Today an iron-nerved passenger could travel by train from Kwantung to London, via the Canton-Manchouli and the Trans-Siberian—a thought daunting beyond endurance, but possible in theory. In these days of the ubiquitous air line, of the passenger-projectile, how much one has forgotten about the limitless capillaries of the railways. (Ah, my Mongolian fire-pot cooker—bought in Peking, ordered to be sent to me by the cheapest possible route; a transaction begun months ago, with the fire pot still on the way, shunting and lingering through Siberia. . . . Maybe I shall see it even yet.)

But these people gave the people the trains, and in the trains they gave them a square deal: that is past argument. In this Number Fifteen there were villagers from Anhwei and Shantung who were traveling as they could never have done before. At each station, always immaculate—what *can* have happened to Asia?—they stood in their formal rows, handing in each others' babies. . . . At the Chen-kiang halt the little trolleys rolled up and down, selling sweets, steam-bread, ducks pressed out flat like flounders in the Nanking fashion, and chickens roasted complete, in a manner for which the neighborhood is famous, still equipped with their calcined, indignant-looking heads. They cost about a dime each. . . . And then the loud-speaker on the train gave tongue again: "Listen, comrades—there is a meal being served aboard the train. This is different from the old days, comrades, when only the exploiters could be served in this way; we work for the people now, and you may eat on the train for three thousand *yuan.* We suggest you do not buy food outside the train; it will have been exposed to the germs and the flies. Please consider your health, comrades. In any case we do not stop long here, and you should not miss your luncheon. The dining car is two coaches from the engine, comrades. *Hurry,* comrades. . . ."

I went to the dining car; they gave me a meal abominable beyond reasonable comparison. All around me people were eating a bowl of rice, seaweed and pork-ribs that looked unendurably appetizing, but nobody would let me eat that. Mine was the special one; it cost a thousand *yuan* more. In their courtesy they had groped blindly towards some vague conception of the European cuisine: a burned piece of cow's flesh on a piece of toasted bread.

I went back to the compartment and tried some more Rousseau. He went tramping up and down to Geneva, incessantly moaning at the ingratitude of those on whom he so grossly imposed; always on the point of writing something; always on the point of going to bed with Mamma; always about to accomplish something, until the next chapter flung him and me back into the stockpot of introspection. It was the worst possible book for escapist reading; already I felt myself thrashing and groping around in a sympathetic maze of frustration. Jean-Jacques thought forever about sex and did nothing about it; he spent his time conceiving terse and apposite paragraphs to which he never gave birth; always he excused his impotence and sloth by some sort of *force-majeure*. How disagreeably like myself, I thought, rumbling through the flat meadowlands of Kiang-su. In the compartment were two officers of the People's Volunteer Army, on leave from Korea; some pig-tailed women soldiers, cosy little bolsters somehow stuffed with blood and bones; a couple of Soviet technicians in the modish bell-bottomed trousers, gently asleep on each other's shoulders. The land outside looked more and more Chinese, as somehow it always did as one approached the coast: feathery trees rising above the floodwaters, rows of bare-legged men in vast hats pedaling at a treadmill water wheel, each turn lifting a few thin pints from the flat gray ocean all around.

The loud-speaker droned on and on; by and by I fell asleep, like a mouse in a power-house, with the cricket in the cage beside me saying *crr-rr-ip, crr-rr-ip*. It was, as the man had said, a pleasant sound; one day, I thought, I shall have a cricket too: the triumph of the gentle noise over the greater one.

Eventually we reached Shanghai.

(15)

The Capitalist Manifesto

THE Shanghai day begins at seven with a sudden crash: in the street below electric bells ring, klaxons blare, bands play, loud-speakers roar out the "One!—Two!" of the People's Physical Training Instructor, the murmur of voices surges into a clamor, and the day is born. Life in Shanghai is turned on like a tap.

From my tenth-floor window in what used to be the old Cathay Hotel, now rather mysteriously renamed the King Kong, the great prairie of roofs stretched around haphazardly in the heavy ochre light, looking as Chinese as Birmingham. Out towards the Whangpoo river front the European skyscrapers jutted up like old teeth, like monuments to the lush commercial past, all dead and gone; the old Oriental empire of the Jardine Mathesons and the Sassoons, the Butterfields and Swires, the *taipans* and the *compradores*. Good men and bad men, traders and tricksters, honest brokers and shady swindlers and millionaires; men of God and main-chancers, philanthropists and tax dodgers, Old China Hands, dealers in stuff and ships and cash and human life and death. What was good for the Chartered Bank was good for Shanghai, everyone said.

And what was left?

Fifth greatest city of the world, they told me, as we climbed to the wind-swept roof and looked over the busy wilderness of yards and house-backs, chimneys and streetcar lines, with the ex-European business blocks punctuating the skyline like overemphatic gestures. This, they said, with strange variations of pride and regret, once had everything—the wealthiest clubs, the most noisome slums, the busiest drinking, the most shameful factories. It had the International Settlement and the French Concession. There was a night life, once—of course, the Long Bar, too. And every year they used to pick thirty thousand dead bodies off the streets, here in Shanghai—in the summer, hunger; in the winter, hunger *and* cold. But at least the foreigners paid no taxes. *Tout passe, tout casse.*

Now that strange skyline is broken again in a new place; a building truly vast and grim stands up swathed in scaffolding, overtopping all the rest—the China-Soviet Friendship Building, the country's most enormous edifice, with its great red-star pinnacle glowing three hundred feet in the sky: Big Brother watching over Big Business.

It had been dusk when I arrived in Shanghai, at a railway station that was probably more crowded, full of denser swarms of human beings than any I had seen before in time of peace. Perhaps the surging mobs in the German stations just after the war . . . but this was different; this was multitude in order, in columns-of-route; the thousands of people who packed the alcoves and approaches to the platforms did so with the strictest discipline, herding behind their barriers, shuffling in tight rows at a steady pace, while the loud-speakers called and wailed and whistled. There was no congestion. I walked through a central concourse like an empty field, between hedges of blue uniforms. It was almost eerie. "Where does everybody *go?*" I asked, but Big Wei shrugged. "Wherever they want to, I suppose." I said that such hosts of people must obviously have waited for tremendous periods. I thought of the platforms of the Indian stations, with the patient armies of peasants camping in turbulent groups, waiting for days. "Frequently they wait a long time," said Big Wei, "not for the train; for the ticket. Once you have your ticket, you have your seat."

"But to leave the city . . . their permits . . . ?" I began to ask, but now we were out in the street; we were shaking hands with whoever it was who was in charge of the arrangements, smiling and looking over their heads at the lights of Shanghai. It was almost odd to see sky signs again.

Once under way, every travel operation in China goes without hitch; there was at this stage of the journey a sensation of being marshalled through a sequence of movements like a child with a nurse; nothing was left to chance. It was all the more upsetting, therefore, when the driver could not start the car. It was big and black, a more handsome and powerful car than I was used to, but it responded to the starter with a churlish whirr, and no more. The driver pushed and tugged at the button; nothing happened; the car gave the petulant gasping sound that announced most clearly that it was not under any circumstances going to start. This was a situation a great deal more troublesome and embarrassing here than it might have been elsewhere. We were blocking the thoroughfare. The driver climbed out and began poking half-heartedly at the engine with a bit of stick. The official who had come to meet me was clearly put very seriously out of countenance. He contained himself for some moments, tapping his knee in increasing annoyance, then barked something at the driver and opened the door. "Wait," he said to me, and strode smartly away, leaving me alone in the car that had suddenly become completely surrounded by an intent and studious crowd.

This, in fact, was quite a new experience. Up to now, during my stay, I had been struck forcibly by the unexpectedly incurious attitude of the Chinese crowds, a careful and courteous absence of gaping and staring or following around; however interested or inquisitive the passers-by of Peking or Manchuria may have felt, they appeared to have far too much delicacy to show it. Here, however, the lesson had not been learned; a pack of faces surged around the car, peering in the window, pressing against the glass, mouths agape, and with eyes that suggested only a bleak curiosity. This puzzled me, since of all cities in China, or indeed in Asia, Shanghai had least reason to consider the European face as a novelty. A long nose in the Imperial City, or the industrial back blocks of the Northeast, could be held to be comparatively unusual, but everyone in Shanghai must have grown up in the visible presence of the white business-man and seen enough of them to be sick of the spectacle. They might resent the European, or possibly even detest him, but at least, one would have thought, they knew all about him. Yet the fact remained: throughout my entire stay Shanghai was the one place where I found it difficult to move about without a crowd.

I was trying rather self-consciously to rationalize the matter and thus avoid the embarrassment of alternately smirking and scowling through the window, when my official came back, obviously in a tearing temper. For me to have caught the transport department out in a disorganization of this kind had probably not lost him excessive face, but it had certainly not gained him any either. He opened the door briskly, cutting a swathe through my attendant gallery, and said, "Shall we get into another car?" sharply, as though it had all been my fault. As we transferred the bags I said sympathetically, "These things always happen, don't they?" He replied brusquely, "They do *not*."

We drove at a tremendous pace through miles of streets that were more crowded than any I had seen in Peking or Mukden or even Canton. It was necessary to be in Shanghai only ten minutes to realize how different was its flavor from that of the capital; even through the darkness something of its other-worldliness, its sophistication, appeared. Its lights were brighter, its shops were newer; there was an indefinable hint of something different in the crowds. This was clearly a city grown out of a concept that owed nothing to the great China of the hinterland; this had been the bridgehead of the West, and the marks remained.

The hotel lobby, too, was a revelation. How long *had* I been away, I wondered, that it should be strange and almost exciting to be in a hotel that had obviously been built as a hotel and was still being run by people who understood what a hotel is?

As I entered the lobby I almost reeled at the impact of the perfume—the lounge was filled with vases of some exotic white narcissus; the place was filled with their heavy scent.

And yet, of course, it was still not a hotel as one knows them elsewhere—there was no reception clerk, no manager; no guests registered, no one was asked for a passport, no one got a key. You arrive in a Communist hotel as you would arrive in an officers' mess, or a nursing home—someone is always expecting you, someone always whisks you immediately away, opens your door and leaves you. *Is* there such a thing as a casual arrival, an unexpected guest in any hotel in China today? I felt not; how would anyone not already in the machinery penetrate the anonymity of those blank official entrances, where there is no supercilious reception clerk nor embittered young woman to say, "Unless you have a reservation, I'm afraid . . ." As one who has beaten against the starched strongholds of three-star hotels all over the civilized world this strange impersonal acceptance was not wholly unwelcome; here they *had* to put me up.

In its day, you could see, it had been a hotel of some pretensions: fourteen floors, excellent beds—and a bath, and water. After Peking it was luxury, after Manchuria it was paradise. Something had happened to it downstairs; the handsome public rooms had been overlaid with an atmosphere faintly recalling a summer camp: there were signs saying "Recreation Room," in English, and "Ping-pong Room" and "Games." A number of Russians moved rapidly from place to place, bustling in from long black cars with heavy brief cases, waiting fretfully for the arrival of the elevators.

Our little party had somewhat grown, including Zig and myself and one or two Indians, as well as the interpreters Big Wei and Quiet Hsi. At dinner, we ate in a private room on the thirteenth floor, a "European" meal, indescribably odious. We were joined by the junior interpreter, the seminarist, as ever tumbling over himself with eager willingness and uncomprehending futility, surrounding the abyss of his linguistic inadequacy with a fence of subsidiary clauses. "Ah, yes," he would say. "But indeed. I may say." He smiled perpetually, engagingly, always in a torment of indecision. I looked out of the window over the tumbled glitter of city lights far below, with the deep vermilion glow of the China-Soviet Building's red star high above, and I asked which direction we faced. "Ah, yes," said the seminarist, "of course. That is north." He clumped his boots together and smiled in anguish. "Or yes—perhaps south. Nevertheless. South. North. Not knowing."

When we all giggled I saw what we had done to him; poor seminarist, he looked vainly around through his spectacles and laughed as though his heart would break.

Shanghai and Peking were in different worlds. It was this sprawling unlovely city of six and a half million people which presented more than any other the unfathomable paradox of Communist China. The difference showed up in small ways: a richer individuality of dress, a brighter splash of neon lighting, a certain uncowed anarchy among the pedicab drivers, a glimpse of lipstick here and there; but also in the biggest possible of ways: Red Shanghai was still, and of design, one of the most considerable capitalist cities of Asia.

It was still a fact, as well I knew, that China's national processions brought forth—among the People's Armies and Workers and cadres and accommodating nuns —the extraordinary revolutionary capitalists' association with its banners and its dedication to "good labor relations." If that seemed symbolic only of lunacy, or perhaps an even less endearing hypocrisy, then the answer was here, in Shanghai. Shanghai was where the policemen in what had been the French Concession still wore French-issue military helmets, where a modish Labor Heroine might even wear nylons under her boiler suit of orthodoxy, where the great Hong Kong and Shanghai Bank building still stood, with the red flag at its masthead. In Shanghai everything changed, every problem was different, every argument modified. Here the Government, which must "explain" Co-operatives to five hundred million doubtful peasants, and dialectical materialism to those who burned paper money at weddings, must now persuade a hive of merchants, who for decades had lived on the periphery of world commerce, to turn their backs on the empty sea and face the enormous land behind.

Chinese private enterprise had always been by definition a good deal more private than most. Now the relations between the Communist Government and China's mass of businessmen were governed by what was probably a good Marxist-Leninist argument, but which nevertheless looked uncommonly like a deviation.

Article Thirty of the Constitution said that the People's Government "shall encourage the active co-operation of all private economic enterprises beneficial to the national welfare, and shall assist their development." Not long before Chou En-Lai had said, "The new state of China relies on the big role to be played by the national bourgeoisie." The words doubtless meant as much or as little as the circumstances might at any time require, but the general position was this:

The Chinese State controlled all banking, virtually all heavy industry and raw materials—about thirty per cent of the nation's total economy. Ownership by provincial or municipal governments accounted for another ten per cent, mostly public utilities. The mixed private-public concerns, an increasing and especially Chinese affair, mostly involving local governments in light industry, was another ten per cent; and the rural Co-operatives, another fifteen. Private enterprise, representing thirty-five per cent of the national economy, *still* continued with the largest share. It had not been what I had expected.

No one expected this interim situation to last more than about another fifteen years at the most. Meanwhile the "capitalist"—from the open-air cycle-repair shop-keeper to the owner of the great weaving mill—continued to live in a sort of economic dreamworld, buttressing his philosophy with the consideration that sufficient unto the day was the evil thereof. Nobody was prepared even to guess when, or in what circumstances, the axe would fall.

Many quite big industrialists, it was said, were tolerated only because of their holdings abroad, useful for overseas currency. One of China's biggest—Wu Tsung-Hi, who employed about twenty-five thousand people in his Shanghai textiles factories—had a rich father in Hong Kong, which in some oblique way I could never quite understand was held to increase the economic value of Wu Tsung-Hi and, therefore, his chances of survival.

Naturally, one of the first things I asked to see in Shanghai was a capitalist in his present-day surroundings —much, I suppose, as one would ask to see one of the more unusual or picturesque denizens of a provincial zoo. The officials agreed with an alacrity that suggested to me that if I had *not* made such a request they would have been both astonished and dismayed. Thus I came to meet Liu Kung-Tsen, who I was told owned a very considerable cement manufactory, employing up to eleven thousand people on the outskirts of Shanghai.

As soon as I called on him, in the center of the great cumulus cloud of penetrating white dust that surrounded his works, humming like a hive with the *Wei-ho! Wei-ho!*

of columns of coolies shuffling loads on to the barges, it was clear to me that Mr. Liu was no fanatical opponent of the new regime. It is fair to say that this occasioned me no overwhelming surprise; it had seemed to me unlikely that my guides would have produced for me a militant leader of the anti-Communist resistance. Nor had they; in Mr. Liu we had a capitalist who had made his adjustments with the least possible pain. He wore the regulation blue uniform of the true believer; the regulation portrait of Chairman Mao was on the wall of the office, which was furnished with the regulation absence of *any* unbecoming amenity. (To the point, in fact, where instead of the routine cup of fragrant tea I was presented with a cup of hot water. I had to visit my first capitalist, I thought, to be entertained with such democratic acerbity.)

Apart from this, the encounter took place under conditions of high good humor. As soon as we were established, Big Wei, who had come with me, said, "Well, since both you gentlemen speak English you won't need *me*, will you?" and sauntered out of the room with what I could not help feeling was a rather ostentatious casualness. Nobody, his gesture said, will be able to say *I* cooked the interview. However, having made his point, he soon strolled back in again, and sat in silence, sipping his hot water with a faint distaste.

Mr. Liu looked young (though you can never tell; I long ago gave up trying to place the ageless Chinese); he was friendly and alert, like a businessman in an American film. "As an industrialist in the new national system," he said, "I can't complain." (Can't, or won't? one thought; always the exasperating doubt.) "This has always been a family concern. My father is the main shareholder. I own some stock, and I manage the place. We are doing very well—three hundred tons a day output; the best we ever did before Liberation was two hundred and seventy tons." He used the word like everyone else, as if it were "Easter" or "last quarter-day."

Mr. Liu's business was now in the intermediate stage, since the Government had come into it as a shareholder. It was all very proper, said Mr. Liu; no shares were given to the Government; they had to invest in an increased capitalization.

"It is the usual arrangement of fixing co-ownership," he said. "The private shareholders still retain the majority of the stock. The system is quite simple: the private parties must be willing, and the Government must be interested—that is, either they need the product or they can convert the equipment. In any case, the company must make the first move and *ask* for State co-operation. It sometimes helps production—the labor works better when it feels it is associated with the enterprise, through the Government." It was an unexceptional remark; perhaps I only imagined Mr. Liu's swift glance toward Big Wei.

"I'll agree," he went on, "that we had considerable anxieties at the time—the Liberation, that is. I had feared that we would be dispossessed, that we might be banished, if not worse. You must know how uncertain things were in those days. We weren't Marxists, you may be sure. But then—first the Red Army played very square with us, unlike those terrible KMT soldiers; they did not demand bribes and indeed began to stabilize prices. Finally the new people announced that they would protect private enterprise—to my astonishment, I will confess—and they are, in fact, doing so."

While I retained my doubtlessly just belief that Mr. Liu was, for the purposes of my information, a put-up job, it remained the case that hardly anyone in his position appeared to disagree with him. It was obvious that the huge expansion in home markets, plus the elimination of all foreign competition (since Russia does not provide consumer goods) had done wonders for the private manufacturer. "In the old days," said Mr. Liu, "gasoline here was so scarce and expensive that I had to use a bicycle. Now I can run my car again."

I remarked that it seemed an odd sort of revolution that put the capitalists back into their limousines, but he didn't bat an eye. "Very satisfactory, indeed," he said.

"Look at it this way," he said; "before Liberation commerce was next to impossible. I had to compete with dumped American cement that sold here cheaper than I could buy raw materials. In 1946, United States cement sold for six thousand KMT dollars a bag; mine cost eight thousand to *make*. I was being forced out of business; so was everyone. As a matter of fact, the United States firm that was destroying me with its beastly dumped cement was the same firm I trained with in California years ago. I knew all about *them*. They were strictly on the side of the corrupt creatures who were running this country. No, my dear sir, I expected to see the Liberation chop my head off; instead it saved my life."

I asked him about his profits, which he discussed most readily. The business made its profit on seventeen per cent of sales—about eleven billion seven hundred million *yuan* or, reduced to comprehensible economics, some five hundred thousand dollars. Of that sum thirty per cent went to commercial taxation (there is no *personal* income tax in China at all). Another thirty per cent went to reserves. Twenty-five per cent went to the shareholders (which now, of course, cut in the Government). The rest went to the Workers' Collective Benefit, a complex affair regulated by law for what they called "incentive rationalism," in other words a bonus system, and part of the State's rigid labor legislation.

I asked if co-ownership made any working difference. "Well," said Mr. Liu judiciously, "the Government appoints a works manager in charge of production and good relations. He looks after the production plan. We have to pay his salary, but he isn't really responsible to us."

The whole economic arrangement seemed strange, oblique and feasible. It was of course not dictated by theory; there had been no managerial revolution in China; the production was required and so far the State just had not got the technicians to run these uncounted businesses. It was part of the elasticity of Chinese Marxism—in this as with the peasants—that the solution had been found in this simple Fabian approach. Private enterprise passes through its penultimate stage, that of State Contractor, a feeder for Government business.

Of course, under the Constitution, Mr. Liu's firm was inevitably to be absorbed in the State. "Quite obviously I'm ready for that," said Mr. Liu. "I give us about ten years. Meanwhile, with all this reconstruction going on everywhere, I just can't make enough cement. The currency is stable, so I don't have to worry myself to death fiddling with gold bars or United States dollars. When we are wholly socialized, I can expect to continue as manager. Which, after all, is what I am now," he said in a way that I would like to have called wistful.

We went out among the beelike porters, still singing *Wei-ho! Wei-ho!* under the sacks.

"One more thing," said Mr. Liu, "I might add that there are *no* disputes with the workers nowadays."

One hundred and ten years before, some fifty British merchants came to Shanghai, opened to trade by the

Treaty of Nanking. Seven of them brought their wives. One imagines them, veiled and full-skirted at the ship's rail, watching with alarmed disapproval the approach of those mudbanks, that flat plain of dull paddies. They were granted a strip of land beside the Whangpoo, a quarter of a mile by three hundred yards deep; on this they might own their own ground, build their own homes, govern themselves by their own laws.

That patch of ground grew to fourteen square miles, and became one of the costliest water fronts of the world. The huge commercial buildings soared; behind the Bund stretched the houses and flats, hospitals and schools, cathedrals and golf courses, mills and race tracks, parks and factories. Air-conditioned offices and cinemas and bordellos and Episcopalian churches and charitable institutions and the back streets where the starving could die without interference. It was the international city of all international cities. When the Communists took Shanghai, the value of British property there, with its noble real estate, its wharves and godowns up the West and Yangtse rivers, was something like nine hundred million dollars.

When the Communists took Shanghai, more than half the prewar British community, which had been some ten thousand, had gone, driven away by the ridiculous and intolerable chaos and corruption of the Nationalist Government, and the catastrophic collapse of the currency. There remained about four thousand, who saw with a sort of relief that the Communists jumped on speculation right away, pegged the four basic commodities of grain, textiles, oil and coal-bricks, and somehow stabilized both currency and prices. All foreign interests would be safeguarded, said Mao Tse-Tung, so long as they kept out of politics.

In two years the four thousand had dwindled to seven hundred.

The foreign interests were safeguarded in a fashion that most European *taipans* recognized as spelling stark ruin. If there was persecution, it was strictly in the double-entry; all foreign business was drastically curtailed; at the same time the plants had to retain all their redundant labor on full wages. It was even difficult to put up the shutters. To wind up its affairs, a firm had to pay its workers three months' wages, plus a month's bonus for each year of service, plus another month's wages for travel expenses home, plus commodity taxes and turn-over taxes. Dying gracefully became a commercial problem; there was "squeeze" even on the funeral.

Shanghai—it all meant something very different now. The Club was no more—it had turned into some sort of institute, with blue-uniformed men and blue-uniformed girls sitting in long unassimilable rows drinking pale pink soda pop out of cups, while the radio droned on about production. The night life had gone—the last cabaret had petered out the week before, leaving in all China a total of none. A handful of Europeans remained, doing a sort of Robinson Crusoe business, torn between the bitter desire to execrate the whole horrible affair and the prudent impulse to keep their mouths shut, lest worse befall.

"Certainly the shops look very full," they said, "but you see, it is a deliberate illusion. Nobody can buy anything." I went into the town's big department store to buy a handkerchief; it was crammed.

"The harbor gets about ten ocean-going ships a month now," they said. "It used to handle thirty a day. Just go and look at it." I did, and a desolate sight it was indeed: a few junks, an antique gunboat and one Dutch freighter. All the Chinese coastal junks carried guns; the emplacements had been mounted forward behind a heavy incongruous sheet of armour-plating, on which was usually painted a reproduction of Picasso's dove of peace. However successful or otherwise Chiang Kai-Shek's blockade from Formosa was at strangling the mainland sea traffic, it seemed to have paralyzed Shanghai.

"That isn't the *point*," the Chinese official told me. "Shanghai is no longer a world port. It is not intended to be. We shall replace it—Tientsin, possibly, which is nearer our heavy industrial belt. Shanghai is *our* big commercial base. Six and a half million inhabitants. Eight hundred thousand industrial workers. Seven hundred thousand students. No more unrelated sections of the city with foreign troops. Do you know that when we came in 1949 more than a *million* people were living in huts made of gasoline cans or cardboard—or nowhere? We have built something like forty thousand new homes since then. But it still isn't easy, I can tell you. . . ."

We went for a long drive through the city; with its autos and buses and streetcars it still looked like a *city*, unlike Peking which still looks like a sublimated provincial capital. Here and there very highly decorated triumphal arches had been thrown across the thoroughfares, apparently for the October First celebrations; they looked good enough to last for years. They were a terrible obstruction to the traffic. We came to a huge gate behind which was a tremendous flurry of construction.

"The old dog-racing track," said the man. "Here we are building a theater to hold eighteen thousand people."

I had heard the flow of statistical information with the usual passive acceptance, but I felt compelled to query this. "A theater for *eighteen* thousand people? An open-air amphitheater, surely?"

"By no means. A building, for the presentation of plays. It will hold an audience of eighteen thousand."

There was nothing with which to argue; if it was so, it was so. I state the fact as presented to me: here on the old dog-racing track of Shanghai, they were building a theater some three or four times bigger than any other on the face of the earth.

Then he took me to the Pioneers' House. This had been the residence of some millionaire British Merchant, now taken over as an educational-establishment-rendez-vous-show-place for the Young Pioneers, the most junior echelon of the Communist youth leagues. It was a large house, of an opulence and uninhibited vulgarity almost impossible to describe; it was all curving rococo stairways and tessellated floors and Empire mirrors and hanging *lustres* of an ostentatious splendor to be seen nowhere outside a super-cinema. Its rooms were all five times too large, its ornamentation five times too florid; where—as in its private cinema, or its personal ballroom for eighty couples—it went in for expensive restraint, it confined itself to gigantic panels of mahogany and enormously obscure groups of statuary in unidentifiably costly materials. Everything about it parodied every decorative idea the world had ever seen. Its creator and owner had shrewdly taken himself off—to Hong Kong, everyone thought, though nobody seemed to care.

"Do not think we just commandeered this imperialist's house," they told me. "On the contrary, the Government pays him a handsome rent of something like fifty million *yuan*."

"You mean you actually transmit him his rental from Shanghai, in money?"

"Not exactly. We appointed an agent for him here.

The rent is paid in Chinese currency, here. We look after it."

For a while I wandered fascinated through this dreadful pleasure dome, enthralled by its polished marble and tortured ebony, its convolutions of gold-plated late-Victorian chinoiserie and its Metro-Goldwyn lavatories, all somewhat unbalanced by the introduction of vast portraits of Chairman Mao in attitudes of celestial contemplation, by little desks in the morning room, and by showcases full of the work of industrious Pioneers; cardboard models of steel-rolling mills, little Mig aircraft made of tinfoil, stuffed doves, more portraits of Chairman Mao embroidered by loyal little hands on the fronts of undervests.

I was about to sympathize with my guide for having to commit the care of sensitive young minds to surroundings of such unparalleled horror, when I caught a strange expression in his eye. "It is indeed a place of great beauty," he said reflectively. "The owner was a reactionary and doubtless a tyrant, but it needed money to create surroundings of such magnificence. . . . Happily it is now dedicated to a purpose worthy of it."

After dusk Zig and I shook everybody off and went out into the windy evening. The road outside the hotel was bordered by hundred-yard-long exhibition cases full of photographs of worthy and inspiring subjects—Labor Heroes throwing fuel into furnaces, handsome peasants mounted on tractors against backgrounds of rolling corn, well-known political personalities smiling indulgently at small children with bouquets. It was not the sort of *salon* to hold one absorbed indefinitely in the chill of an autumn evening. We intercepted a passing pedicab (the

Shanghai version, unlike the Pekinese pedicab, holds two)
and tried to say, "Wo *yao tao*. . . ." but he didn't care
where we wanted to go; he pedaled gaily through the
streets, whistling and calling out ribaldries to passing acquaintances.

He took us, inevitably, to the Bund, and there we
walked about through the kind of crowds one might normally see outside Wembley Stadium before a Cup Final.
Every hundred yards or so the multitude coalesced into a
group, opened itself out into a ring, and began to dance.
Sometimes there was a mouth organ or a flute, but usually
there was nothing at all; the boys and girls merely beat a
rhythmic measure with their palms and hummed. A dozen
youths would link arms and tread out a sort of *yang-ko*,
the rural harvest dance which has latterly acquired a sort
of Revolutionary symbolism.

It was impossible to observe unobserved; very soon
we were surrounded by the biggest group of all—no longer
silent and wordlessly curious; the onlookers laughed and
pointed and seized one by the arm, with obscure but
friendly gestures. By and by they formed a ring around us,
and in no time at all the clapping had begun, and the
humming of a song; a dozen of them formed a figure in
the circle. Somebody seized my arm, and I was there too,
groping for the measure, being passed from one linked
arm to the next among the laughter, turning and wheeling under the lamps to the murmur of a tune I had never
heard before.

(16)
A Night at the Opera

To THE crash and hiss of many gongs and a crescendo of little drums, the Emperor Liu Pang stalks across the scene—most richly bearded stark white face (white, the color of duplicity), enveloped in his robes of yellow silk (the yellow of imperial majesty). Above the painted scrolls that mark the royal brow towers the tyrannical mitre, aglow with scarlet beads and rimmed with swinging jewels. No one can ask, "Who is this?" for every line and hue and gesture proclaims him: Liu Pang, apotheosis of dramatic grandeur. He may not move without a storm of cymbals; his voice is echoed by the roll of that special drum called *hsia ku*. He sings of war to war itself—the General Han Hsin, Marshal of all the Tartars, so bedecked and hung about with cuirasses and sumptuous brocades, so violently painted and caparisoned that all humanity is lost in a blaze of martial symbolism.

Now All the Emperors in the World are chanting to All the Soldiers in the World. Somewhere behind the bamboo wall waits the faithful Concubine—with her wailing strings to sing for her, the tiny silver bells—but for the moment this is an encounter of Red and Black, the rasp of beaten copper and the thud of drums. In a moment the Emperor will ride away on a wisp of horsehair. Always, in

237

the end, he does. But the show goes on—hour after hour, day after day, year after year.

The Theatre House was almost everywhere; from outside it was a crowd of people, an open door; densely full, surging with devotion. I had seen the opera before, among the Chinese people of Singapore and Hong Kong; this was far better. There was nobody here to drop in because it was quaint. Chinese people do not drop in to the theater; for some part of the day it could almost be said that they live there. Nor is it quaint. It is fantastic, barbaric, rude; it had always been so, and splendid too. The Chinese adored it; in a world that changed around them, this, at least, did not. I sat back, in my island of ignorance, and let the sounds bounce off my skull.

One does not go to the theater in China to see how the other half lives; one goes because it *is*, to some degree, China. To say the Chinese are a theater-loving people is to say that the people of Australia enjoy an occasional cricket match, or that those of Seville have been known to attend the bull ring. The theater has been part of China since the records began. Today, throughout China, an average of three *million* theatergoers see some kind of play or opera *every day*. Some three hundred thousand performers are professionally occupied in the classical theater alone. When an important *artiste* performs anywhere, the house is sold days in advance, and parties of dedicated Trade Unionists and Democratic Leaguers converge on it much as supporters on Hampden Park or the Yankee Stadium.

The Chinese Opera, for all its vast popular appeal, is far from simple entertainment. It is an esoteric formula in primary colors and brutal sound. It is an acrostic, an enigma, an occultation, a code. It is also a pantomime, a drama, and a ballet. No one understands the inner meaning who was not, as it were, born on the playhouse floor. Practically no one was, though many have come near to it. Therefore the inner meaning—as I was once told by an intelligent European who knew the Opera well—was something to be taken or left alone; anyone could still *look*.

Outside the theater, China's face is set with the effort of political reform, higher education and economic production; inside, life is still concerned with the passionate eccentricities of emperors and princesses, generals and war lords, brandishing their emotions in a blaze of tinsel against a background of illusion which, in contrast, is practically nonexistent. The personalities appear, announce their names, their characters, their thoughts, their intentions. This is an accepted piece of supererogation; their very appearance has already conveyed it all to the audience through the conventions of make-up: the *chin* is a face slashed with black and orange lines of ferocity —the general; the *chon* is the whiskered grotesquerie of the clown; the *tan* is the white mask of the heroine. The heroine is the star, played always by a man (except in a variant of Shanghai opera where, for some perverse historic reason, the men are all played by women). The most famous living Chinese performer, Mei Lan-Fang (still occasionally to be publicly seen on occasions of especial grandeur—like Ulanova, he now performs only for princes), has perfected this strange technique of portraying feminity in a fashion apparently impossible for a woman. He can no longer walk, he undulates; his body is one lissom seductive arabesque; no female voice could reach the shrill heights of his falsetto; never for a second are his hands still, manipulating the yard-long overfall of his silken sleeves, the precise arrangements of which are part of the intense stylization of the play.

The Emperor declaims. From the wings saunters a stagehand in a blue boiler suit, hands him a horsehair switch, and strolls off. From that moment on, every one knows, the Emperor is mounted. A storm arises—two blue-suited employees put down whatever they were doing and casually appear, waving flags. The actor treads with exaggerated gesture over an invisible devil-step: he is now indoors. Each player, entering or departing in a ritual sequence, is instantly identifiable by the basic color of his face: red for the good and honorable, black for cruelty, white for feminine virtue or for mourning, green for a somewhat oblique characterization familiar to the Chinese, the good bandit—as we might say, Robin Hood.

And all the time every mood, every line, every gesture, is pointed and underscored by the music—strident, savage, monotonous; to the uninitiated the noise is tremendous, meaningless, almost terrible. The accompaniment is improvised, following always a line or two behind the singer, with a whine of fiddles and screech of brass, with every situation a significant phrase announced by a thunderous crash of gongs. It was an undying astonishment to me that subtlety could be produced in such a fabulous din.

All this has not escaped political attention.

"In the past," said the accepted work on the modern stage, "the theater served the interests of the feudal ruling classes. Although the form of drama and opera came from the people, the content was provided by their masters. It is typical of the feudal structure that, although theater was so popular among landlords and mandarins as well as the people, those that provided it were at the bottom of the social order. Actors, dancers and musicians constituted, with shoemakers, barbers, and prostitutes, the 'untouchable' class, ineligible even to sit for the imperial civil service examinations. . . . The opera extolled the virtues of patience, submission to despots, filial piety. . . . The form of traditional theater is being given a new and progressive content. Scenes which laud servility, submission, and long suffering are eliminated; those which depict courage, patriotism and struggle retained and developed. . . ."

The actor who plays the faithful concubine, Yu Chi, glides across the empty stage; two banners of black silk droop beside her, therefore it is night. Her master has betrayed her; her piercing artificial voice, unbearably shrill, wavers among the semitones in a fortissimo lament. She dances a formal, funereal measure between two swords; her sleeves sway and flutter like butterflies until, impaled ritually on the steel, she sinks, while the gongs clash and ring triumphantly around her.

And then, one night, real drama entered.

In Shanghai there was—as there always had been, under all the variants of imperialist domination, Japanese exploitation, Kuomintang tyranny and Communist liberation—an establishment called the "Great World," which must be one of the strangest places of entertainment on earth. At one time, they said, it used to be considered far from the most decorous center in Shanghai, a place of shows, side shows, eating houses, music halls, and diversions even more curious. The new Government cleaned it up, so that by the time I saw the Great World it was no more bizarre and extraordinary than, say, a three-ring circus directed by Salvador Dali.

It was an enormous building of indefinable design on many floors, all loosely interconnected by arcades and galleries and sweeping flights of stone stairs, full of flashing lights and steaming rice and wailing music, a rather riotous contrast to the rather gray spirit of redemption all around. But the feature of the Great World that I feel must be unique is its collection of five separate theaters, all going full blast at once, and practically within earshot of one another.

In the overcharged atmosphere of the political China then it had a lovely unreality. For two thousand *yuan*—about eight cents—the proletariat of Shanghai could spend hours wandering through a rich choice of opera in the Peking, Szechuan, Shanghai, or Ningpo styles, a play or two, a cross-talk show and a cinema, all staged with delightful Chinese bravura, all superbly done.

By that time I was almost within sight of the sophistication necessary to enjoy the exquisite formalities of Chinese opera—the interplay of gorgeous costume and stylized behavior, the random crash of cymbals—it began to have for me the proper chaotic and dreamlike quality. As usual, the traditional postures and interminable songs were in no way distracted by the casual appearance of stagehands and musicians with cups of tea, which they would frequently leave absent-mindedly lying about the scene. In any case nobody listened very intently to anything. The audience had adopted the fashionable attitude of relaxation, lolling on the benches, chatting, feeding their babies, smoking, spitting, heating their dinners; while peddlers strolled noisily around selling sugar cane and bean curd, sunflower seeds and sesame cakes. It occurred to me that it was the nearest thing left alive to the old Elizabethan theater of London. If you loved China in all its noise and anarchy and visual sensitivity, this was the way to love it.

Nothing, that night, seemed further from the tight political minds and stern slogans outside; the Chinese Government is good about retaining the merrier moments of the past. The Great World was one of the few places left where the Wicked Emperor was hated only for his beard, and the Distraught Princess admired for her beauty. I watched it all with immense pleasure and refreshment; it was the first time I had not been exhausted for many weeks.

Even Big Wei, my interpreter, broke down and enjoyed it. He was, as I have repeatedly suggested, a reliable Party functionary, a cadre, and an inflexible man, indeed. Sometimes I thought he was a sieve; whatever jovial Chinese heresies might be expressed came through filtered into the limpid formulas of orthodoxy. It had taken me a very long time to discover his Achilles heel: he was devoted to the theater. A night out at the Great World had, indeed, been his idea. Now he was mellowed enough by this splendid silly place to agree willingly when I said, "Let's go behind and meet the players."

We chose one of the shows at random. It was even odder backstage than in front: a rickle of flats and canvas palaces, an empty dressing room like a kitchen. Among the litter of grease paint and glorious costumes was a blackboard. You get used to blackboards in China. There was a message of some sort chalked on it in Chinese characters—there usually is; something about production statistics or the necessity of liberating Formosa. I casually asked Big Wei to read it, without being tremendously interested in what it would say, and he began:

" 'At the Discussion Group this morning I was made aware of my shortcomings, thanks to the proper criticism of my colleagues, to whom I am indebted. The comrades helped me to realize the burden I had forced them to carry through my failure to confess to my errors of thinking. I was made to realize that my fear of arrest and punishment was responsible for this. . . .' "

My interpreter, as I endlessly repeat, was a man of the Book, but he paused and drew a sharp breath.

" '. . . I was aware of the suspicions of my comrades, and conscious of criticism.' "

Outside the music soared and banged; someone on stage sang out pentatonic romance. It was terrible; it was like breaking into the confessional. I said, "Go on."

" 'I have been enabled by the Group to purify my thinking and repudiate doubts and questionings. I now . . . I now acknowledge the debt we all owe to the self-less leadership of Chairman Mao and the People's Government . . .' and he signed his name."

Big Wei paused, and began, "You will understand . . ." I said, "Let's go away, quickly."

I do not know, nor ever shall, which of the graceful mummers or tumbling clowns was the comrade whose burden was so bitter, whose anxieties so horrible, that this desperate immolation was the only way out—and whose secret was now exposed, not just to me, but to the Government official whose appearance that night he would forever after be certain was designed and significant.

I walked out through the capering colors of the Great World into the even greater, and somehow the show seemed less gay, and the thing outside less remote.

The People's Court of Shanghai sat in a dim drear Edwardian relic of a building that was no dimmer nor drearier than the usual county court. Moreover outside the building someone with a gong and a fiddle was rehearsing operatics, which is more than one gets in a county court.

Over the judgment seat were two red flags and the usual portrait of Chairman Mao, which was perhaps no less appropriate than the Royal Arms of the Old Bailey and rather better than the cigarette advertisements tacked in front of the Bench that you find, say, in South Africa.

I did not know what the case would be. It turned out to be a commercial squabble over the sale of a store. Nothing more clearly pointed the ambivalent position of Shanghai, still full of petty industrialists and a few big ones, too. The *modus vivendi* between the capitalists and the Communists became daily more absorbing.

It is possible that anywhere but here the thing would have been a bore: an old man, manager of a shop, was accused in some circumlocutory way of fiddling the books, misappropriating the proceeds of the sale of the shop, and evading taxation thereon. *Nothing* here, however, was a bore, least of all the elaborate Communist juridical procedure to determine which of a crowd of palpably undesirable bourgeois traders was in the right over a deal that was certainly about as Marxist as Wall Street.

The presiding judge was one of the ubiquitous young-old experts of the new regime, cool and quick and fair. He sat between two civil assessors—there was no prosecuting counsel; the judge led all the examinations himself, and the defending attorney said never a word except a mitigating plea at the end. A score or so of onlookers filled the benches—the same old blue uniforms on the Bench and off it; a court of boilermakers, like a trade union conference, with no implications of right or wrong. The old man in question was the one individual there who seemed to have absorbed but an imperfect understanding of what the Revolution had been all about. He was a testy old character who spent his time tut-tutting at the witnesses, quite clearly tiring of the technicalities. Yes, yes, he kept on saying, naturally he did this and that; who didn't? What did they all suppose he was

in business *for?* When they urged upon him that a new
and incorruptible world had dawned he said, "Very well
—why fuss? All this trifling affair had happened *before*
the Liberation. Does anyone here know anything *about*
this sort of transaction?" He sat down, shaking his shaven
head in exasperation.

It was all intensely fair and reasonable, and I felt a
considerable warmth towards the keen young professional
jurist presiding over the case. Once, when somebody murmured the words, "political situation," the judge snapped
back, "Please understand there are no such things as political considerations here. We are investigating the truth
or otherwise of certain allegations, none of which remotely concerns politics." Whenever issues of conflicting
evidence occurred, the Bench did an odd thing: he recalled both witnesses together, on opposite sides of him,
and made them argue it out. The old man kept shrugging,
clearly anxious to get back to the shop. From time to time
the judge would call out to him, "You see? What do you
say to that?" and the irascible old man would growl, "If
people will tell lies, what am I supposed to do?"

I was considerably sold on the fairness and expedition of the proceedings. Then—it always happened; the
fly devoured the ointment, the great truth became distracted, the blue note intruded on the pleasant chord—
after an hour or two of exemplary hearing the judge asked
the parties concerned if they felt they had another word
or two to add. One side said, "I want my money back."
The old man said, "Nonsense."

And then a man with a notebook rose briskly from
the public benches and moved into the well of the court
and said, "I represent the business community of the district in question, and I consider it my duty to make reference to the great work done by the People's Government

of China in protecting the interests of all, both great and small. I would like to commend the work of the People's Government in bringing such men as this to trial for wrong thinking and antisocial behavior, and I trust that the sentence about to be passed upon him shall be a warning to others who do not follow the teachings of our leaders." With that he folded his notebook, slipped it into the pocket of his blue suit, and returned to his place.

This staggering intrusion—which for irrelevance, assumption of guilt, contempt of court, and generally intolerable interference with an otherwise impeccable hearing would have had the man arraigned in two minutes anywhere else—was to my astonishment accepted by the intelligent and shrewd young judge without a word.

"And we hope," said this sinister visitation from the public benches as he regained his seat, "that the accused man will repent."

The judge pursed his lips, and made no remark.

And quite suddenly, then, a commonplace little case of fraud turned into something with implications too sad to be borne. That was all there was. The old man was sent up for two years, still grumbling; somehow he did not seem to matter any more.

It was weeks later, far from Shanghai—enclosed and bored in the cabin of a river steamer, in fact, with all that past and far away—that I went through my notes on new China and the law. The country was making a big effort to speed legal processes throughout its unmanageably huge territory, to standardize a system of justice in a country that had for centuries defined the law as the unpredictable whim of whoever happened to wield the ocal stick at the time. "The main task of the nation's judiciary," said my piece of paper, "during this transitional period, is to strengthen and employ the judiciary weapon further to consolidate the People's democratic dictatorship and smooth progress towards the realization of a socialist society in China." To this end they had established two thousand new mobile circuit courts to tour the country-side, exercising both civil and criminal jurisdiction, acting as investigating and prosecuting agencies in cases of "non-co-operation" or "opposition to Government." The proceedings, it said, in public squares, take the form of public meetings. . . .

Then Big Wei knocked on the door and came in, as he sometimes did, with that air of vague and purpose-less indecision that always presaged some awkward and pointed discussion. This time I was wrong; he merely wanted to ask the question put so often, with a motive so obscure as to be usually invisible: Was everything go-ing all right? Of course, I said; everything was arranged with great efficiency.

"Naturally we are always obliged for your comments —criticisms," he said. He often said it. "Has anything cropped up since we left Peking that struck you, one way or another?"

I was very tired, my head had begun to ache again in the old way; I felt incapable of a sustained debate on the progress of the People's Democracy in China. I said every-thing seemed all right to me.

"I don't think so," said Big Wei. "I think you were distressed in Shanghai." Never once since we left had he mentioned Shanghai, nor any detail of our stay. "I think you did not like the case in the People's Court. There was something . . ."

I said, "All right. I did not like it. I thought that by allowing the thing that we both of us remember, you bitched up something that you could otherwise have been very proud of."

He was in no way upset. He nodded, looked at his watch, and strolled towards the door.

"Funny thing," he said, "but I knew you would say that. I did not forget, either."

(17)
The Mountain City

THERE were by that time so many Chinas in my mind
—the cold and the hot, the long past and the yet to come,
the beguiling and the exasperating, the splendid and the
sad. I suppose it was only proper that I should see the
brave new world before going back into the middle ages.

Early one morning they took us to the airfield in
Shanghai and put us in a plane—bare aluminum, projecting hooks and stanchions, a pile of mailbags, rigid bucket
seats with webbing backs along the bulkhead; it was like
the war all over again. We flew through steaming cloud
like a Turkish bath over the invisible province of Anhwei.
I tried to read, but Jean-Jacques Rousseau bounced about
in my hands; I lost patience with his endless complaints;
the interminable fencing with physical romance that
came to nothing. Then Hangkow—a good terrain, well distributed with parked Mig's, beautiful little cocktailed aircraft, and the bus taking us to lunch round the wide circuit of the perimeter so that we should not approach
them too closely. Then another lift into the steam over
a landscape almost completely aqueous—rivers merging
into lakes, lakes dissolving into floods, trees and houses
projecting wanly from vast gleaming expanses of shallow
water—it was as though China was some enormous scullery floor, waiting to be mopped up—with the mopping

up a national problem that had never been solved. Where was the mechanical sponge that could deal with a saturated neighborhood the size of Belgium?

We dropped down again at Ichang, in the province of Hupeh—a place that forever more will have no meaning for me at all, except that it was there that I lost my *Confessions*. We were taken to drink tea in a sort of an airfield shed, and when I got back into the plane I realized I had left Rousseau behind. It made no difference; something the less to irritate me. (Yet nearly a fortnight later, after many thousands of additional miles, I passed through Hangkow on the way back to the North, and a courteous stranger in a blue suit approached me on the steps of the plane with the wilted paper-backed book— the same book. He said, "I believe you left this on Ichan airfield some time ago." How far away was Ichang, and how long ago, and how did they know it was I who had lost it? Nothing, but *nothing*, can ever be abandoned in China.)

Then we flew some more, and the land below began to writhe and weave itself into patterns of fantasy and bizarre beauty; the mountains came crawling out of the mists ahead in a fashion breath-taking in both senses. How alarming, from four thousand feet, are the lovely peaks of five thousand! Somehow we wriggled down among the slopes and terraces to Chungking. Mist everywhere, swirling and pouring through the valleys like something artificial; a smiling little man on the tarmac waiting to be introduced, as usual, as the man from the All-China Journalists' Association. Sometimes, in moments of absent-mindedness all over this huge country, I would think it was always the same man. Maybe it was.

A dockyard among the mountains; a harbor in the deepest hinterland; great cargo junks fourteen days' sail from the sea—here in the rocky heart of Southwest China, twelve hundred miles from the ocean, was the Port of Chungking. One can never quite get used to this extravagant compartmentalization of China. However was unity of *any* kind imposed on a nation so hugely spread, so tenuously linked? Here in Chungking were nearly two million Chinese toiling in a steep, stony city that until the other day, as it were, had no road, no rail, nothing to associate it physically with the rebirth of its own immense surroundings but the river, indispensable artery of China, crawling from the foothills of the Himalaya to the China Sea, three thousand miles of highway through this endlessly sprawling land. From Peking to Chungking was from London to Rome—and that was a simple step in China—twelve hundred miles and a generation separated the Communist capital and this, the last great city to know what was now called "Liberation." All of China had a two years' start on Chungking.

With or without the Revolution, life here was hard indeed—a big town, clinging to hillsides so precipitous that half of it was caves and the other half balconies, still emerging from chaos, shifting mountains with nothing to help but two hundred thousand pairs of human hands. This was the final redoubt of Chiang and his Kuomintang Government: Chungking was the dateline for the wartime communiqués; Chungking was where the handful of uncertain diplomatists hung on through those final troglodyte days under the Japanese bombs, maintaining the polite international illusion that this was China. So Chungking became the last mainland enclave of the one Chinese whose name in China now was a curse. When it fell in the end, most of China was already "reformed"—and Chungking ruined. You could see it still.

Here among the terraced hills of Szechuan was the

China of one's old imagination, the China of the ancient
scroll paintings and the silken screens, a place of surpassing beauty. It was as though every miniature formal Oriental garden in the world had been united and magnified
to the size of Britain; a composition of rivers and moun-
tainsides and mists, curious trees and torrents—yet somehow *inhabited* as nowhere else .You could travel for mile
after mile and find barely a square foot of land that was
not cultivated, walled in, fussed over almost by the fingers. What looked from the air like an intricate mosaic
was a thousand patches, hoed and tilled and growing:
vegetables, a pool of rice, a row of beans, a drill of corn;
thin ribbonlike strips of gardening adhering somehow to
the slopes, with somewhere a small man bent double,
plucking weeds from between the stones. China counted
its land by the ten thousand miles, the Chinese by the
mou—the unit of personal possession: one-sixth of an
acre.

Chungking might once have been a capital for what
might once have been a government, but which was now
called by formula the "Traitorous Clique"—that was
to say: Chiang, Mrs. Chiang, and the financial operatives
of the Four Families. The last days of Chungking must
have been fantastic indeed—embassies bivouacking in
cantonments among the hunger; three different currencies, inflation, speculation, unemployment. In 1946, the
price of a *tan* of rice—about eighty-five pounds—jumped
from twelve dollars to twenty-one dollars. By 1949, it
cost five thousand three hundred and ninety million gold
dollars—each one of which was worth three million of
the old ones. Clearly there was a sense of doom—and,
they say, panic. Who would cling for a second to cash
when he might change it into something durable, like cotton or rice or gold? Who would produce anything when

he might invest in it? If you had no capital, you went hungry.

All this, while disastrous at the time, makes eloquent argument for the new men of today. Not until 1949 was the Kuomintang driven from Chungking, leaving a city bankrupt and starving. It showed it still. Here was the first place I had seen in the new China where poverty looked you straight in the face—not the clean business-like austerity of Peking or Hangkow, with its rather self-conscious monastic implications of moral self-denial, but hard, bare-footed want, with angry eyes, with the scalp-scars of impetigo, inheritance of hunger and necessity.

And yet—since everything in China said, "And yet" —even this was revealed as a challenge. Long before, when I had protested at being shown only the model examples of progress in the country, they had shrugged and said, "We would obviously prefer you to see the things we are proud of. Szechuan, so far, is not a good example of de-velopment, but if you particularly want to see it . . ." There I was, anyhow, among the thin people, bowed under monstrous loads. At its worst it was better than the past, in that it contained hope—and *they* knew you knew it.

To the end, of course, there would always be para-dox. I was taken to lodge in what was spoken of alterna-tively as the "Guest House" or the "Auditorium"—an edifice of quite indescribable ostentation and overdeco-rated vulgarity, an enormous piece of rococo chinoiserie suggestive of three Albert Halls united in some night-mare concept of the Second Dynasty. It contained an opera house seating four thousand five hundred people, divers salons and administrative blocks, and the row of rooms in one of which I lived, which brought to mind a prison cell capriciously established in the Oriental Room of the Victoria and Albert Museum. The whole proposition seemed so out of character, reminiscent of all the spendthrift pomp that the Communists so deplored in Chiang Kai-Shek, that I could scarcely believe it to be part of the new Puritan regime. But it was. It had been completed only two years before. It was impossible not to hint at one's doubts about this barbarous gold and scarlet fantasy erected among so much difficulty and hardship. Very clearly this was not the first time the authorities had been faced with the same objections; the defensive facts were ready on the tongue—the place was used for public business; it occupied only 1.3 per cent of the area of new building; it had cost only 1.8 per cent of the Southwest China Council's income; it was not financed by agricultural taxation. . . . Evidently some hard words had been said from on high; Marxist self-criticism in China did not stop at the Street Committee.

It was a strange and almost touching aberration for these starkly realistic people, a throwback—among all the drab moral excellence—to the Chinese adoration of color. It was hard to keep complaining. But I did not enjoy my quarters. I loved Szechuan, the most splendid eccentric landscape in China, but I did not love the Auditorium: the great, gaunt, darkened opera house, the ninety-five exhausting steps up from the front gate to the terrace, the laborious elaboration of the exterior with its carved and painted eaves, and the shoddy nastiness of the bedroom, with the plaster already flaking away, the plywood furniture, the enameled bath stained and crusted below the dripping tap.

Everything else was full of interest.

The visit to Chungking had been my idea, not theirs, but very soon they were profiting by this chance for another statistical session. We drove around the mountain-

ous streets to what seemed to be the municipal headquarters, a walled compound with riflemen at the gates,
one of the few occasions I saw armed guards anywhere
in China. The mayor—I think it was the mayor; the introductions never made it clear—pressed the appropriate
button in his brain and explained civic progress between
sips of tea. By 1950 prices were stabilized; by 1951 private
business was back to its 1946 level; by 1953 reconstruction was begun; and today Chungking was a city of a
hundred and thirty-eight State firms, forty-four joint
State-private enterprises, seventy-five Co-operative, ten
thousand nine hundred private firms. . . . The mayor, if
indeed it were he, knew it all; without reference to a note
he detailed his saga of renaissance, smiling and urging
round the tea. There were, he said, still far too many un-
employed.

"When we took over, there were exactly eleven
broken-down buses for a million people." And now the
big red Skodas ground up and down the formidable hills.
How did they *get* here, with no roads or rails? The answer was, of course, as for everything else: They were carried here—first of all by the Yangtse some of the way, for
the rest by hands, and backs and shoulders. One forgets
the hopeless immobility of machinery when deprived of
its working medium: How does a three ton bus move
from place to place—with nothing to move on? It was
built to move men, but finally it is men who must, and
bodily, move it.

We drove along, then, by the Kialang River—tremendous by any European standards, but a slender tributary
on the map of China. There were the mountain-movers.
We came upon them first by scores, then in hundreds,
then by the thousands, and more again than that. From
a distance it might have been one of those terrifying films

of the movements of irresistible tropical ants, a dreadful
corporate industry, apparently undirected except by some
invisible communal impulse—the sort of busy multitude
to be seen nowhere else but in China, moving and crossing and trudging under their loads: the men with the
bamboo shoulder-rods that bear all the burdens of Asia,
restless units in some boundless pattern of determination. They were building a road.

Nor was it only men; in Szechuan the women too
lift the loads and strain against the harness, turning the
wheels and heaving the rocks. It took fifteen humans to
move in an hour what one truck could do in ten minutes
—but there were no trucks, and men were abundant. They
were also building a siding, and a housing estate. They
were scratching away the contours of hills. They were
equalizing the fall of valleys. Give one man a chisel, and
a hammer, a small bag of rice and a great deal of time, he
can cut a hole in a mountain that—with a thousand men
doing likewise beside him—is pretty soon big enough to
carry a railway train. That is indeed what had just happened. In this fashion they had finished the celebrated
railway, the first the Province had known: Chungking to
Cheng Tu; three hundred miles in two years, dug and
hammered out by hand, tunnels and bridges and all.

And there it was. Trains used it—with every truck
and carriage, every tremendous locomotive having been
borne up the river, and manhandled over the hill.

There were, again, various aspects of fantasy. I stood
on a pile of shaped masonry while the toiling crowds
trudged around below, each with his stone, each with his
timber prop. Was this the way the Pyramids were built?
As one looked at these people, one knew one was living
among the greatest sea of humanity on earth. A slender
Chinese paused, lowered his shoulder-bamboo to the

checker's scale—two panniers weighing ninety-five *cattis* each—that being an approximate total of two hundred and forty pounds, the dead lift of one heavyweight boxer, to be carried uphill. For that: forty-two cents a day. He loped off, humming the *wei ho, wei ho* of all China, into the mass that somehow was not and could not be just a crowd of coolies, but a colossal and nearly incomprehensible concentration of individuals. The Chinese were without end, but to the last man they were individuals. They passed by in teams of six, harnessed to carts like mules; they neither stood up nor did they lie on their faces; very slowly they progressed up the slope with their bodies making an angle of forty degrees to the ground, their weight straining on the ropes, their eyes shut, the wooden wheels whining in slow rhythmic squeals to the pressure of their pull.

As I stood on the pile of stones, a man came up; he was dressed in a faded parody of the cadre's uniform—blue, but tattered and faded to the semblance of a miller's overall. He looked up and smiled and to my tremendous astonishment said, "*Est ce que vous parlez français, par hazard?*"

I said with pleasure that yes, I did; who and what was he? Oh, nothing much, he said, he was by way of being a sort of *contremaitre* on the roadwork, but once upon a time he had been to a convent school in Shanghai and—one knew how it was; here in Szechuan one saw nobody at all. It was interesting to speak French again, said he, with an appealing hesitancy. "But who are *you* . . . ?" And then—there was the man who had brought me there, helpful and smiling in his blue uniform. "Is everything satisfactory?" he asked, and cast a brief word in Chinese to the man from the Shanghai school, who at once said, "I am glad to have met you, but I must get back to my work."

Wei-ho, wei-ho, sang the men, bending under the bamboo shoulder-poles; the road progressed a yard or two; a new house rose a foot on the hilltop estate; somewhere along the new railway an engine howled. In the history of China are recorded the change of a great many historic regimes, many monarchial families, punctuating the interminable story of the race. Each change of dynasty has been marked always the same way: by a bath of blood either greater or less, by a prodigy of civil engineering—a river dammed, a new road built; ten thousand people bent to the task of impressing *somebody's* will on the shape of the land. The Chinese people have fought geography since the dawn of their records; there are more of them now, and geography remains.

I was tired beyond definition; I had moved too much, not just here but over a long time; I had reached the point where the thought of bed was equally desirable and terrifying. Perhaps the Opera House room did not help.

My Chinese friends were both helpful and considerate. Deciding that my weariness was not wholly the effete languor associated with the capitalist races, but not impossibly due to insomnia, they suddenly decided to give me a momentary rest from good works. One day they said, "Let us go into the country and have a day by the Hot Springs. We can bathe, and look at the mountains."

Nothing seemed to me at that moment a more desirable proposition. We piled into a car and set off up the valley of Kialang.

There are possibly few drives in the known world of

greater charm and beauty than the thirty-six miles between Chungking and—whatever was the place we visited. I paid absolutely no attention to its name—it had no political or economic significance; it was associated with no serious development of historic importance; this was a day off. I made no notes at all. This was an error; it was the one place in the province I recall with undiluted delight.

During this journey I kept awake long enough to realize that this scene—now skirting the profound valley of the river, adrift with great sampans and barges propelled by spidery oars; now rolling round the shoulder of a mountain most delicately set about with terraced fields, most cunningly diverted with crooked trees that nature could never have gnarled so artistically—was probably the loveliest thing I had ever seen in all my life.

It seems to me that in the rest of the world we too arbitrarily compare the qualities of untouched landscape with that contrived by man—unlike the realist, Cobbett, who assessed natural beauty only in relation to its human usefulness; I must say a most healthy point of view. Who wants an attractive desert? But here—there was everything. Not only was the setting so curious and original, the bizarre sweep of the hillsides so elegantly complemented and emphasized by the intricate pattern of fields and paddies, but the very groups of casual trees had entered into the spirit of the composition—they had leaned this way and that, and held their better branches in such and such a fashion so as to give the prospect exactly that flicker of the grotesque which would take it from the delightful almost to the sublime. . . .

I do not want this enthusiasm to be construed as an unquestioning act of faith to Chairman Mao and the selfless leadership of the People's Republic. It is not impossible that all this visual delight existed even in the days of the Four Families and the Traitorous Clique. It might well be that it was there in the days of the Empress, and before her of the Ming and the T'ang and every other dynasty far back into history. That is the wonder of China: you look at that wall, that contouring of the hillside, and you feel that its owner will never know how many grandfathers ago it came about. I rode through this country with the Communists, and we talked about the strains of rice. The breed of trees, the names of the turtles who bobbed with tireless curiosity on the ruffled ochre surface of the great river; we talked about the advantages of painting with a brush made of dog's-hair over spreading the color with the nail of the second finger. By and by we came to the Hot Springs.

There was nothing much to them—in Japan these things are done with infinitely greater finesse and charm. There was a sort of guest house, but they had built it in such a fashion that groves of unattractive bushes hid the superlative bend of the Kialang River from sight; the mountain behind was lost against a windowless wall. It might have been anywhere. The bath itself was a dank steaming pool, with the hot mineral water spilling through a mossy orifice into a shallow tank; it was warm and relaxing; everything smelled agreeably of sulphur, like the anteroom to Hell. Outside the main pool was a smaller, and considerably warmer one that seemed to have been planned especially for women. They sometimes shared the main pool, too, but it did not make much difference; everyone was most heavily and decorously clad in costumes such as one sees in picture postcards of Coney Island in 1904; we might have been a party of Baptists.

We ate a sandwich lunch and set off home.

Halfway on the journey home we suddenly said, "Let us stop off *here* and look at a village." (The enduring urge somehow to catch somebody out, perhaps; to see something that had not been organized days in advance. I think it was possibly rather futile; it satisfied nobody but ourselves. It invariably seemed, however, a good thing to do.)

When we saw a cluster of roofs over a breasting field we stopped; we all got out and made our way towards it along the narrow mud parapet dividing two flooded paddies. The interpreters led the way a trifle grumpily— "You can't just break in on people like that; we had better go ahead and ask if they will welcome us." We said jauntily that it didn't matter; would we not see a truer picture of the rural China if we merely strolled in? And then, of course, we lost our point, inevitably: it wasn't a village at all, only an isolated farmhouse among the fields; the elaborate curves and falls of its outhouse roofs had looked more important than they were.

We peered through the outer door: a wall surrounding a courtyard; a three-sided arrangement of buildings made of baked mud, but solidly and attractively made, with delicate up-pointing eaves. Big Wei pushed hastily to get in first; I knew that these impromptu encounters worried him until he had made introductions, established who we were and, perhaps, who he was. I do not think there was anything very sinister in this, but he liked good impressions and had a concern about misunderstandings. But this time it seemed the joke was on him—when the farmer came out, he could not understand anything Big Wei said; his Szechuan dialect had nothing in common with Big Wei's precise Mandarin. The farmer stood looking at us in mute incomprehension—the grotesque Big Noses, and the obvious cadre in the neat blue uniform.

Big Wei was sadly put about by this development, and had to go back and call the car driver to interpret for *him*.

In the end, it was hardly worth all the trouble: I spoke to Wei, Wei spoke to the driver, the driver spoke to the farmer; then the farmer spoke to the driver, the driver to Big Wei, and Big Wei to me. One would have required a very serious point at issue to have justified such a palaver, but there wasn't much to talk about, and the old man was clearly mystified, when he was not bored. His wife ceremoniously brought out wooden stools for us to sit on; the farmer rubbed his hands on his knees and said yes, he had got this plot with Land Reform. He had farmed it for years, as a tenant. How much better off was he now? "Well," he said, "I've got the land, as I've said." Had that improved his condition financially? No, he wouldn't say so; not that he had noticed; instead of paying levies to the landlord you paid taxes to the Government. This sort of story was not wholly to the taste of Big Wei, who preferred rather more enthusiasm, but it seemed to be faithfully enough interpreted, filtered through two translations, while three or four small children stumbled and groveled round the yard, and a great water buffalo stamped and snorted in the byre. In the dusk of the cooking-place a young blind girl nursed a fretful baby.

I asked how old the farmstead was, and the old man looked up, quite at a loss. Why, he said, how could one tell? It had always been there. When this was queried jocularly, the farmer grew suddenly testy; we were wasting his time anyway, without arguing about natural facts. The farmstead had *always been there*, and that was that.

Big Wei laughed, in his short way, and explained, "That is what they say about anything that was there before they were born. I should say that this building is about ninety years old. If you require an accurate answer, I can have enquiries made at the records office."

I assured him hastily that the question was of the greatest possible unimportance. "Just ask him whether he thinks the old days were better than these."

The farmer stretched out his hands, which looked like the roots of fossilized trees. Of course they were not. Had he not explained that now he owned his own land? As for progress towards socialization—they had a mutual-aid arrangement with the neighbors, but of course they were spread at some distance. He began to look at us dubiously; without any translation at all I could follow the train of his new thought: This was some sort of official enquiry, he was being investigated, it was bound to end in taxation. He became restless under the impact of this idea, and I felt it was high time to produce a new Liberation for him. We said our goodbys and went out; it is possible that to this day the old farmer waits anxiously for the new tax assessment which, I hope, will never come.

Evening came early in Chungking, drifting in among the mountains with the thickening mist. There was not much to do—a walk through the town, but it had little charm; it showed the face of a city that had been in the wars too long, beaten up by isolation, by corruption, by mad economics, by loneliness, a history of rather dreary confusion finally culminating in the bombs. The new buildings that were going up were flat and stark and characterless—people weren't again to be led into fanciful glory and expense like the Auditorium. There was a smart new place which looked as though it might have been a club—indeed it was a club: the Seamen's Institute. Chungking is probably the only city in the world buried a thousand miles inside the mountains that has such a place, a Seamen's Institute without any sea. It was used by the river crews. We went in and looked around, but there was nothing much to see except rooms full of patriotic posters and wall newspapers and huge graphs. In two of the rooms groups of uniformed seamen were having committee meetings, sitting around long tables while someone addressed them—*hsueh-hsi* meetings, the study groups that are held at every level throughout the country, and at which the Party line's bearing on various aspects of affairs is discussed and explained.

After that there was nothing to do but stroll towards the water front—which was everywhere; Chungking lies at the apex of the V between the Yangtse and its tributary the Kialang; wherever there were not mountains, there was river. I found a steep path leading towards water, but not to the docks, only to a stretch of the Kialang bordered with rocking shanties made of wattle and matting, with a pattern of sampans slowly drifting about on the river far below, some people fishing, a squadron of ducks, and the wreaths of mist writhing down from the mountains all around. It reminded me of the great Mekong river in Indo-China. I had waited on such a bank as this, on such a night, in the town of Luang Prabang in Laos; it had been beseiged by the Communist armies and was about to fall, everyone said, while the sampans bobbed gently about and people fished and dozed and ducks scavenged. It did not fall; the Communists shrugged it off and went away somewhere else—to Dien Bien Phu.

Back again through the gray streets. . . . What problems arise in a country that has no bars, no cafés! There were teahouses of a kind in Chungking, dim caverns full of smoke, but they were also full of men sitting waiting in a watchful silence—for what? You could not stroll in on them any more than you could into the Racquet Club. At the street intersections the policemen stood on pedestals, looking exactly like little fairy-book gnomes in their green padded jackets and trousers, their round caps; almost spherical little men under their concrete mushrooms. They did not look in the least sinister or even repressive; one felt the guns inside their little holsters must be made of chocolate. When we crossed the street they leaped into gestures of alert efficiency, holding out rigid arms to stop the traffic—but there was no traffic, not a car in sight; the empty streets climbed upwards into the empty dusk.

Then at last was made the discovery of the day. Behind a gate and a ticket office, life went on, there was music—it was a place like the Great World in Shanghai, only far smaller, far less opulent and crowded; a pleasant plain gray courtyard with diversions all around, a theater here, a teahouse there, a kind of music hall in the corner, with the sound of gongs and singing. For a thousand *yuan* you could buy yourself out of the bleak inhospitable streets and find color again, and noise. Who knows what you might find? I thought, remembering Shanghai.

The first entertainment was a superb and wonderful success. The teahouse tables stood in groups under a kind of pergola, and at the inner end was the stage—perhaps fifteen feet across, surging sound and alive with the projection of color and animation. It was a puppet theater, I think the most wonderful puppet theater I have ever seen, though this may not be true; a thirsty castaway might find a bottle of average beer and wholly overestimate its qualities as a drink. I felt, sitting there with my cup, almost full under its lid with the fat green leaves of tea, constantly replenished with hot water from a can, that these noble little three-foot marionettes were the

only true and unchallengeable stuff of drama. . . . The
performance was a Chinese opera in the Szechuan style,
full of magnificent emperors and war lords, gorgeous creatures roaring out grandiloquent wickedness, martyred
princesses squealing their laments of abandonment, while
the drums thudded and the cymbals crashed to point the
unendurable drama of each tremendous entrance.

There were no strings; somehow the actors were ma-
nipulated from below. It was not quite possible to see
the floor of the stage, to see how these little wooden people contrived their splendid attitudes, the delicate co-
ordination of their movements when they twisted and
whirled around each other in the intricately stylized conventions of their ballet. They would make their appearance through a patch of curtain at the rear, minute arms
holding back the brocade, heads bent and crowns
flourished in the fashion that, to those who understand,
means triumph or challenge, danger or despair, the im-
pending arrival of climax or comedy. At the proper moment some unseen agency would hand the little character
his *mah pien*, the symbolical switch of hair that indicates
the entrance of a horse—when he held it this way, he
rode; when he held it that way, he ceased to ride. A throne
appeared, by magic, from the floor; where there was nothing there came a palace arch. Here in the puppet theater
there was illusion, legerdemain, everything that the Chinese human theater so materialistically avoids, with its
visible lethargic stagehands, its tea-drinking musicians.

After a while I persuaded someone to take me
behind. Here at least could be no repetition of the Great
World, no sad and unexpected revelations from the heart.
The little wooden emperors would remain emperors, without political confusion or distress.

The scene, enchanting from the front, was quite fabulous from behind. In a pit no bigger than a small room were the company, the orchestra, the voices, the manipulators, all playing and banging and blowing and dancing in a tremendous congestion of highly disciplined chaos, and, it seemed, enjoyment. There was, of course, *no* floor to the stage. The puppet masters held their dolls arm-high above their heads, the control strings hung below the sumptuous puppet robes; but the manipulators did not make their figures dance and bow and declaim and pirouette; they *themselves*, down there out of sight below the lights, performed the movements of the play—singing, revolving, nodding, circling in their drab blue cotton uniforms, while the dolls above their heads reproduced their movements exactly. . . . It was as it were one of those elaborate draughtsman's instruments where a line drawn big is recorded small; there was a strange moment, in that howling crowded little space, when one wondered which of the two sets of players was in fact in charge, the whirling blue-suited people down below, or the vivid dynamic automata bowing and gesticulating in the lights above.

After that, nothing seemed to remain. Yet there was one more surprise.

From the puppets we drifted over to another theater. After their miniature perfection it seemed vast and coarse and draughty; it was in fact a simple playhouse with benches; some acrobats and *jongleurs* were playing with ropes and spangles and the diabolo. We sat down behind two figures, one dressed very rakishly in a deep-brown robe and a gold-embroidered Tibetan fur hat, the other, a shaven-headed Lamaist monk in a saffron gown. Such figures are by no means rare in this part of the Southwest, always the communication link between Sinkiang and Tibet and the heartland of China, but among the

dull blue-cotton-clad audience they might almost have
been in fancy dress.

The man in the Tibetan hat saw us first. He turned
round in his seat, rested his arms on the back of the bench
and stared over them at us, with a deep reflective consideration. He was without the slightest social inhibition; he
completely abandoned the spectacle on the stage—this
was something far better—and studied us reflectively over
the back of his seat, as though we had been in an aquarium.

After a little while he suddenly said, in these exact
words, "I wonder if you speak English."

In the circumstances, nothing he could have said
would have been more astonishing—as though I, one
night in the Palladium, had turned to the nearest stranger
and repeated the magic words of the Lamaist liturgy:
Om ma-ni pad-mi humh, so sacred that the very expression of them puts a devout Tibetan in a condition of
grace. The man in the fur hat repeated, "English language
—do you speak it?"

I said, "By all means. I am from England."

At this the man in the hat rose from his bench,
pushed his way along the outside aisle to my side, thrust
out his hand and said, "I am really *delighted* to meet you.
I do not know when I last met one from England. So
many years."

There was nothing for me to do then but to rise too
and shake hands, and so did we all, with the entire auditorium looking on; for a minute or two we constituted a
practically unchallengeable competition to the unlucky
jugglers, left unwatched on the stage, balancing piles of
saucers on sticks.

The ensuing scene remains confused in my mind, a
strange interlude of greetings, explanations, personal in-

troductions and broad smiles. I recalled the collapse of
the French-speaking *contremaitre* on the roadworks, but
the man in the fur hat owed nothing to Big Wei or any
other Government officials; he was a citizen of the autonomous province of Tibet, and his own boss in every sense
of the word. He had come, he said, from Lhasa—two
months on the way so far, but at Chungking he had heard
that there were flying machines that could take him to
Peking. He had it in his mind to see the Chairman Mao.
There was much talk of Chairman Mao, he said, in Lhasa.
But his primary function was to act as guide and interpreter for his companion, who had never before left Tibet
nor spoken anything but Tibetan.

"I come," he said, "with my friend, the Living
Buddha." He indicated the shaven-skulled young monk,
whose attention was neatly torn between our own curious
Western selves, and the performers on the stage, now
desperately standing on their heads and balancing odd
shaped objects on their feet.

"My friend, the Living Buddha," said the other man,
"most anxious see Peking, see Mao Tse-Tung, see our
leader, Dalai Lama. My friend, the Living Buddha, not
of this world, of course. Living Buddha *most* big saint. I
want you to meet Living Buddha," and he beckoned to
the young lama, who obediently joined our act in the
aisle, which had by now completely absorbed the whole
theater. "A friend of mine, from England," he said. "Now,
please meet my other friend, the Living Buddha."

It was an odd situation; the young monk shook
hands with great cordiality, nodding and smiling with
inarticulate good will. There was left nothing whatever
for me to say, grasping the holy young creature's hand,
but, "How do you do, Living Buddha?"

"Important thing, shake hands with Living Buddha,"

said the older man with satisfaction. "Makes holy. *I* am a bit holy, but him first-class. See—he likes you." And indeed the Living Buddha was now shaking hands with himself with energy and enthusiasm and nodding his bald young head.

It seemed that the man in the fur hat was called Hsuen-Ming Teh, and he had learned his English years before at a mission somewhere in Yunnan. I think he was very largely Chinese himself, but he lived in Lhasa and had at some point attached himself to the Living Buddha as a counselor and interpreter for this arduous journey from the Eastern fringe of Tibet to Peking—a monumental journey in the winter. He asked me, "You have a name?" I said yes, as a matter of fact, I had; I told him what it was, but he asked again, "Will you give your *name?*" It turned out that he meant a card. I gave him one; it disappeared up his long Tibetan sleeve with a dexterity as professional as anything being shown by the lonely people on the stage.

"I shall write to you," he said, "and so will Living Buddha. Oh—*such* a pleasure."

He was one of the most engaging men I ever met. He shepherded the Living Buddha back to his seat, rose again and waved his hand; the little monk shook hands with himself with increasingly vigorous ardor as we moved away.

The odd thing was, he *was* the Living Buddha; the even odder thing was, we were to meet again.

(18)
The River

WE WERE going to be able to leave Chungking by
the boat: four days' sailing by the river steamer down
the Yangtse to Wu-chang, and then—somewhere—it did
not matter, that could be determined later; the boat trip
was the thing. I do not know for how many years of my
life I had wanted to sail down the Yangtse Kiang. It was
one of those symbolic journeys, meaningless except for
some sentimental suggestiveness: the Orient Express,
the Golden Road to Samarkand, a schooner to Waikiki,
by elephant to the Palace of Amber—I had done them
all, or most of them, and retained memories of exasperation and disenchantment. There remained, a matter of
great anticipation, the Yangtse River steamer.

That afternoon Big Wei announced in his gray,
abrupt way that we must board the boat either at midnight or at four A.M. I asked if that meant we could go
aboard any time between midnight and four in the morning, and he said no; one went on the ship at twelve exactly, or at four. When was she expected here in Chungking? I asked. He said that, so far from being expected,
she was already in dock and had been most of the day.

Then why, I asked, could we not go aboard immediately after dinner and save four hours of useless waiting
in that horrible guest house? Because of the regulations,

he said, growing impatient; if you prefer not to go aboard at twelve, you are welcome to get up early and go aboard at four in the morning. Eight o'clock would not do, nor twelve thirty, nor two. . . . It was one of the occasions when I grew ill-tempered at a troublesome and capricious order for which I could divine *no* possible reason, and I began to grumble, in the halfhearted way of someone who knows he stands no chance at all, like a child resisting a strong-minded parent. Big Wei said, "Well, shall we say twelve, then?" and walked away.

The docks of Chungking—the great docks twelve hundred miles from the sea, buried in the mountains, as far from the ocean as Kansas—were half an hour's drive through the steep and empty streets, to the top of a huge dramatic flight of stone steps that plunged into the gloom. Far below an oily flicker of light and a quiet slap of moving water suggested a quay. We humped our bags down this great stairway, and there it was—the ship. It was hard to see what sort of ship it was, except that it was a good deal bigger than I had expected; it lay out on the riverward side of a great flat barge; I could see a tall funnel, some electric lamps playing on two or three terraces of decks. It looked like the sort of ship in which one might well go from England to the Channel Islands. At the end of the gangway sat a dim nocturnal-looking man busy with his chopsticks and a bowl of stew.

It was, as one might have known, precisely midnight.

As soon as we got aboard the ship we began stumbling and tripping over bodies. They lay in neat arrangements along the decks, resilient corpselike cocoons bundled in blankets. Clearly *they* had not been presented with the twelve-or-four-o'clock ultimatum; they looked as though they had been there for days, bound like mummies in their quilts, surrounded by minute parcels, pots, baskets. Almost every cylinder had a small spherical infant head protruding from one end or the other.

Almost at once we fell into a superb state of disorganization; no one knew where our rooms were, and for at least twenty minutes we tripped and blundered up and down over the uncomplaining forms on the deck, like latecomers on a battlefield. Finally we disposed ourselves here and there. I found myself, almost with a sense of guilty disapproval, in a room marked, in English: "Special Class Stateroom No. 13." I hurled myself into a small truckle bed, and perversely went at once to sleep.

Not, however, for long.

The process of getting a ship under way anywhere, in any circumstances, seems always to involve the maximum expenditure of noisy energy—there are peremptory cries and thuds and splashes; nothing is ever successfully accomplished at the first attempt; co-ordination in the matter of ropes between those aboard and ashore is achieved only by strident cross-talk and loud metallic clanks. It was no different on the Yangtse Kiang, in the landlocked part of Chungking.

Finally, however, our engines began to rumble comfortably below and we were off, into the darkness of the stream. Five thirty in the morning. Long live Peace.

Precisely one hour later, at half past six, there broke out the daybreak pandemonium of which, in the next few days, I was to live in almost neurotic dread. It was like Shanghai over again, only this time I was not ten floors up, but imprisoned in the very heart of the uproar. . . . There was no sort of preliminary warning—all of a sudden the loud-speaker immediately outside my cabin broke into the thunderous overture of some quite unusually robust march, with a beat of drums and clash of cymbals. It is a banal and unoriginal thing to say, but I nearly

fell out of bed with the shock. The sensation was exactly
that which would be experienced by some irresponsible
and simple-minded millionaire who, in drunken aberration, had arranged to be awakened at dawn by half a
dozen military bands gathered in his bedroom.

Startled into life, I heard the music then change, by
formula, into the measured beat of the Physical Culture
class, with the ringing commands of the radio instructor,
whose vibrant one-two in Chinese—which is EEH!
URRH!—made him an even more unsympathetic personality than his morning counterpart of the BBC.

All over the ship the inert bundles began to stir
about the deck and unravel themselves from their quilts;
one or two of them even began to flap their arms about to
the music in a desultory way. A tremendous chorus of
spitting broke out everywhere; for some time it sounded
as though the ship were crashing against sharp-pointed
rocks. A man began to walk outside, ringing a little bell,
an event that happened at frequent intervals throughout
the trip, for no reason I could ever detect. The Chinese,
I have had many occasions to remark, are not the noisiest
people in the world—the Italians and even the Scots
make a far greater din—but they are without any conceivable doubt the greatest lovers of noise in the world.
By far the majority of the passengers slept, ate, read, fed
their children, and chatted on the railed-off corridor that
served the ship as deck space, and the really sought-after
spot on that deck was the part of it immediately under
the loud-speaker. There they would sit or recline in sociable groups, discussing whatever it was they had to discuss
in absorbed and intimate tones, while the air round them
vibrated and shuddered to the clang and screech of mechanically reproduced Peking Opera. It was not as though
they did not notice it because, in the only too rare mo-

ments of silence occasioned by the change of a record, they would themselves pause and look disconsolately round until it began again.

One can foresee nothing; I had expected the river trip to be the high light of my whole journey, an interlude of peace and relaxation. Instead, it drove me to a condition bordering on the manic-depressive. Apart from Special Class Stateroom No. 13, which sounded a great deal more spacious than it was, there was practically nowhere to go. There was no upper deck, or if there was, no one was allowed upon it. The corridor outside the cabins was some four feet wide, and almost impassably congested with the sleeping bodies of those who had even less resources than I. There was one public room, the eating saloon, which was worthy of note if only for its decoration: for some incomprehensible reason the authorities had seen fit to cover its walls closely with posters designed by the Ministry of Health to inform the people of the less frequently discussed aspects of personal hygiene. There was a large revelation of the human digestive tract, with each convolution of bowel affectionately depicted, both in the healthy and in the constipated state. There was an inhuman picture of a six months' fetus; another, in startling close-up, of the accepted method of eliminating crabs; yet another poster the sole object of which was only too evidently a demonstration of successful and unsuccessful ways of emptying the bowels. It might be that I was unnecessarily finical about these doubtlessly educative works, but I found them poor company for my stewed pork strips and rice. I found myself at mealtimes going with ever-diminishing enthusiasm to the dining saloon; as one stared, fascinated, at these instructive visceral themes the chopsticks faltered over the bean sauce; it was like living in two dimensions of time.

All these small disadvantages, however, were amply made up for by the Yangtse Kiang itself.

For the first night we stopped in the river at Wan-hsien; ahead lay the great Gorges, which could not be negotiated in darkness. As we came to rest, we were approached by several very beautiful sampans with swinging lanterns at their prows. Each sampan was loaded to the gunwales with fruit. This was in the heart of China's reputedly best citrus-growing area; the boats were piled with superb oranges, tangerines and enormous pomelos. The boatmen clung to the side of our ship calling out their prices. They were absurdly cheap by any standards I knew: a basket of sixty fine oranges for the equivalent of fourteen cents, with the delightful bamboo basket thrown in. The growers had, I was told, very few methods of distributing their crop in this transportless neighborhood. Every time a deal was signaled, the boatman would hoist the basket on a tall pole; someone on the crowded deck would lift it off and put three thousand *yuan* into a little bag tied to the pole. Anyone who had chosen to remove the oranges without paying could most easily have done so, but of course nobody did. These were incidentally the only commercial transactions I think I ever saw in China where no receipts changed hands.

Somehow that hour at Wan-hsien remains in my mind long after many more important things have slipped away—the black river sliding past, the glow of the swinging oil lamps on the glowing oranges, the upturned faces of the boatmen, the strange patterns of the probing poles; it was beautiful.

So was the river next day. I suppose the Yangtse Gorges must be one of the most memorable and gripping riverine sights available to man. All day long we sailed at what seemed to be an immense speed over a current that had become fast and turbulent, the huge river now compressed between narrow and enormous banks. On each side soared the spectacular hills, climbing into unreal and dramatic pinnacles, rushing into strange writhing valleys; we sped along between sheer cliffs of rock stratified like layer cake, worn into a monstrous wall by this timeless river over more centuries than the mind could imagine. Sometimes in a patch of green halfway up some precipitous mountainside would appear a pattern of minute terraces, a tiny crop of something or other, a group of cottages—no road, apparently not even a track, nothing to link them with any other kind of human life but this river.

But the river itself was life of a kind; the sampans moved up almost imperceptibly against the stream, hugging the bank to avoid the current's full power, ten or fifteen men jerking at the oars. The boats looked like water beetles, grasping rhythmically at the water. Every time the bank shelved for even a hundred yards the men would leap out and drag the sampan along by a towrope. It must have taken them many weeks, traveling west, to get anywhere at all.

And everywhere the landscape washed in the curious pale Chinese colors—white and gray and green; with the river tumbling and eddying in its haste to be through the Gorges, dense with silt; whorls and tumults exactly like boiling chocolate. How many thousands of tons of China is swept away to the ocean in the solution of these vast rivers, swallowing the earth through which they move?

Once we passed a tall pinnacle of rock, a natural obelisk as high as a cathedral and somehow on its summit had been built a pagoda, itself of great height, with nine graceful roofs superimposed one on the other—an idealization, almost a parody of the Chinese symbol. I could have studied this bizarre and lovely thing for hours, but we swept by, and soon it vanished round a bend in the stream.

So we sailed on through this superb place, while the loud-speaker roared and chattered on, telling us what to do, what not to do, informing us of the progress of some especially diligent factory in the neighborhood, reminding us of the unsleeping concern for us all of Chairman Mao and the People's Government. It is fair to say that I conceived a dislike of the little man in the amplifier booth that in the end amounted almost to an obsessional hate; I would go and stand outside the door of his little box, willing him to stop, to relent, to lose his voice, to have a seizure, to commit suicide—anything to purchase peace from those chattering and meaningless words. Whenever he caught sight of me, he would smile and give a pleasant wave. From seeing me there so often he must have been under the impression—than which no human fallacy could have been greater—that in me he had won his only real admirer.

Sometimes I would walk from the port deck space, full of doll-like children and old ladies with bound feet, to the starboard side, where there was a very pretty girl wrapped up in a pink quilt who seemed to spend every hour of the day writing letters. The children would be always struck dumb at my approach, staring open-mouthed until I moved away; the old ladies greeted me with quiet murmurs; the pretty girl paid no attention whatever. Twice a day the greater part of the ship's crew would assemble in the macabre dining saloon for *hsueh-hsi* meetings, and would be addressed in quiet urgent tones by the captain. Once I caught them learning the words of a song. They were reading the characters from a sheet, with the captain beating time. On the second day I asked if the captain would allow me momentarily onto the bridge (since from nowhere else was it possible to see the view ahead), but his answer was no.

So there was not much for it but to return to Special Class Stateroom No. 13, stuff my ears with cotton wool damped from the water bottle, and try to read. The absence of J.-J. Rousseau at this point was a very serious matter; not that I am any fanatical admirer of those interminable *Confessions*, but their very endlessness had been a boom. To allow myself to get caught short in the vital question of reading matter is one of those indefensible pieces of bad organization to which I seem somehow prone—those terrible waits in abandoned airports, those deadly nights in remote hotels, scratching around for old newspapers used for lining drawers! To counter this I have made it a practice over the years to carry, as a piece of more or less permanent luggage, some work of classic dimensions, some book of enduring but exacting worth, something, in short, that I should have read but would never dream of attempting except in circumstances of genuine desperation. Thus, over many thousands of miles in Southeast Asia, had I come at last to complete *Tristram Shandy*. I recall a crisis on the coast of Tanganyika, alone in a Greek hotel with nothing but the late Emanuel Swedenborg's *Heaven and Hell*, than which I know no more numbing work. In this fashion I had come—at last, and far too late—to Jean-Jacques Rousseau and his life of frustration.

Now I had Jane Austen. This aberration from the rule can be explained by a visit I had paid to the International Bookshop in Peking—a very good store indeed, though not the place, on the whole, for anyone seeking an hour's furtive respite from the doctrines of Engels. The English shelf contained some very stiff stuff indeed. It included, however, a good deal of Thackeray. (Will anyone *ever* explain to me the curious affection shown by the Marxist mind for Thackeray? You find him in left-wing bookshops everywhere; you find him in Moscow, even in Siberia; sooner or later most foreign Communists bring him up.) But I didn't want Thackeray. Imagine my gratification, therefore (as she herself would have said), when I came upon Miss Austen. And if I add that I had never read *Sense and Sensibility*, it speaks badly of my reading, but extremely well of my luck on this occasion.

"The family of Dashwood had long been settled in Sussex. Their estate was large, and their residence was at Norland Park in the centre of their property, where, for many generations, they had lived in so respectable a manner as to engage the general good opinion of their surrounding acquaintance. . . ."

Outside the great river rumbled between its grotesque, enormous banks, the sampans toiled upstream; beside my ear soared and wailed the denunciation of the War Lord's Concubine. It seemed a long way from Jane and her little bit of ivory, from the passionate virtuous Marianne Dashwood, Willoughby with his pointers and his curricle; no doubts, no speculations. . . . "Let other pens dwell on guilt and misery," she said. "I quit such odious subjects as soon as I can."

The old women sat under the loud-speaker, cleaning out the babies' ears with bits of wire; in the saloon the crew debated production beside the posters of people's insides; far away in Sussex, Elinor conducted her cool courtship between the water colors.

By the time the third dawn exploded, the Gorges had gone; the Yangtse was broad like a small sea, like the middle reaches of the Amazon, a great street of beaten copper between the low rims of shelving banks: the flood area. It went on all day; the river was fatigued with its struggle through the Gorges, drifting and spreading all around under an ochre sky. By midnight, we reached Hangkow.

How strange that one should have credited the myth that the Chinese are fatalists, that they are "passive"—the Chinese who live in a land so incessantly exacting, an enormous land so endlessly carved into minute gardens, where a man must tread a waterwheel all day to irrigate his paddies, that must be forever preserved and nourished with the products of his own body, that demands every sort of quality *except* fatalism.

But he is durable. Nobody in the world but the Chinese peasant has survived so much grinding poverty, such generations of bad government, such ages of physical toil, corrupt administration, personal hardship, civil war, hopelessness.

Most of all, he has survived his rivers. Not by fatalism.

I stood on an embankment outside Hangkow, level with the river, twenty feet above the land around. In front was the great mud-colored tide, with the junks and sampans moving behind square matting sails like driftwood tied to vast dead leaves; behind were the farms, the roads, the market of the province of Hu-peh. If the rampart of earth on which I stood had collapsed, it would have been all up with all of them, and indeed, with me. A parapet of compressed mud and osiers and balks of timber held China's greatest river from its immemorial enemy, the land.

The Yangtse Kiang is one of the great rivers of the world, one of the most indispensable, cruellest, most capricious. The three thousand miles between its bubbling beginnings in the Himalaya and its broad and sullen meeting with the sea have been for forty centuries a matter, literally, of life and death. Two hundred and eighty million people—half the population of China—depend on and worry about the Yangtse River. I had come down through the miles where it is domesticated, gathering its strength. Here, in its great Hangkow loop, where it meets its major tributary, people have always lived as other people live on the slopes of Vesuvius. When there is too little water, there is drought, and people starve. When there is too much water, there is flood, and people drown. The river, they say, hates people.

In Peking exists the Government department with a gentle fluent name and an urgent cast-iron responsibility: the Ministry of Waters. Never in its existence before this year, which was 1954, had there been a year of such forebodings, desperation and finally triumph.

That year, one may remember, produced over Europe a weather that was bizarre in its beastliness—a sunless summer, an almost permanent rain. People shook their heads and spoke angrily of human interference in the meteorological processes; most of them, knowing nothing about it, blamed the Bomb. Some spoke rather smugly of a natural retribution on the overadventurous scientists. Were that the case, the retribution fell upon the just and unjust alike, for things, it seemed, were even worse in China. The floodwaters of the Huai and the Yangtse rivers were higher than had been recorded for a century. Here, where I stood by the Hangkow bank, the rainfall during the three wet summer months had been ninety-one per cent higher than had ever been recorded in history before.

Down by the Hangkow docks a plate let into a wall marked the highest level of recorded flood, made in the disastrous year of 1931—31.08 yards. For months the city was under water. There, where the Yangtse faces and sometimes rejects the rushing confluence of the Hanjan River, the situation was—as was plentifully recorded at the time—appalling: twenty-seven million acres under water; enormous numbers of people drowned. In one town, of two hundred and ninety thousand inhabitants, only seventy thousand were saved. This year—as was less amply recorded, since there was no one but Chinese to record it—the floods were far worse. The Yangtse has no sense of proportion. Here they said, "Heavy rains mean a major flood; light rains a minor flood; no rain means a drought." All over China the rains were worse than they had been for centuries, and the Yangtse was the worst of all.

For a long time, during that frightening summer, the Chinese said little about it, fearing no doubt that the effects might be uncontrollable and that the river would win. Astonishingly, the river did not win. When they were sure of this, the Chinese told the story of the floods and of their own sensational victory over them; the river had risen actually nearly three yards *higher* than in 1931, and Hangkow had remained dry. Where about two thousand people had been drowned, nobody had been drowned. In 1931, there had been twenty-seven million acres under water; in 1954, they had kept it down to thirteen and a half million. It was, indeed, a story of organization, improvization and the mobilization of multitudes—of twenty-five million cubic yards of stone and eight hundred thousand cubic metres of concrete, of moving so much Chinese earth that, piled a yard high and a yard wide, it would have gone seventy-three times round the Equator. Farfetched statistics, it was clear, were not the monopoly of the capitalist brochures. The Huai River Project became such a triumph of complex hydraulics that it was a high priority on the list of delegates' musts.

So I did not go to the Huai River, but I came to the Yang-tse, at Hangkow.

By that time the worst was over, but one could see something of this fabulous use of a manpower that, in emergency, could be for all practical purposes unlimited; that could—as I had seen in Chungking—literally move the surface of the earth by swarming all over it with little baskets and a bamboo rod. At one time there had been several scores of millions of Chinese peasants working on the river projects, fighting off the floods.

Of course, it had not been easy. I had heard about it in Peking from Li Bo-Ning of the Ministry of Waters. All peasants are individualists and the Chinese, as he agreed, most of all; outside his family the economics of the world did not exist at all, and its physical problems came only to the edge of his garden. He would go to the river-work simply to earn the relief grain to send back to his family. At the very most he accepted the proposition that he was working to stop the floods on his own piece of land, or on that land to which he might succeed on Land Reform. In his mind, said Li, he expected to mark out a piece of land, dig it away and carry it off to the last half-inch of what he cut. When the projects became immense, however, he was compelled to change his methods, if not his attitude. On a ramming job he could work only with a team—the first suggestion of co-operative work. The watchful organizers saw to it that the peasant's leisure was well taken up with meetings and "explanation." They appear to have been full of sense, demonstrating that hundreds of miles away other peasants were also building dams and sluices which would protect him, as his protected them.

"In this way," they told me, "he acquires a world outlook."

This I doubted, but it was incontestable that he had, at least, partially and at least for the moment, mastered the Yangtse Kiang. The river flowed, still high above the land, but fettered within the huge dykes. A couple of hundred yards away lay a small village; the curling eaves of its tiled roofs were level with that huge idling surface of water.

"It is in their interests," said the man with me, "to keep an eye on the security of the dyke"—an observation which seemed to me laconic to the point of irony.

Nevertheless, all around stretched the floodwaters that had not, presumably could never be, controlled. We drove back between flat fields of waters; hundreds of men sat in long lines at their edges, fishing. Some were far out into the water, sitting on little stools exactly level with the surface; it gave an extraordinary impression of tiny bouyant men afloat on the floods. I could not imagine what possibility there was of catching anything in waters so very casual and impermanent—a film of flood over a rice field—yet when I looked there were indeed little fish flapping wretchedly beside the stools, or stiffening into dry corpses with indignant glazing eyes.

Down by the river front, where the Yangtse joins the Han, the junks were tied up in long, gently undulating rows. I stopped at one—it was old and worn and rather beautiful, planked with some ancient gray wood; its yards were festooned with rows of dried fish of all sizes, and from the mast hung three dried ducks, split and spread-eagled and rigid as boards; they looked exactly like pterodactyls. The smell was frightful.

The crew were taking their ease all over the deck; they were only too pleased to talk. There were eight of them, including the man Liu who owned the junk, his wife and child. I could see the baby, a spherical tot of about a year, loosely tethered to a stanchion, crawling vigorously about the after-platform chewing on a dried carp. Yes, they all lived together on the boat; it was called the "Boat-from-Chan-Sha-Hsien," or at least they had never heard it called anything else. Mostly they carried grain for the Government, up and down to Shanghai—two months for the return trip.

Did they think they were any better off now—under the new system? Most of them laughed, with a blinding glint of gold teeth: Oh yes, now they could keep the two hundred and eighty thousand *yuan* they earned a month instead of giving most of it back to old Liu; what was more they were not obliged to submit when he felt like beating them. Anything else? Well, yes; there was the Seamen's Union. But other things, less practical things—what difference had communism made? They hummed and hawed and laughed: perhaps not much—except the business with the Bo-Yan Lake, of course, said someone. It seemed that in the Bo-yan Lake, through which the channel ran, there lived a Turtle God, who would bring about contrary winds and bad weather unless propitiated with the customary money sacrifice. It was necessary to burn a specific quantity of money each time—not genuine money, of course; the usual paper imitation used for such purposes; who would waste *real* money on a Turtle God? —still, it was a bore; furthermore, it was obligatory to kill a chicken and smear the blood on the hull; when the water washed it off, the Turtle would be conciliated. It was all most tiresome. Since the Liberation, naturally, it had no longer been necessary.

But, I said, was the Turtle God satisfied with that arrangement?

Somebody laughed uproariously and said, "Why not, if the Turtle was liberated too?"

Of course, when a storm came these days, there was now *no* way of dealing with it. . . .

Nine hours in the train to Chang-sha—practically nothing by the standards of the last weeks. Rolling all day through the flat watery lands of Hunan, where the Center becomes the South, staring out of the window at a vague, dim, gently meaningless landscape of tiny fields, listening to the loud-speaker, trying to pick out of the vocal jungle the few words I knew—it was stupid; we were in the South, where they would not use them anyhow. I would shut my eyes and try to sleep. Two hours later I looked out; we might have been in the same place. By the side of the railway track sat a very old man and a woman; they were so old I thought for a moment they were something carved. They sat there side by side, quite immobile, while the train clattered by almost over their feet. They had all of China to sit in—why did they sit there mysteriously, silently, immobile, within a couple of feet of rumbling death? Then *they* had whirled away; there was nothing left to look at.

Back to Jane. " 'No, no,' cried Marianne, 'misery such as mine has no pride. I care not who knows that I am wretched. The triumph of seeing me may be open to all the world. Elinor, Elinor, they who suffer little may be proud and independent as they like—may resist insult, or return mortification—but I cannot. I must feel—I must be wretched—and they are welcome to enjoy the consciousness of it that can.' "

The water-man came into fill the tea glasses; the sweeper-girl, masked like a surgical bandit, brushed up the single splash; back in eighteenth-century London the brokenhearted Marianne Dashwood was jilted by the infamous Willoughby, and her splendid tears welled up through the past over the rice fields of Hunan Province. I lay back on the smooth dusty leather of the railway seat and thought about home.

At Chang-sha that night the guest house had been the provincial governor's home. "A bad man," they said, "who would need a home like this?"—a broad shabby courtyard, narrow stairs on each side to high verandas, rooms set out in rows like bathhouses. So the provincial governor had gone—somewhere; one did not ask; and the new one had taken up his quarters in a housing estate. It was right, completely in character.

The bedroom was like a tomb, an aquarium, stark and bleak, dimly lit in a ghastly way by one small electric bulb that was incomprehensibly painted green. Amazingly, there was a radio set in it—connected up, and working. Moreover, a short-wave set. I had an idiotic impulse to go and find someone and ask if I might use it. . . . *That* would be too ridiculous, I thought. I spun the dial and, with considerable surprise, fell straight upon the BBC—the overseas service, relayed from Hong Kong. It may strain credulity to snapping point, but I must attest, with three witnesses available to support me, that as I intercepted that oleaginous organ from the ether it was playing "A Slow Boat to China."

For a second dose of the extraordinary, there began a commentary of a football match—Arsenal against Moscow Spartak—the well-pitched cultivated voice rising at moments to a shrill but always gentlemanly hysteria. . . .

When it faded Peking Radio swelled over it, in English: ". . . Government working indefatigably . . . only by stronger efforts . . ." And in a moment, a resonant American voice on a harsh admonitory note: ". . . only by that shall you be saved! Only by that'!" But he was just a revivalist preacher; you heard the long-playing

Heavenly Host behind him; somewhere in California long ago they had probably turned up at the studio in seemly white gowns to record their modulated praise, to be shipped in a can to Manila, to be projected at last over the China Sea to me, in a green-lit bedroom in Chang-sha.

It was the sugar around the aloes; by and by the real man began to talk, the Voice of America, in the fierce declamatory style that gave authority to the news—but it wasn't trying to inform; it was trying to subdue.

". . . said that the American people could no longer tolerate . . . Defined it as an example of naked aggression. . . . Senator Knowland said. . . . Lives of American boys . . . Opinion of the Free World . . ." It was all about them—the ones all around in Chang-sha, and Hunan and Peking. The ones in the next bedrooms. One imagined them listening to it also; maybe they deserved it all, but did that self-confident man at the microphone ever listen to a playback—or was he impervious to the simple menace in his *tone,* if not his words? "This newscast comes to you . . . There can be no further compromising with such provocation . . ." On and on it went, minatory and truculent. The Chinese would always tell me, "The Americans are aggressors," and I would always say: How can they be, geographically? But if you only listened with your emotions it *sounded* aggressive.

Then Peking would drone on about its indefatigable efforts, its selfless leadership—jargon to right of you, jargon to left of you. And the BBC drip-dripping the golden syrup from the organ pipes, the spurious dramatics of the football match.

Chang-sha was remote and strange and—odd, somehow; you wondered what the difference was until you realized it had no cars, none at all. It was a big city, and the streets were wide and well paved, but nothing moved along them but people. There were thousands of them, trotting under the bending bamboo poles, for there were not even many wheels. There would be a few carts, monstrously heavy laden, and harnessed to the shaft five or six men, straining against the ropes, maintained—it seemed permanently—in a position neither upright nor prone, but dragging along at an acute angle to the ground, barely moving. There seemed to be no other beasts of burden.

I asked why they did not even make use of mules, as they did in the North. The man said, very seriously, "A man eats less than a mule."

The village birthplace of Chairman Mao Tse-Tung lay far enough away into the hinterland of the province to make the thought of going there a penance, but it was clearly of enormous importance to the mythology, and they would have been bitterly hurt if I had actually refused to go. I hinted—but they looked wounded and said, "But after coming all this way. . . . Besides, it is very beautiful."

So next day we climbed into a bus—where they had produced it from, in that car-less town, I could not guess —for a four-hour trip south. It was a terrible bus, by any standards. It had a homemade Chinese body on an old Dodge chassis; it was designed with consummate skill to provide the maximum of physical discomfort in any position possible for the human frame. It rattled and bounced and groaned. It had curtains of pale green *crêpe-de-Chine*.

For two hours we bounced and thudded over the earth road until we came to a ferry over the Siang River, at an enchanting little town called Siang-tan—it was made of pale weather-worn wooden houses all built on stilts, like something in Malaya. Then we bounced along some more on the other side. I grew desperately thirsty, and asked my guide if there was any way of getting a drink. He said there was not. I said nothing more—and then, ten minutes later, the driver suddenly stopped the bus, hopped out, ran up the road, and came back with a pocketful of oranges for me.

We reached the birthplace of Mao Tse-Tung in the late afternoon—they were right; it was beautiful. It was more than that, it was almost perfect. It was called Shao-San, and it lay in a valley of which the proportions of slope and shadow, of elegant mountain and delicate stream were superbly composed: entrancing. Here and there life moved through it: a wheelbarrow, squeaking horribly, but of a shape so rough and charming and grace-ful—indeed the barrows, like so much else in China, like the roofs, the sampans, the gestures of a little boy play-ing in the dust, everything had a *line*, a kind of *style*. The sun, preparing to set behind a pleasant little hill, spilled its last lemon-colored light on the pointed eaves of an old temple. I remembered an old saying I heard in Peking. "Is it true," I asked the guide, "that the Government had to search the province for several years to find such an ideal place for the birthplace?"

"Oh, no," he said seriously, "not nearly as long as that."

But he had not understood. Big Wei would have made no such faux pas. Nor would the Town Clerk of Stratford-on-Avon.

This was in fact the birthplace; sixty-one years ago Mao Tse-Tung had been born in a farmstead up the stream; here he had learned to read.

That evening we walked up to the place itself. It was

reverently marked by signboards all the way: "Here Was Born Mao Tse-Tung," in big red characters. "Down this path," said the guide, "Chairman used to walk to school. This is the duck pond where Chairman kept his father's ducks; the ducks, of course, are no longer the same, but descendants. And here"—we breasted a little hill—"is where Chairman lived."

It was a place rather finer than I had imagined—a very graceful farmhouse built round the usual square, the typical house of a Middle Peasant of the time. An elaborate sign outside said that it had been taken by the Kuomintang "and completely destroyed." This was a restoration faithfully copied, and with the original furniture. We went round the shrine, speaking with hushed voices—and it *was* an attractive house, with some of the inviolate atmosphere of a model home in an exhibition. In the bedroom was the big *kang* bed of brick, with the fireplace below; on the wall the enlarged photographs of Mao's parents taken in 1919; typical peasant faces; they did not look at all like the plump dimpled countenance one saw in every public place in China today. The old bamboo chair—that had been his mother's dowry; in that separate four-poster bed Chairman had been born. In a glass case, two of the arithmetic books from which he had learned. Out in the courtyard hung a glass frame in which was a strange battered object six inches long of iron that looked like a comb—it was a comb, and underneath it was an inscription which said: "This article has a brilliant history. Fifty years ago, Chairman Mao often handled it, to comb the fleas out of his father's cows. At the time of the Kuomintang struggle it was buried in the earth, but it did not rust away. It shall never rust away!"

We climbed on a knoll behind the house, beside the carp pond, looking over the valley in which the little farms and steadings lay so exactly placed, a perfect harmony between man and nature. How was it that a man became a revolutionary *here?* The place was a picture postcard symbolism of quietude and peace; how did it come about that the destiny of China should be reshaped so violently in such a lovely valley, with two rice harvests a year as well as a crop of wheat? It was as though the English Revolution should be conceived in, say, Dorset. And that recalled Tolpuddle, which had been another pretty and fertile place. . . .

For all its rural beauty, Shao-San had somehow acquired the slightly smug and glossy look of famous birthplaces. It was probably unique among all the villages of China in that it actually had its own guest house, for the convenience of pilgrims and the devout. Not many foreigners came so far.

We dined that night as the village guests—a local meal, built up from very powerful combinations of peppers and chilis; one dish that glowed green and orange was hotter than anything I ever tasted in Madras. There was also a dish of sautéed frogs from the village stream, pigs' lungs, and the best steam-bread I ever tasted. I also noticed that in Hunan Province we used chopsticks that were much longer than anywhere else—for a curious and simple reason: in Hunan, they told me, the tables have always been a little bit bigger than elsewhere; when you eat in Hunan you need just that little extra reach. The logic of China is complete to every detail.

The village Co-operative (for naturally Shao-San had not lagged behind in the programme of socialization) had its headquarters in what had been the local Temple of Ancestors. Inside, the shadows on the gray stonework were chased violently round the walls by a couple of oil lamps; on the ceiling still remained the strange painted winged beasts and monsters of the days when this was where the people interceded with the shades. (Where do the ancestors go? There is no fund for refugee ghosts. Most of them were Maos—even now, sixty per cent of the villagers of Shao-San were called Mao. I asked if the Chairman had any surviving relatives in the neighborhood; they told me no, the last one had died some years before. (Yet the next day, back in Chang-sha, I met two Indians who had visited the birthplace only a few hours before we had; they had been introduced to an old man, the Chairman's uncle, who actually lived, they told me, in the same guest house where we were lodged. They even had his name: Mao Yue-Chao. Could it be that the duty-uncle knocked off at six? Was he an uncle, or wasn't he?)

Now, the Temple of Ancestors was hung about with the banners and pennants of production and loyalty; every emphasis of the slogans denied the faded emblems on the ceiling—the future, no longer the past. They told me that 616 families lived today in Shao-San; 2,918 people. In the old days there had been nine landlords, of the rich peasant class. Where were they now? They survived; they got their share of the redistributed land. They were now "sincere." Yes, they lived in the village—indeed, said the energetic lady who was President of the Co-operative there is one of them now, and pointed out an old man by the doorway, who quickly smiled and slipped out. Yes, they were "sincere" now. But of course they could not expect their civic rights back *yet*—by and by, no doubt, they would get the vote.

It all seemed idyllic enough. The village was run on the normal pattern—a head of the village administration, a secretary, and the leaders of the Co-operative. They lived well enough; three meals a day of rice and vegetables, meat once a week and an occasional fish from the co-operative stewponds. Nobody ever ate after five because of the difficulty of the light. Yes, they drank from time to time, when work was especially hard; they brewed their own rice wine. Cigarettes? No. The men and the older women smoked the *suya-wei*, the water pipe. They maintained the traditional village trades: the barber, the joiner, the porter, the smith, paying them annually. Nowadays they paid them in cash, not in grain.

They kept the main country feasts too—the great Spring Festival, in February, and the *Twan-Wu*, when everybody in the district celebrated the memory of a great poet, in June, between the two harvests. They made decorated paper boats and sailed them on the stream. They did that still? Well—yes, said the President of the Co-operative, a little dubiously; yes, a bit. But the really feudal customs had been abandoned, very properly. For a wedding, now, it was just a question of the couple going to the *hsiang* office, signing their names, saluting the picture of Chairman. Sometimes they would make a speech, telling how much better it was to make a free choice after Liberation, and denounce the methods by which their parents had met. In the old days it had been ridiculous—a ceremony in this Temple of Ancestors, with gongs and trumpets and paper money to burn; you couldn't marry your children without running into debt. Now, it costs *nothing*. In fact it saved money—two allocations of land could be united. Money? Of course they used money, and saved it. What they saved was deposited first in the village Co-operative, which then put it into the bank, where it accrued two per cent interest. They could withdraw it whenever they liked. (This wholly contradicted every story I had been told by experts in Europe and by the diplomatic colony in Peking, who alleged that peasants were prevented from withdrawing their deposits unless they provided a satisfactory reason. But everything contradicted something.)

Someone brought in an immense vacuum flask of hot water and refilled the teacups. Outside the Temple of Ancestors a scurry of bats whirled and danced through the lamplight like black confetti.

Perhaps after all, I thought, it was Chairman Mao who had made the really big sacrifice.

(19)

The Twilight People

BACK to Peking, back to the Pei Ch Ko, back to the
Press Club. It is strange how, for those who must be forever on the move, almost anywhere can seem like home
after a day and a night . . . the subconscious reluctance
to pass by, I suppose, to exchange the devil one knows for
the devil one doesn't. It was this way with the Pei Ch Ko;
already it had acquired all the lineaments of familiarity;
coming back was momentarily like the end of term. At
least, no more trains for a while.

The young Information was waiting at the airport to
meet us, full of smiles and handshakes; in my weary state
this struck me as the acme of genuine friendship, and I
began to reproach myself for all the testiness and impatience I had shown him in the past. Even the bleak aus-
terities of the Press Club gave out a very thin, minor
chord of welcome—on the lobby blackboard still hung
the notice advising us of our departure-time, weeks before.
It was probably the nearest thing to a memorial I was
likely to leave in China.

Then a most astonishing thing happened. I was riding with Zig in a pair of pedicabs along the broad main
avenue of the city, idly watching the columns of blue
suits padding steadily up and down before what had once
been the Legation Quarter. Abruptly I chanced to see,

among all this multitude, a hint of yellow among the blue, a shaved head, and a tall fur hat. I reflected that it was mildly interesting to find a couple made roughly to the same formula as that which we had met in the playhouse of Chungking. I looked more closely; it *was* the couple from Chungking; without any doubt at all it was our friends from the far west: the Tibetan and his charge, the Living Buddha.

This must be considered one of the classic coincidences which tend to happen often enough to make the accepted laws of chance a matter for serious suspicion. To have met an English-speaking Tibetan and a Living Buddha at all could not be held to be an everyday thing; to meet them again—among the six hundred million people of China, and in a city of three million people a thousand miles from the original encounter—suggested a natural caprice too curious to ignore.

I was perhaps guilty of a certain irreverence—I pulled the pedicab driver to a skidding halt and shouted out, "Hello there, Living Buddha!" This had no impact at all on the priestly young man, to whom the words were doubtless as meaningless as though they had been Chinese but they were at once picked up by the Tibetan in the fur hat, who stopped and turned, saw us, and seized the Living Buddha by the arm. They broke into enormous smiles, and advanced on us open-armed.

It was a splendid reunion, and some four or five minutes had passed before we had finished our mutual handshakings, the Buddha beaming with every kind of speechless good will. There was nothing for it, then, but that we had to return with them to their lodging.

This was in a remote part of the city to which I had never been; indeed the city had almost faded away before we reached a little Lamaist temple buried behind a series of gray brick walls. "We stay here," said the Tibetan, Hsuen-Ming Teh. "Living Buddha, he likes living in temples," and sure enough, we were hardly inside a sort of living-room annex when the young man hopped nimbly onto a low dais covered with a rug and decorated with a holy *thankha*, crossed his legs, wrapped his robe around him, and assumed most expertly the attitude associated with his kind, maintaining, however, the same alert and interested smile.

Very soon there entered an extremely picturesque young man dressed in a loose Tibetan coat, a silken tunic, and high embroidered boots; his long braided hair made a vivid contrast with the Buddha's shaven skull. He produced tea. Nobody made any introductions.

"He's brother," said our first friend. "Living Buddha's brother. He serves him. Living Buddha needs slave; uses brother."

I asked whether this relationship was encouraged, or indeed even countenanced, in the newer circumstances of today. Really, I asked—a *slave?*

"Oh, sure," said our friend. "Things not change for Living Buddha. Living Buddha, where he come from, abbot of—how many people?" He translated the enquiry to the young man, who murmured something. "He say: thousands and thousands and thousands. Brother not a bit holy, do you see?" I looked at the brother in his rakish habit, leaning very much at his ease against the wall and chewing a straw; there seemed no need to contest his lack of holiness. I remembered that the Chinese, in some access of poetic delicacy, had once given the Tibetans the exquisite name of the "Shy People." It seemed to me to say a great deal for their lyrical sense; rather less for their descriptive accuracy.

I questioned my friend quite keenly on the changes

that he had seen in Lhasa since the arrival of the Chinese authority, but either his sense of security was much greater than I had imagined or in fact he did not know; he shrugged his shoulders and said that it seemed much the same as usual, except for a few more soldiers. It lacked, of course, the Dalai Lama. That was why they had traveled all this long and difficult way: it was necessary for Living Buddha to refresh himself spiritually by a moment in the presence.

It was then that I recalled—with one of those flashes of inspirational good fortune that customarily occur only in daydream situations of one's own invention—my own brief meeting with the Dalai. I mentioned this casually, and produced as an afterthought my envelope bearing the signatures of the Dalai and Panchen Lamas.

The effect of this was gratifying in the extreme; both our friend and the young man studied this with a reverence that was soon, I felt, transferred at least proportionately to me. "Oh, very holy too," said the Tibetan. "Dalai Lama writing—yes; well, well," while the young lama's face became a wreath of what I could only feel were congratulatory smiles. "If Dalai Lama *touch*, though—that make man into Living Buddha too," said Hsueh, in an effort to maintain some sort of sacerdotal ascendancy for his friend and colleague. I remembered the limp handshake the Immortal had given me back there among the trays of vodka—it seemed unnecessary to recall it; perhaps the theory was incorrect; I might have *not* been made into a Living Buddha after all.

There was a murmured consultation between the two, and then the Tibetan said, "Living Buddha say: he so happy to meet you. You first foreign men he ever seen, except Chinese. He say: could you make picture?" and he pointed to the camera Zig was carrying. "He like picture of you in your strange costume. . . ." We were wearing rather threadbare lounge suits, second-day shirts, and dusty shoes. It was probably the first time in their existence they had been compared favorably with a saffron robe, a silken tunic, embroidered boots, and a hat made of the fur of a bear.

We left in a glow of mutual affection, shaking hands and exchanging addresses. This is usually a vain and disappointing thing anywhere; here it seemed more doomed than anywhere else. I have the paper still, however—my only address in Lhasa. And who knows?

That month, at all events, the Mountain Road went through. It became possible, at last, to drive a truck over that enormous desolate plateau, that freezing belt of inhospitable hills, into Tibet.

It had never happened before. Tibet was always the great land barrier between China and the Western world. Tibet stood not only between China's potential conquerors and China, but between China and what was, in fact, the rest of the world. No great aggressor had ever managed to cross this mass of icy highlands; for several generations China sheltered from the Western barbarians behind Tibet. And yet—this uncrossable plateau also cut off the overpopulated South from the empty North; it debilitated any Chinese resistance to the steady pressure of Imperial Russia on Turkestan, on Mongolia.

But now the road was made—at extravagant cost, at an almost fabulous expenditure of material, of men—thousands upon thousands of men, driving through the frozen rock faces, bridging the snowy rivers, laying their length over the feet of glaciers.

Now, when it was ready at last, the Chinese said that the Tibet Road was the greatest single endeavor of all her engineers in history. It was, they said, a more impressive feat of labor than the Great Wall.

That, it seemed, was the way the Living Buddha would return. He, and the engineers, and the commissars, and the meteorological experts, and the administrative consultants, and the cadres. Then there would be Radio Lhasa. Then there would be. . . .

The next day I went up to Tsin Hua University, which is one of the establishments most highly thought of in Peking. It was so like every other technical college anywhere else in the world that it has left on my mind a vague impression of rectangular buildings, concrete stairways. . . . I met Chien Wei-Chan, the Dean of the University. (He was called the "dean"; they used the word as they used the words "freshman" and "sophomore"; in truth I feel that Tsin Hua resembled a Middle Western College more nearly than it did anything else.) Chien Wei-Chan, like everyone else in authority in modern China, looked as though he himself were just on the point of leaving school. When he took over, at the time of the "Liberation," there had been twenty-three hundred students; now there were fifty four hundred. By 1957, he said, they hoped for ten thousand.

For what? Technique, he said, technique, always technique. The university was changing rapidly over to an engineering school. Already they had seven departments—two for machinery, one for electricity, one each for building and architecture, one for water conservation, one for radio. They were five-year courses—except for architecture, which lasted six years. We went through the architectural section—walls lined with drawings of consummate skill and sensitivity, portraying architectural conceptions of unparalleled banality.

"Well, yes, as a matter of fact," said the man who showed us round, "there is another side"—and produced a room where the old methods of roof-laying and tile-designing were practiced; interlocking lathes and beams culminating in curling eaves and fabulously decorated pilasters. "It is hard to adapt this style," he said, "but it is necessary to keep it up. It takes *years* to learn to build a Peking roof."

It was a student life on a model quite new: everyone did twenty-four weeks practical work in factories, or on special projects. "This of course was never possible under the old style," said the man, "but now the State owns the factories *and* the colleges. Moreover there are no secret processes and manufacture patents to safeguard. We see to it that study and production are closely integrated. . . .

"There are of course no fees. On the contrary, there is a standard pay scale, applicable to both men and women. Every student gets a hundred and twenty thousand JMP a month" (it was about four dollars and a quarter) "to cover their food and pocket money. As for us, the teachers—we have more than six hundred here; we are paid on a scale considered sufficient to let us, as adults, maintain a family of five, with, of course, free accommodation. We have our trade union. The students have theirs. . . . Both sides understand the vital importance of the production of good cadres. . . ."

"Cadres? Or technicians?"

He shrugged his shoulders. "Where is the incompatibility? There is of course a political course—four hours a week, and it is by all means compulsory. In this current year there have been two hundred and sixteen thousand students throughout the country (*far* too few, but it increases all the time), and I should say that every one of them goes out imbued with a spirit of patriotism, the Marxist-Leninist principle, and a knowledge of their subject."

"In that order?"

"There is no order. Certain courses are common to all schools and are taken by everybody reading everything. They are the history of the Chinese Revolution, the principle of Marxist-Leninism, and modern political economy. Also a foreign language."

"Which is Russian?"

"Generally. It is more convenient. The bulk of the technical textbooks are in that language, so most students prefer to learn it."

"There are also other languages?"

"Naturally, there *are* other languages. There are many schools and universities where these are taught— English, French, German."

"But here in Tsin Hua, the only foreign language taught to technical students is Russian?"

"That is correct."

We went out for a stroll through the playing fields —a magnificent expanse of open ground, dense with young men and girls leaping and jumping and skipping and throwing balls about, filled with the random energy that seems to penetrate all modern Chinese on playing fields. It was called, I was told, the "campus." As soon as our presence was remarked on the sidelines of this activity the students would pause and clap with a nervous formality that became engagingly friendly and gay whenever one stopped and smiled. It was the most meaningless piece of spontaneous good-will gesture I ever saw.

I said, "Why do they applaud *me?*"

"They are pleased to welcome a foreign friend here in the name of peace."

"But how do they *know*. . . ." I began, but it wasn't any good; it was pettish and futile to feel resentful at precisely the sort of thing one spent one's time at home advocating. "Do you think they really mean it?"

"The youth of China is filled with the love of peace."

And I suppose they were; they looked as though they were—who doesn't? I thought of the three-year-olds in the nursery schools who also clapped the arrival of any obvious European—can you be filled with the love of peace at the age of three?

"As you see, the history of imperialist tyranny has left them only with a sense of the brotherhood of man."

The brotherhood of man rushed gaily around kicking footballs, throwing things, scoring goals in nets.

"Really," I said, "what balls it all is. Why, even I . . ."

"Exactly," said the teacher, "the love of sport is part of the nature of the new generation. Health, for example . . ."

But they were charming youths, and without their boiler suits even the girls looked like girls. I walked for a while around the living blocks—dormitories stark and clean and austere, with a standard of the sort of bleak discomfort associated with the better English public schools. In fact the whole atmosphere was, if anything, reminiscent of that, with the students cheering peace as readily and as automatically as, ten thousand miles away, other round-eyed youths were cheering someone's winning try. . . .

Did they, one wondered, have a "Commem?" In the year 1908 the University of Tsin Hua was founded on moneys paid as indemnity after the Boxer Rebellion to the United States. The United States relinquished their claim on the indemnity on condition it was used to establish a college, for which they would supply a grant and the teachers. It is possible that this fact will not even be recalled in five years' time. There is unlikely to be a Commem. for Tsin Hua University, the People's College started by the people of the United States.

There were one hundred and eight institutions of higher learning in China, not including secondary or technical schools. They were: fourteen comprehensive universities; thirty-eight engineering colleges; twenty-five agricultural colleges; three forestry colleges; twenty-nine medical schools and teaching hospitals; fifteen fine arts schools; four physical training academies; eight schools for foreign languages; thirty-one teachers' colleges; six schools of economics; four institutions of political jurisprudence; three minorities institutes.

Thirty per cent of the contemporary enrollment was composed of girls. Five years before the figure had been rather less than one per cent. In the whole of China there were some thirty-three thousand professors and lecturers. The new age had struck China unprepared, with an aching vacuum of education.

"We need *everything*," they told me, "technicians, of course. And administrators. How would *you* run a country like this?"

China was perhaps the one country in the civilized world that suffered from a tremendous shortage of civil servants. Most of the administrative posts were filled with Party cadres, full of zeal but ill equipped academically, or former Kuomintang officials who had been passed most rigorously through the mangle of a re-endoctrination course. The Ministry of Higher Education had been charged with the task of producing at least two thousand new trained civil servants a year: a daunting prospect.

The candidates were chosen by entrance examination from a selected list of cadres and workers with an interestingly flexible political and educational background. Those eligible were "revolutionary cadres with more than five years' service, and industrial workers with over three years' service, both with a cultural level of the junior high-school grade, or cadres with less than five years service in revolutionary work but with a cultural level of the senior high school." The candidates had to be sponsored by their respective branches of the Party, or their factory managements. Ordinary workers received seventy-five per cent of their wages during training. ("Model Workers" got one hundred per cent.) The Party cadres were paid only the most minimum pocket money, in order to maintain the manifest frugality and austere standards of living that— it must be said, without exception—characterized every Party worker in the country. There were no cakes and ale being a Communist in China.

There were not, of course, very many of them. The figure given for membership of Kung Chan Tang, the Communist Party of China, was six and a half million— a membership deliberately limited, just as the reservoir of Party Youth Organizations was stimulated. For the sixteen-to-twenty-five age group there was the New Democratic Youth League, with nine million members. (About eighteen per cent of the population was in this age group; one in nine, therefore, was in the League.) For the school-children there was the Pioneers, or the Young Vanguards —one saw them everywhere, with their red scarves and their little chevrons of rank on their pinafores—with seven million. Promotion went from group to group. There were thus some twenty-two million Chinese enrolled in this or that form in the Party complex.

And they started very young.

One day I went to Number Two Primary School affiliated with the Peking Teachers' College. It sounded like an unpromising expedition; it turned out to be absorbing.

I had already spent a great deal of my leisure in the kindergartens and nurseries—of which there were four hundred and thirty-five in Peking—for no particular reason except that the appearance and behavior of Chinese children under the age of ten is the most bewitching thing to be found in the entire country. After the age of ten, it seemed, behavior became more self-possessed, more calculated, but the sense of discipline remained, the air of being in charge of every emotion.

The Number Two School was—naturally—a model school; I supposed it to be the best in the city, as they had been at me for some days to go and see it. It was as handsome and well-designed a school as could be found anywhere—sunny and bright, its sage-green walls touched here and there by just the proper splashes of color; the scheme was brutally wrecked in places by the glaring posters portraying, as usual, the gross villainies of Chiang Kai-Shek and the sublime benefactions of Chairman Mao. I have seen such schools all over the world, and this one—apart from its size; it had a thousand and sixty pupils in twenty-six classes—seemed to me to embody no strikingly new principle; it appeared to be simple and unexceptional. It had, however, a headmaster who was certainly not unexceptional, and far from simple.

"Until the fourth grade," he said, "we just teach them figures, a bit of art, some music, and physical culture. After that we add history, geography, and"—the interpreter hesitated for the word—"natural phenomena. Experimental? I suppose we're experimental in the sense that the students from the Teachers' College can come here to try out new educational theories. But nothing bizarre. We have a *tremendous* lot of educational leeway to make up. . . .

"Politics? Why, of course not. How could you teach politics to children like this?"

I vaguely indicated the great signs demanding the liberation of Formosa, the display-photographs of Chou En-Lai and the Chairman. He smiled (he was a good-natured man). "Those? Those are part of the *décor* of the land," he said. "I am told that in British schools there are frequently portraits of the Royal Family, and that in the United States the national flag is not altogether unknown. No," he said, seriously, "we don't teach politics, as such. However, facts are allowed to teach them. . . .

"For instance," he said, "if you put salt into water, it dissolves. If you boil the water away, the salt remains. That is a law of nature. We call it a natural phenomenon. Its value to our children is that enough of that sort of demonstration eliminates the background of superstition that is still a trouble to our country. *All* facts have a political meaning of some sort. We say: it's *natural* that children should love their parents, obey their teachers, respect the property of the school. It's natural too, we say, that they should feel an impulse to help old and weak people. These things seem to me to be intensely political matters. They involve the feeling of the group—which ultimately, of course, adds up to the State.

"Moreover, most of these children's parents had a pretty bad time in the old days. After the Liberation the change was visible—even to them, or if it wasn't it could be explained to them. Our argument is that these things are a natural law too—like the salt and the water—and therefore they're politics.

"Certainly we teach them about other countries. We

teach them—I can show you the books if you like—that among the imperialist capitalist countries, of whom we disapprove because they threaten us, only a minority nevertheless are of an aggressive turn of mind. Most of the people in your country, I'm sure—and so we teach them—are pretty much the same as ourselves. These things are also facts, we maintain, and therefore they are politics. That is, politics by implication. I really don't understand how else you would teach them. . . ."

In a classroom next door a class was having a singing lesson. I noticed that they were using exactly the same doh, reh, mi as is used in Europe.

". . . . teach them love of labor, too, and diligence. We can demonstrate to them factually that the reason why our living standards are rising and our international status is improving is because of the example of work and zeal shown by the Communist Party. It isn't propaganda; it is merely factual. . . . So is history: we teach them the incidents of ancient and modern history, things you can't distort. Such as the corruptions of the Manchu Dynasty, the past aggressions of the Imperialists. That the peoples of all countries want peace, but that there are influences. . . ."

When I asked him if any noteworthy new educational methods had been evolved by which these factual matters were imparted, he said, "Well, naturally we use Chinese methods, which are simple enough. As a matter of fact we make quite considerable use of the more advanced techniques used in the capitalist countries: the principles of Froebel and Montessori . . ."

At this point rather a curious thing happened. From the pattern of his queer Chinese tones I had somehow disentangled the words "Froebel" and "Montessori," partly because I was interested in them in any case. Big Wei, who was interpreting, translated them as "Flaubert and Montesquieu."

I had worked with him for some time, and no one knew better than I the virtuoso grasp he had of almost all technical expressions in all fields; this was the first time I could ever have caught him in an error, and that by the merest chance. It offered a really fascinating glimpse of this talented, indeed cultivated mind—his learning went genuinely deep down certain defined shafts of knowledge. And now the words "Froebel" and "Montessori," associated by one of his automatic reflexes with learning, emerged from his lips in the character of two not dissimilar names grouped equally in his mind with culture. For a Chinese—with part of his mind, the active part, doubtless reflecting on the works of Engels and the liberation of Taiwan—to have reached into his subconscious and pulled out Flaubert and Montesquieu struck me as both extraordinary and admirable.

But I never quite trusted him again.

It was never a good plan to excuse oneself for anything by the convenient hint of indisposition, nor was it advisable ever to suggest a physical malaise of any kind, because the most casual inference of this would bring medical care around with almost embarrassing speed. Several times I watched fellow visitors, who were clearly doing nothing more urgent than making small talk, mention vaguely that they had a cold, or a sore throat, or a cigarette burn. Before they knew where they were a doctor was in attendance, and a little blue-uniformed nurse with a box of dressings. With my own eyes I saw my friend Bill, who had suffered some difficulty in breathing in the humid swamps around the Yantse Kiang, whipped off to a hospital in Hangkow with an expedition marvellous to behold. Once committed, there was no way of escaping medical attention; it was a situation both deeply reassuring and at the same time, in its way, inhibiting.

I had been interested to learn something of the new developments in this field, since everyone knew the Chinese had for centuries pursued a path of medical research very divergent from that of everyone else. Throughout Southeast Asia, wherever a Chinese doctor was available, people had spoken of him in terms of mingled bewilderment and respect; they were generally known as "needle men." This was largely because of the Chinese concentration on the ancient art of acupuncture—the practice of driving needles into specified parts of the body in order to stimulate, or alternatively to numb, the nerves connected with a disordered organ possibly very far away. It was a branch of superficial surgery that was, everyone said, completely understood in China and nowhere else; I had made many inquiries about it in the past. Many centuries of experiment had rationalized the whole process: it was invaluable for facial spasms, for bed-wetting, for various forms of indigestion. In tonsillitis, for example, or specific forms of laryngeal pain, the needles driven in between the thumb and forefinger were considered to relieve the pain; chronic bed-wetting could be cured by a needle deep in the region of the cervix.

The science of acupuncture was closely allied to the general practice of traditional Chinese medicine, which was herbalist and to some degree homeopathic, with a succession largely hereditary, and full of peculiar mysteries seldom committed to writing. In every way, one felt, irreconcilable to the new Marxist ethic. I had the good luck to corner two doctors together—one of the old school, one of the new. I met them on a visit to one of the just-built Peking hospitals—another great great building, so new that the wards were being filled upstairs while the bricklayers were still packing up on the ground floor.

The old herbal doctor was Kiang Chien-An, who had followed his father, who had been a herbal doctor, who had followed his father, who had also been a herbal doctor. . . . And with him was Sun Yin-Hua, an energetic young woman graduate of the Peking Medical College six years before. They were *both*, I found, on the staff. It seemed to be part of this subtle and insidious new system that a considerable effort was being made to co-ordinate the two opposed schools of medicine, rather than set them in competition.

There was not a great deal one could ask Dr. Sun; she represented something equally easy to encounter in Europe, or America. But the presence in this gleaming new hospital of the herbalist—he was far older, and could with artistry have changed his blue suit for the long gray robe of the leech.

"Why should they interfere with our work?" he asked. "We are not even considered to be quacks. It takes an herbalist *far* longer to qualify than the orthodox comrades. There are at least three thousand separate prescriptions to memorize, for example. Two thousand eight hundred years ago there were books on our medicine— works on anatomical subjects for example: the length of the larger intestine, the weight of the liver and the various major organs. There were no autopsies in those days; one did not approve of the mutilation of one's ancestors; but it has since been found that the figures were almost exactly correct."

"Indeed, yes," said Dr. Sun, "to within an ounce or two."

It was curious, I thought, here as before: the moment the new Chinese start to rationalize the old things they begin to uphold them; they are a people engaged almost perpetually in denouncing the past, and constantly praising things because of their antiquity.

"Our diagnosis was—indeed is, I might say, since nothing significant has changed—much the same as theirs," said Dr. Kiang, "except of course we never believed that illness, any type of illness, could exist in isolation. We diagnosed in terms of group disorders. Finally we check the pulse—there are, you may know, exactly twenty-eight distinctive kinds of pulsebeats; from that we can check on the diagnosis. I *could* tell you how, but it would take some years. You mustn't imagine this is something we thought up overnight. Back in the Tang Dynasty our herbalists knew, for instance, that the diabetic urine gave a sugar reaction, the processes of uterine contraction. They even used the same materials. Why, we *invented* ergot. Isn't that so, Dr. Sun?"

"Indeed it is, Dr. Kiang," said the lady with respect.

The unexpected thing about this extremely modern hospital was that it had been built to accommodate a clinic run on the traditional methods, and patients on entering were permitted to opt for whichever technique they preferred. There were frequent consultations, and in cases of medical failure, the orthodox staff would hand over to the herbalists for experiment. Each side was permitted and indeed encouraged to attend the ministrations of the other.

There was also a separate, and highly thought of, Acupuncture Clinic. Dr. Sun, the modern doctor, spoke of this in terms of great enthusiasm, as one who had been admitted to something outstandingly new.

"We don't like to emphasize this," she said, "but not long ago we *thought* we'd achieved some sort of success with a poliomyelitis case. We on our side couldn't do anything with it, so we handed it over to the acupuncture people. They couldn't make it any worse, was what we thought. Not even they had ever thought of curing polio by pricking the patient—however, they did, with a large number of needles on either side of the spinal cord, and some in certain parts of the leg. The patient began to improve; indeed he may yet recover. We have had three cases like that. Naturally, one can't make claims on such a narrow basis, but one day we may. . . . Those needles; they are tremendously fine. You can scarcely feel them. And now, at least, they're sterile. What is more," she said, making the inevitable gesture, "it has been decided that acupuncture is a principle wholly compatible with the theories of Pavlov."

I asked the herb doctor whether he did not feel an impulse to resist many new specifics—the antibiotics, the sulfa drugs? He said, "Well, no. Chairman Mao said some time ago that we were to co-operate with all new developments in clinical work, so we co-operate. I might have personal reservations. . . . The new medicine, that is to say Western medicine, is really founded on autopsy; these people got their knowledge from thousands and thousands of post-mortems. We believed that an organ is a very different thing when it's dead. We considered what it did rather than what it looked like."

The first twenty-two medical classics that were then being officially printed in Peking included the *Mei Ching*, a treatise on the pulse written in the third century by Wang Shu-Ho, and the *Pen Tsao Kang Mu*, an enormous encyclopaedia of plant drugs compiled by the sixteenth-century pharmacist *Li Shih-chen*—which they had furthermore translated into Russian, French, Latin, English, German and Japanese.

"We still think in terms of herbs, you know," said

Dr. Kiang. "There are hundred of plants and grasses and barks. . . . I can give you an herbal remedy for a fractured arm, do you know that? I can pick you a small plant on the Western Hills that is ten times more effective than quinine. . . . But of course," he said, "the time is past for making competitive claims. We work together now. Eighty per cent of China's doctors are still herbalists. But it took the twenty per cent—and, of course, the Liberation, to provide hospitals like these. . . ."

I said that one thing only bothered me about the traditional physic: was it true, I asked, that an infusion of the *jing-pen* root, for sale throughout the land, gave one back his youth?

"As to that," said the doctor sadly, "I only wish I knew."

The present of Peking lay in the busy streets, the whisper of three million felt-soled shoes on the pavement; the future lay in the mushroom growth of building all around, awaiting expression behind the high red walls of the Inner City, in the solemn bureaus of the People's Government. The past—or so they would say—lay in the Liu Li Chang, the alley that once upon a time, many years ago, had been known as the Street of Beautiful Articles. It was a place to which one found oneself returning over and over; it was very sad.

This had at one time been the celebrated beaux-arts center of Peking, the street where every shop was an antiquarian: a dim and shadowy door opening into a room aglow with richly colored things, opening into yet another room where were stored things that even the dealer thought good—that silk-robed, wispily bearded shadow who offered scented tea in a translucent porcelain cup, and would never speak of money. There were some left now, but not many. The survivors had a farfetched job, presenting for sale the relics of a feudal, reactionary, vicious and somehow secretly admired yesterday among the relentless solemnities of a Marxist today. Here and there they remained, merchants of ancient manuscripts of classical calligraphy, the *roulade* paintings—over four yards of endless repetitive incident, an elaborate precursor of the comic strip—the brittle kakemonos, some pieces of ceramics, seals of jade and jasper. There would be suddenly striking shelves of apparently priceless stuff—funerary statuettes of the Ming and Tang epochs, pottery goddesses, old bronzes. But of course, they weren't real. They were nevertheless astounding—every flaw delicately reproduced, the scars of age and fire and burial conceived on them the other day with almost impenetrable accuracy; they were magnificent, and they cost a few pence each. They were presented for sale without comment: nobody claimed them to be real; there was nothing about them to confess they were false. They were there to be bought—by whom? Who in Peking today patronized the shops of the long-forgotten tourists?

The answer was: practically nobody. The antiquarians were now, like everyone else, part of the State machine. Not the smallest article of virtue in any shop but bore its price-controlled ticket—there was no more bargaining, no more cups of fragrant tea. The State had, they said, an inventory of everything that could be considered a work of art or of antiquity in Peking—but they hadn't, it turned out. Towards the end of the visit I was called to the house of a friend, who had summoned a friend of *his* in the antique business, who brought with him, for strictly private sale, ivories and jades, carvings and paintings that he had somehow not been compelled to declare to the Ministry. . . .

I got back to the Pei Ch Ko to find that Andrew Condron was waiting to see me.

We were getting to the end of the journey now, and
to things that became increasingly difficult to recount
and explain. Andrew Condron was one of them. He is a
real and a living person, and his family in Scotland are
real and living people; it is necessary to speak of this encounter without comment or emotion, although it was
a thing not without emotion, and steeped in some tremendously elusive significance.

I have mentioned before that we asked the authorities in Peking for many facilities, some obvious and some,
we considered hopeless. Not infrequently the obvious
and banal took longer than the apparently difficult.
Among the representations made—rather impulsively,
and near the ending of our stay—was a caprice of Zig's:
could we, he said, be allowed to meet the prisoners from
Korea?

It had been more than a year since the day, after the
cease fire along the Parallel, when a dozen or so soldiers
of the United Nations forces, captives of the Chinese in
Korea, had chosen to reject the offer of repatriation, and
had elected instead to remain on the side of their conquerors because, as they were reported to have said, they
thought the Communist cause was the just one. It had
been a strange story, invested with all manner of denunci-
ations and bitter explanations—these soldiers, with their
perverse and unexpected decision, had dislocated the
propaganda machine; it became necessary to project them
in a hundred conflicting lights, uniformly unfavorable.
The accepted epithet was "traitor," tinged with "mad-
man."

There was clearly going to be no chance of putting

this matter to the test; it was unlikely to the highest degree that the Chinese would reveal the whereabouts of these men, still less the men themselves. Among them, we knew, was one British Royal Marine, whose name was Andrew Condron and who, since his momentary burst into melodrama in Korea, had vanished from the sight of man.

The day after we made our request to see him, Andrew Condron turned up to see us.

This was one of the fantasies of the Chinese method with which there was no coping on rational grounds. It is illustrative of the strange mental labyrinth in which one worked that the first impulse was to consult our liaison Government friend, in case there had been some bizarre and unprecedented mistake, likely to cost everyone dear. His reaction was bland enough: "That is quite right. We were sure you would be glad to know each other. And as a matter of fact, since you speak each other's language, after all, we thought you would not mind if you dispensed with an interpreter today."

That meant that the final rationalization of the situation had dissolved; they did not even want to supervise the meeting. As it turned out, we met, went out together, ate together, and spent the day together, without as far as I knew the Chinese either knowing or caring where we went nor what we did.

Andrew was an upstanding young man with a West of Scotland accent; for a long time, it seemed to me, he was struggling between his eagerness to be with people of his own race and his acquired suspicion of those very people. For a long time we spoke banalities—of his home in Bathgate, of the Arsenal-Spartak match, of the wintry cold that was slowly beginning to grip the city of

Peking. We went for lunch to the Peace Restaurant in the Eastern Market; it served European food from a menu trilingually printed in Russian, English and French; it was thoroughly odious, as "European" food always was in modern China, but the young man said he had still not become accustomed to Chinese food. I took the most exquisite pains to say never a word that could be held to be a leading question or a personal enquiry; for at least an hour the atmosphere was charged with a terrible delicacy. By and by we spoke, with a freedom that was erratic at first, and gradually built up into a sort of confidence that was strange and in the end full of all sorts of mutual hidden pain.

There is no point in elaborating the nature of this talk; it was commonplace, built of the sort of remote banalities that claimed significance only in this weird context. He had chosen to stay with his captors ". . . because it seemed to me they were the chaps who wanted peace; everyone said so; I saw it for myself. If you'd seen the way some of our lot went on, over bye in Korea·. . ." And I had, of course; I had not been without my own tormenting troubles and dilemmas in the same place, for the same reason. It had been easier for me; I had had—or thought I had—the means of expressing the quandary without this terrible committal; I had held it possible to maintain one side was wrong without agreeing that the other was right. The young Marine from West Lothian had been racked too soon, with too few resources.

". . . anyhow, I'd been so near dead I reckoned I knew the right way of it. I still think I did. I did what I thought was best—not just for me, see, but for the lot of us. And so . . ."

And so, here he was. He now lived in the People's

University of Peking, studying Chinese. ("Man, that's a real problem. Whiles I think I've got hold of a hundred characters—but it's not a language for a man like me. Still—it's got to be done, if I'm to do any sort of a job in China.") The Chinese Red Cross paid him three hundred thousand *yuan* a month, about twelve dollars; he had to pay about three quarters of that for his food and lodging. . . . And his politics now—was he, for example, a Communist?

"In the Party? No fears. You can't get to be a member that easy. Why, man, it's a real tester; they'll not admit you. I'm not sure I'd even ask—that's something else, see; I've a long way to go before I could sort that sort of thing out in my mind. I expect you'll not understand. . . . This thing I had to do wasn't because I *was* something but because I *wasn't*" (Ah, that dilemma of the negative decision!). "It wasn't a question of coming over to get into something but to get out of something. I was right, do you get it? I wouldn't change it, even now. . . ."

I am wholly inhibited about these revelations, and for several simultaneous reasons, which will be apparent to anyone who puts himself in this unhappy situation. As I say, half of this young Marine remains in Scotland, but a vulnerable half remains in China.

Suddenly he finished his beer and said, "Would you not like to come home and meet the lads? We're all in it together. They'll be tickled to death to see you."

It wasn't what I expected. We went back to the enormous block of the People's University, and there in a row of dormitories were the others, the fellowship of the irrevocable choice—about a dozen of them, all Americans, among them a couple of Negroes, sitting around the camp

bed beside the stoves reading, studying books of characters, mending their cotton-padded suits against the cold.
. . . It looked like any scene out of an American campus
movie. They grinned, they hi-ya'ed, they made room on
the beds. They made expressions of comical exasperation
at the Chinese books, they larked around and kidded one
another with esoteric family jests. It was wholly unreal.
There was no practical way of explaining it. They were
not Young Communists of the familiar pattern; they
spoke never a word of politics nor asked one question
about the things I must know and they not; they sat there
in the desolate heart of this remote planet, buried, it
might be, forever in this insulated political vacuum and
they talked like second-year students of Princeton and
Glasgow and Durham and St. Andrews. . . . I knew then
that there was nothing I could ever write about it, though
I was the first Westerner ever to set eyes on them since
those grisly Korean days. Should I say they were simple
and apparently goodhearted boys without neuroses or,
apparently, fear; should I say that they were brain-
washed to a point where they had reverted to the characteristics of naïveté; should I say they were traitors or
fools or idealists or imbeciles or decent men or nonde-
scripts? There was no choice; in the curious circumstances
of the contemporary world anything can be deduced by
implication; I said nothing. I still do not know what to
say.

They came out to the roadside to see me off, with
the dusk soaking down over the ashen-colored city. I said
good-by to the young Marine, and asked, "Are you home-
sick?"

"Whiles," he said, "there are things I miss. But I'm
happy."

"Do you never think of coming home?"

"Maybe," he said, "that I'll do. When the time comes."

The next day I left China.

At the airport I found that Shen Chen-Tu and Li Ping had got up to come and see me off—it was half past five in the morning and they had come a long way. We sat talking sunrise platitudes among the empty seats and the piles of yesterday's papers and the pictures of Stalin and Chairman Mao, with their confident smiles and their empty eyes. I found I had two hundred thousand *yuan* in my pocket which I was not allowed to take away. I gave it to Shen.

"What can I buy you?" he asked, "to remind you of China?"

I said, "The little green monster third from the left on the topmost roof of the Forbidden City."

"It is a deal," he said, "but failing that?"

"Buy me a fire pot," I said. "I can get the charcoal."

"First a devil, then a fire pot," he said, shaking his head. "I think I shall send you a dove. With a whistle."

Then I got into the airplane and we climbed up over the gray sleeping squares of Peking, over the Western Hills, over the Great Wall of China, snaking like a stone string across the ridges, over the Mongolian border, over the icebound emptiness of the Gobi Desert to Ulan Bator, among the fur-coated camels and the leather men in the town of felted tents. No more China; over into Siberia into a white dead solitude—the day and the night and the day and the night; Russia below, and the world growing colder all around.

Appendix:
The Machine

This vast, durable, lovable, alarming country; perverse and disarmingly reasonable at the same time, is today administered by an intricate system that is by now very nearly proof against all argument. The shape of this can be detailed only in a fashion so formidably unattractive that I have kept it aside from the rest, on the considerate principle that keeps one from deliberately including a piece of salt pork in a cheese soufflé.

The People's Republic of China came into existence with the Organic Law of September, 1949, based on the findings of several commissions which had been at work for a year or more. The point that has to be borne in mind is that it got off to an historically unparalleled flying start. The Communist Party of China, unlike that of Russia thirty-two years before, achieved power as a going concern, with thirty years growth behind it, having come through the testing fire of a very long war, with a mature army, and considerable administrative experience. It did not mark its accession to power, as so many people believe, with a purge (the drastic eliminations were yet to come); on the contrary the enormous new officialdom was compelled to absorb administrators of almost every kind of political background. A political virtue was made out of this practical necessity; since so many known non-Communists and defecting Kuomintang civil servants were placed in prominent administrative positions, this was held to be in keeping with the proclaimed ends of Mao's "New Democracy," which was ostensibly a coalition. To a degree that principle was maintained even after the Constitution; to this day China can look the world in the face and say: We have not a hundred per cent Communist Government.

To say that the effective administration was not loaded in favor of the Communist hierarchy, however, is to say that the Republican National Committee does not contain a certain number of accepted Republicans.

China began its new career ruled by three chains of command: the Party, the People's Republican Government, and the Revolutionary Military Council; with the functions of all three unified through a small group of accepted leaders, dominated by Mao Tse-Tung himself.

This tripartite structure operated to begin with through an administrative system of six Area Governments, plus the autonomous Area of Mongolia, and Tibet. Each area was headed by an administrative Commission—usually, but not in all cases, led by an accepted military personality. Below this level were the Provincial, County and Village administrations—a pattern, indeed, traditional throughout Chinese history, which after four thousand years is not, as one may imagine, without administrative precedent. The difference now was that the Central Government penetrated local affairs down to the smallest unit in a way that had never occurred before. The interlocking of Party and State functions was nothing particularly new to China either; it has always been a feature even of the Chiang Kai-Shek Government, insofar as that Government's writ had ever run.

During those five preparatory years power was gradually concentrated more and more at the top, to centralize Government and avoid the historic Chinese tendency to produce regional overlordship of greater and greater influence. For the rest, administration was on the classic Soviet pattern, with State and Party operating parallel and overlapping systems.

From the very beginning the methods applied that I have in previous chapters been able to describe, rather inadequately and rather misleadingly, as the "persuasive system" were applied, in a fashion almost institutional—that is to say, the first appeal was made to those communal sections that had always been debased and dispossessed: the wage earners, the youth and the women. For all of the group specific organizations were created: for the workers there was the Federation of Labor (which is now known as the All-China Federation of Trades Unions); for the youth there was the New Democratic Youth League (with the "Pioneers" for the children); and the All-China Federation of Democratic Women for this enormous and newly liberated group of female people.

This principle was rapidly extended to other sections of the Community—the All-China Students' Federation, the All-China Federation of Literature and Art; indeed very soon there existed no social, professional or ethnic division of life that had not its own organization, directed by cadres of the Party and dedicated to transforming the pattern of life not from above, but from within. It seems to be a fact that the early objective of Mao Tse-Tung's Government was to reduce to the minimum the number of groups who might one day act against him—to win them not by suppression, but by recruitment.

During this period the membership of the Communist Party soared. In 1937 it was said to be forty thousand; at the declaration of the People's State in 1949 it was one million three hundred thousand. By 1954, it was six million. It has put on perhaps half a million since then, at which point it is held to be at its optimum for discipline and efficiency. (This is of course exclusive of the Youth Leagues, whose part in the Party pattern was mentioned earlier.)

In 1954, the whole affair was *mis en ordre* by every ostensibly Democratic endorsement: Congress passed the Constitution.

The newly elected Congress was convened in September 1954 to adopt and promulgate the Constitution. For the first time in its enormous and incalculable history China was knit together as a "united multinational State." The sanction for this fabulous development was an adult franchise with the biggest electorate on the face of the earth. However cynically one may regard the effective practice of this matter, it has to be recognized that— to give the process its minimum value—people did, in fact, vote.

However, the electorates were so arranged that peasants and workers and acknowledged revolutionary elements got a considerable weightage at all the levels of the People's Congress. To begin with, two hundred and ten thousand representative Congresses at the *hsiang* (or basic rural) level elected a representation of 5,669,-144 deputies; these deputies electing Regional and Provincial Congresses, which in turn chose members of the National Congress. Except for the primaries, therefore, all elections were indirect (and even the primaries were generally conducted on the basis of a show of hands, because of the voters' illiteracy). There was in fact provision for a ballot at the next two stages, but (since this demo-

cratic process was new and untried) most of the hand-
picked candidates got in on a unanimous vote.

So . . . at last the Constitution of the People's Republic was promulgated in September, 1954, to coincide
with the celebration of the Fifth Revolutionary Anniver-
sary—a stirring moment, as I can personally attest,
though it had to be admitted that whatever details in
the administration were changed, the framework of the
structure remained untouched. What did one expect?

At the moment of writing, then, the situation is that
effective power is firmly held in the hands of a comparatively small group of Revolutionary giants, of whom the
unchallengeable star billing must go to Mao Tse-Tung,
Chu Teh, Liu Shao-Chi, and Chou En-Lai.

Here we have a situation quite unique in the contemporary revolutionary chronicles, in that the hierarchy
have common ties, experience, and doubtless personal
affection that go back to the early 'thirties, with many of
their associations dating back a decade beyond that.
These people have lived, fought, wrangled, argued, and
planned together for a very long time; there is not one of
China's responsible political leaders who is not a middle-
aged man, solidified in the crucible of insurrection and
common planning, adjusted long ago to the principle of
administrative responsibility. It is tremendously significant that at no time has Mao Tse-Tung felt it necessary
to conduct any sort of purge in the Party hierarchy at its
higher levels. There has never yet arisen a Chinese Trot-
sky, a Chinese Beria (which is not to say that there may
never be). Such changes, demotions and promotions as
have occurred have been strictly administrative; however one observes the career of Mao Tse-Tung one fact
emerges without challenge: that he has endeavored to

maintain a spirit of security and mutual responsibility among his colleagues, relying for cohesion upon his personal qualities of leadership and authority. Mao Tse-Tung has, over and above his peers in the history of revolution, this singular advantage of prestige without competition: he existed, and exists, as the symbol of successful projection of military leadership and theoretical command of the movement—for the Chinese it was important not only that he could in fact win battles, but that he could thereafter analyze them, and in a fluid and beguiling prose. These factors are not so stupid as they sound.

However, we have now reached the consummation of the endless war and the repetitive revolution: the Constitution. From this we find that the apex of the pyramid consists of two supermen: Mao Tse-Tung and Chu Teh, the Chairman and the Vice-Chairman—for it is by those titles alone that they are accepted through their huge country.

Yet on examination of the Constitution it can be seen that both of them enjoy the most limited constitutional powers. Chairman Mao, as Head of the State, is vested with the most formal ceremonial duties. Chu Teh has even fewer responsibilities; his function is only to relieve the Chairman when so required.

In effect, however, their constitutional authority is heavily overridden by certain other political functions. Mao is rather more than Head of the State; he is also Chairman of the Central Committee of the Communist Party of China, which—since this organization is in fact the controlling influence of the country—is no inconsiderable post. Chu Teh is head of the Army, and thus manipulates the motive power of the whole machine—of which Mao, as Chairman of the Republic, is *ex officio* the Supreme Commander. Mao is also Chairman of the National Defense Council, with the right to nominate not only the Vice-Chairman but all the members. For Vice-Chairman he nominated Chu Teh; and for members he nominated all the prominent Field Commanders of the People's Liberation Army (the "volunteers" who fought in Korea), including General Peng Teh-Huai, the "Hero of Korea," who is also Minister for Defense. It can thus be suspected that Mao Tse-Tung and Chu Teh hold, between them, no inconsiderable part of the leverage of power.

The second buttress is the Standing Committee of the National People's Congress. The Congress itself (whose manufacture we have briefly examined) is described by the Constitution as the sole and supreme organ of State authority. Since it meets once a year only, and only for a few days, it could be held that this authority is transitory and almost evanescent. It is its Standing Committee that discharges all its legislative duties—enacting decrees, supervising the work of the Cabinet and the Courts, appointing Ministers and Ambassadors, ratifying and abrogating Treaties. The man in charge of the Standing Committee, therefore, is perhaps the only man in China whose authority could be said to parallel, if not challenge, that of Chairman Mao himself, and that man's name is Liu Shao-Chi.

Liu Shao-Chi is, in fact, next to Mao the most powerful and significant man in China. If there could be said to be an *eminence grise* in this closely knit ruling group it would be Liu, who is held to be the foremost Marxist theoretician in the land, and whose technique in dominating every aspect of the country's administration is to stay always three paces in the background.

The State Council (the Council of Ministers) consists of the Premier, the Vice-Premiers, Ministers, Chairmen of Committees and Secretary-General—all of whom, again, must be approved by the Standing Committee. There is no question in any circumstances of what might be called a "collective Cabinet responsibility." The Premier is technically "assisted" by the Vice-Premiers when they meet together as a State Council, passing orders for the Ministers to carry out. The Vice-Premiers, therefore, enjoy what might be considered "Cabinet rank"; ordinary Ministers and Chairmen of Commissions remain in the status of consultants, and, of course, executives.

The Premier is, of course, Chou En-Lai. It is unnecessary to describe this short, compact, beetle-browed young-old Chinese politician, graduate of many years in the Revolutionary wilderness (and several years in an engineering shop not far from Paris), the man who on his brief appearance at Geneva created the simultaneous double effect of a nervous constriction in the diplomatic hearts and a violent sexual impulse in the persons of almost every European woman who clapped eyes on him. This is both unusual and immaterial, politically, but might as well be noted. Like Molotov of Russia, Chou is a far bigger figure abroad than at home. He is frequently rated overseas as the Chinese Number Two; in fact he scrapes in domestically as Number Four.

After Chou En-Lai there are ten Vice-Premiers, twenty-nine Ministers, seven Chairmen of Commissions, and the Secretary-General.

One other leg, or buttress, of the Constitution is the Supreme People's Court, the judicial arm of the Executive. It is fair to say that in China the judiciary does not act independently of the executive, since constitutionally the "people's justice" is described as part of the dictatorship of the People's Democracy. There is no *prima facie* case for thinking either less or more of it on that account. However, the posts of Presidents and Members of the People's Courts are treated on the whole as political appointments; the constitution provides for their election every four years, and the Standing Committee can fire any or all of them at will.

The Supreme Court consists of an elected Chief Justice, or President, two Vice-Presidents, and fourteen members. Below it exist the People's Courts at a great number of levels—provincial, county, district and village (the *hsiang*, of which we have been always talking). They tend to be manned in general by Party cadres.

This network is technically—and indeed in fact—spread all over the land, under the control of the Procurator General, with the function of ensuring strict observance of the law not only by the citizens but by all Government institutions and public functionaries. The Procurator-General's office may initiate investigations and if necessary prosecutions on complaints or suspicion. In the early years it had a hard, exacting, and bloodstained task; of late it has operated unexceptionally.

The Constitution of the new China describes the nation as a "unified and multinational State"; it contains *no* provisions for regional autonomy. That is to say, for the first time in four thousand years it makes an administrative unit out of the greatest concentration of human beings on the face of the earth.

The old six administrative regions have now been sliced into twenty-six (the twenty-sixth is Formosa); with the three autonomous regions of Inner Mongolia, Tibet, and Changtu (which is Sinkiang and Tsinghai), and the three municipal administrations of Peking, Tientsin, and Shanghai. These administrative units are in turn subdivided into 2,116 Counties, 163 and 821 Municipal Districts, and 220,446 *hsiang*, with in addition 65 "organs of self-government" above the county level in the National Minority Areas.

The democratic application throughout this enormous and variegated area is, of course, both new and fumbling. The People's Congresses at their various levels elect their own People's Councils—governors and deputy-governors, mayors and deputy mayors, county heads and deputy county heads, away down to the *hsiang* stage; all of these bodies are responsible for the administrations in their areas "in accordance with the rule and condition laid down by the State Council."

At the primary level, the People's Congresses consist of 5,669,144 elected deputies, who in turn elect deputies to the Congresses one stage higher, leading finally to the electing of the National People's Congress at the Center. Half a million deputies, an estimated hundred thousand office holders at various levels . . . and at the center, below the glazed green roofs of the Emperor's city in Peking: Mao Tse-Tung, Chu Teh, Liu Shao-Chi and Chou En-Lai.

It may sound complex. It is a complex country.